Manufacturing
National Park Nature

The Nature | History | Society series is devoted to the publication of high-quality scholarship in environmental history and allied fields. Its broad compass is signalled by its title: nature because it takes the natural world seriously; history because it aims to foster work that has temporal depth; and society because its essential concern is with the interface between nature and society, broadly conceived. The series is avowedly interdisciplinary and is open to the work of anthropologists, ecologists, historians, geographers, literary scholars, political scientists, sociologists, and others whose interests resonate with its mandate. It offers a timely outlet for lively, innovative, and well-written work on the interaction of people and nature through time in North America.

General Editor: Graeme Wynn, University of British Columbia

Claire Elizabeth Campbell, *Shaped by the West Wind: Nature and History in Georgian Bay*

Tina Loo, *States of Nature: Conserving Canada's Wildlife in the Twentieth Century*

Jamie Benidickson, *The Culture of Flushing: A Social and Legal History of Sewage*

William J. Turkel, *The Archive of Place: Unearthing the Pasts of the Chilcotin Plateau*

John Sandlos, *Hunters at the Margin: Native People and Wildlife Conservation in the Northwest Territories*

James Murton, *Creating a Modern Countryside: Liberalism and Land Resettlement in British Columbia*

Greg Gillespie, *Hunting for Empire: Narratives of Sport in Rupert's Land, 1840-70*

Stephen J. Pyne, *Awful Splendour: A Fire History of Canada*

Hans M. Carlson, *Home Is the Hunter: The James Bay Cree and Their Land*

Liza Piper, *The Industrial Transformation of Subarctic Canada*

Sharon Wall, *The Nurture of Nature: Childhood, Antimodernism, and Ontario Summer Camps, 1920-55*

Joy Parr, *Sensing Changes: Technologies, Environments, and the Everyday, 1953-2003*

Jamie Linton, *What Is Water? The History of a Modern Abstraction*

NATURE | HISTORY | SOCIETY

Manufacturing National Park Nature

Photography, Ecology, and the Wilderness Industry of Jasper

J. KERI CRONIN

FOREWORD BY GRAEME WYNN

UBC Press • Vancouver • Toronto

21 20 19 18 17 16 15 14 13 12 11   5 4 3 2 1

Printed in Canada on FSC-certified ancient-forest-free paper
(100% post-consumer recycled) that is processed chlorine- and acid-free.

Library and Archives Canada Cataloguing in Publication

Cronin, J. Keri (Jennifer Keri), 1973-
    Manufacturing national park nature : photography, ecology, and the wilderness
industry of Jasper / J. Keri Cronin ; foreword by Graeme Wynn.

(Nature, history, society, ISSN 1713-6687)
Includes bibliographical references and index.
ISBN 978-0-7748-1907-7 (bound); 978-0-7748-1908-4 (pbk)

    1. Jasper National Park (Alta.). 2. Nature photography – Alberta – Jasper
National Park. 3. Place marketing – Environmental aspects – Alberta – Jasper
National Park. 4. Ecology – Alberta – Jasper National Park. 5. Nature – Effect of
human beings on – Alberta – Jasper National Park. I. Title. II. Series: Nature,
history, society

FC3664.J3C76 2010   971.23'32   C2010-906813-0

e-book ISBNs: 978-0-7748-1909-1 (pdf); 978-0-7748-1910-7 (epub)

Canadä

UBC Press gratefully acknowledges the financial support for our publishing
program of the Government of Canada (through the Canada Book Fund), the
Canada Council for the Arts, and the British Columbia Arts Council.

This book has been published with the help of a grant from the Canadian Federation
for the Humanities and Social Sciences, through the Aid to Scholarly Publications
Programme, using funds provided by the Social Sciences and Humanities Research
Council of Canada.

UBC Press
The University of British Columbia
2029 West Mall
Vancouver, BC V6T 1Z2
www.ubcpress.ca

Contents

Illustrations

"that fatal breath of 'improvement'"

Graeme Wynn

When the Canadian Pacific Railway began carrying passengers through the western mountains in 1886, the "awful grandeur" of the rugged terrain west of Calgary became the focus of much admiring attention, not least by agents of the railroad, anxious to recoup enormous construction costs by capitalizing on the scenery through which the rails ran. Given impetus by the country's first prime minister, who was persuaded, after an early trip along the transcontinental line, that although "there may be monotony of mountains as there may be prairies ... in our mountain scenery there is no monotony," a concerted publicity campaign "sold" the region to the world.[1]

The Canadian Rockies were a titanic sculpture. Here "serrated peaks, and vast pyramids of rock with curiously contorted and folded strata" were "followed by gigantic castellated masses down whose sides cascades fall thousands of feet." Glimpses of "glaciers and other strange and rare sights" were available from the luxury of the railway's Pullman cars.[2] Fine fishing and magnificent shooting could be had a short distance from one or another of the stops along the CPR line. Glacier House offered accommodation at the foot of the Illecillewaet Glacier, in the shadow of a peak considered the equivalent of "a dozen Matterhorns," and by century's end Swiss guides were employed there to lead climbers into the mountains, sometimes described in promotional literature as constituting "fifty Switzerlands in one."[3] At Banff, which Prime Minister Macdonald believed beyond compare in its combination of "so many attractions" and its possession of "all of the qualifications necessary to make it a great place of resort," tourists were invited to enjoy hot pools with curative properties, beautiful scenery, a national park, and, after 1887, luxurious accommodation at the Banff Springs Hotel, soon recognized in the *Baedeker Guide to Canada* as one of the five best hotels in the country.[4]

By contemporary measures, the promotion of the region was a considerable success. Some three thousand people visited Rocky Mountain (later Banff) National Park in 1887. By 1891, over seven thousand did so. By 1888, a thousand visitors had stayed at Glacier House; a decade later the tally exceeded twelve thousand. Early in the twentieth century, over 4 million passengers (many of whom were tourists) rode the rails through the Rockies. In 1903, approximately as many guests (five thousand) were turned away from the Banff Springs Hotel as were accommodated there.[5] But as the tide of tourists sojourning in Banff, at Lake Louise (where a small log chalet was built in 1890), at Glacier House, and at Mount Stephen increased, as tents and little chalets gave way to large hotels, and as trails were pushed to new points of interest at stops along the CPR line, some of those who had come, in the early years, "to value at its true worth the great un-lonely silence of the wilderness and to revel in the emancipation from frills, furbelows and small follies," felt their Eden despoiled. With "jealous eyes" they watched "the silence slipping back, the tin cans and empty fruit jars strew [their] sacred soil, [and] the mark of the axe grow more obtrusive."[6]

Among them (indeed, the person who put these sentiments to paper) was Mary T.S. Schäffer. The daughter of an affluent family from Pennsylvania, she had met her husband, Charles, a medical practitioner from Philadelphia, at Glacier House in 1889 while holidaying there with members of the Vaux family from the same city (who had first visited the area two years before). For a decade after 1891, the Schäffers returned to Rogers Pass each summer to pursue Charles's interest in the botany of the region. When Charles died, in 1903, Mary continued his work with Stewardson Brown, curator of the herbarium of the Philadelphia Academy of Natural Sciences, and contributed her own watercolours and photographs of plants to the volume published as *Alpine Flora of the Canadian Rocky Mountains* in 1907.[7] Enduring the deaths of both her parents in the same year as her husband died, Schäffer found herself increasingly "lost and lonesome," amid the early-twentieth-century influx of visitors to the southern Rockies. Nostalgic for earlier summers, when "99 percent" of those who came to the area "flitted across the country as bees across a flower garden, and were gone," she listened to the tales of hunters and trappers, who told of "valleys of great beauty, of high unknown peaks of little-known rivers, of un-named lakes … a fairyland" to the north and northwest, and resolved to venture into this territory.[8]

Thus it was that barely a century ago, two remarkable women spent a couple of summers travelling on horseback along "old Indian trails" in the Rocky Mountains of Canada. Accompanied by guides and outfitters, they rode northward from the Canadian Pacific Railway line at Lake Louise into the upper reaches of the North Saskatchewan and Athabasca river valleys. Soon they entered remote and rugged country little known to Europeans. Fur traders and early explorers had traversed these fastnesses. A Roman Catholic missionary party passed this way in the 1840s, as did the artist Paul Kane, and surveyors seeking a suitable route for the CPR had followed thirty years later. But even in 1913, Canadian government officials would express frustration at the conflicting information about and scant knowledge of the territory immediately east of that into which the intrepid women travelled.[9] Both Quakers, both Americans, Mary Schäffer and her companion Mollie Adams (who taught geology at Columbia College in New York) high-mindedly proclaimed their intent "to turn the unthumbed pages of an unread book" and to "learn daily those secrets which dear Mother Nature is so willing to tell those who seek."[10] More prosaically, but no less importantly, they were in search of Chaba Imne, an almost "mythical lake" at the centre of rich game country, known by hearsay to some local guides and visited historically by members of the indigenous Stoney Band.

After reaching and exploring Chabe Imne (Beaver Lake) in July 1908, Schäffer was ready to declare it "paradise."[11] Miles and miles of lake were bordered by "exquisite bays and inlets" closed in here by "a magnificent double-headed pile of rock," there by a "fine snow-capped mountain down whose side swept a splendid glacier" and yet elsewhere by a "fine waterfall" bursting from a fissure hundreds of feet above the lake and turning into a veil of spray "waving back and forth in the wind, long before it touched the rocks below." Veritable gardens of "vetches crimson, yellow and pink … spread away in every direction," the crashing sound of avalanches interrupted the stillness and "the distant yapping of coyotes" broke the night. "How pure and undefiled it was," this "heaven of the hills."[12]

Yet change was coming, and Schäffer knew it. In September 1907, after her first summer on the trail, the Canadian government established Jasper Forest Park under the authority of the Dominion Lands Act. Encompassing an enormous area east of the Continental Divide, including all the southern headwaters of the Athabasca River, and extending north to 53°35'N, this initiative anticipated the construction of a second transcontinental railroad through the Rockies at Yellowhead Pass.[13] As the rails approached, the entire eastern slope of the mountains from the international boundary to a point north of the 54th parallel was reserved to protect the water supply and produce timber for settlers on the prairies. But when the Dominion Forests Reserves and Parks Act was introduced in 1911, it distinguished between forest reserves "withdrawn from occupation" and forest parks that could be "occupied for the purposes of pleasure." By a subsequent order-in-council, Jasper Park was redefined as a strip of land twenty miles (thirty-two kilometres) wide along the route of the Grand Trunk Pacific Railway, which brought passengers to Jasper in 1912, crossed the Yellowhead Pass to reach Tete Jaune Cache in 1913, and arrived on the Pacific coast in 1914. This left many of the area's most strikingly beautiful sites, including Chabe Imne (which Schäffer had renamed Maligne Lake), beyond the boundaries of the park.

When she was asked to survey the lake for the Geological Survey of Canada in 1911, Shäffer was convinced that "nothing could hold back the tide of 'improvement'" that would follow the python-like advance of the railroad into the hills, and she regretted that "inch by inch, our pet playgrounds are being swallowed up." For all that, she rode the railway from Edmonton to its early 1911 terminus in Hinton, before proceeding by horse and pack train up the Maligne River "where pythons could not penetrate and 'progress' was unknown." Driven onward by her commission, and her memories of the beautiful lake, she acknowledged "an ever increasing desire to see it once more before it too fell under that fatal breath of 'improvement'."[14]

Although the publicity that followed Schäffer's survey, and her efforts to convince federal officials that both the magnificent scenery and the wildlife breeding grounds of Maligne Lake warranted protection, helped secure the inclusion of this area in an expanded Jasper Park in 1914, improvement's hot breath was not so easily deflected. Yes, hunting was prohibited within Parks, as it was not within Forest Reserves. And yes, the narrow corridor that was Jasper Park after 1911 was inimical to effective wildlife protection. But the Dominion's parks had been conceived, since their beginning, as "pleasure grounds, for the benefit, advantage and enjoyment of the people of Canada."[15] Wilderness protection and tourism development were conjoined enterprises. As the first head of the National Parks Branch of the Department of the Interior had it, "nothing attracts tourists like national parks."[16] Whatever else they stood for, Canada's mountain parks were intended to be tourist destinations.

In Jasper, this meant, first, the construction of an imposing building opposite the railway station to serve as the headquarters of park administration, and then the development of scenic roads to local attractions, including Pyramid Lake and Mount Edith Cavell (named, in a moment of imperial patriotism, in honour of the English nurse executed by German soldiers in Belgium in 1915).[17] Outfitters began to guide wealthy tourists into the mountains and to the shores of several lakes. Soon there were tea houses and a campsite with permanent tents and a log kitchen and dining hall in the park. Early in the 1920s, the "tent city" was superseded by Jasper Park Lodge, a $2.5 million investment where visitors could "rough it" in "rustic log cabins in a spectacular mountain setting" while enjoying the "service and facilities associated with luxury resort hotels."[18] After 1925, guests could play golf on the new, carefully designed eighteen-hole course at the lodge, construction of which had entailed blasting away rock outcrops and bringing in forty freight-car loads of topsoil. By 1935, "about one hundred miles of excellent motor highways" ran into the park in various directions from Jasper Park Lodge. There were three-day excursions by automobile, motorboat, and horseback to a chalet on Maligne Lake. There were opportunities for boating, fishing, hiking, and riding in the backcountry and cross-country skiers also began to use the growing network of trails in the park.

Government spending on public works during the Depression years produced an all-weather highway from Edmonton to Jasper (which also opened access to the Miette Hot Springs at the eastern entrance to the park) and the spectacular Banff-Jasper highway (now known as the Icefields Parkway). In 1941, a New York magazine described Jasper Park Lodge as the "gathering place of Summer sportsmen, society and vacationists ... a top-notch caravanserie that combines the luxuries of a tycoon's Adirondack camp with the informality of a first class Dude Ranch."[19] But improved accessibility also encouraged the rise of automobile tourism, the development of autocamps, and the promotion of new activities such as "boat racing, surf board riding, water skiing, and a rodeo" within the park.[20] By 1950, the Jasper town site boasted a new recreational facility with "an outdoor swimming pool, dressing rooms, tennis courts, bowling green and sports field."[21]

Given the extent of the park – in excess of ten thousand square kilometers in 1930, after a series of boundary adjustments – these developments were hardly fatal to the "great garden of the mountains" in which Mary Schäffer had sought solitude, peace, and comfort only a few decades earlier. The breath of improvement, the transforming wedge of progress that she identified and lamented in 1911, moved inexorably, permeating dozens, scores, then hundreds of "secret places," and ensuring that they "would be secret no longer," but it also moved slowly, especially at first. There were ten thousand visitors to Jasper National Park in 1920. It took almost twenty years for this number to double, and it remained above twenty thousand for a mere three years, before falling through the remaining war years to approximately twelve thousand. Then the onslaught quickened: almost seventy-two thousand in 1947, eighty-five thousand in 1950, over one hundred thousand in 1952, and almost one hundred and fifty-four thousand in 1955. Still, these numbers were modest compared with Rocky Mountain/Banff National Park, which had more than one hundred thousand visitors in 1924, counted over seven hundred thousand in 1955, and fell below one hundred fifty thousand only four times after 1927, in the depth of the Depression of the 1930s. In comparison with its southern neighbour, Jasper was a "sleeping giant" until the mid-1950s. Then its popularity increased dramatically. Between 1957 and 1962, the Jasper visitor count averaged almost three hundred and fifty thousand each year. By 1966, it approached six hundred thousand (Banff topped 2 million in that year). [22] Schäffer, who died in Banff in 1939, may have discerned a pattern in the loss of mountain wilderness, but with the acuity of hindsight it is clear that the trajectory of loss unfolded quite differently across the vast and varied space of the Canadian Rockies, and that it begs interpretation from a number of perspectives, all of which reveal the tensions inherent in human-nature interactions in the modern world.

By PearlAnn Reichwein and Lisa McDermott's account, Mary Schäffer's embrace of the western wilderness drew from the nineteenth century Romantic movement, which "sought the sublime and picturesque in wild landscapes," and from those nineteenth-century New Englanders "who found joy and divinity through transcendental communion with creation." [23] For Schäffer, the wilderness was a fount of peace, health, and happiness, but in her experience it was also a fragile place, one whose redemptive qualities were continuously under threat from the clamour and clutter of "modern materialist society." Anxious about the impending despoliation of the wild mountains and of the wildlife habitat around beautiful Maligne Lake, she sought to protect these places while urging those who shared her attitudes toward the wild to visit them while they remained unspoiled. Extending the boundaries of the park would help maintain wildlife. But saving habitat meant fencing it in, managing it. Protecting wild spaces this way inevitably meant that they were less wild. By the same token, mapping Maligne Lake helped secure its inclusion in a reconfigured park but also gave it a place in the minds – the mental maps – of untold numbers who had never seen it. Writing evocatively of the lake and its surroundings gave power to Schäffer's pen as she implored readers of *Old Indian Trails*, a book that she described as "the key to one of the fairest of all God's many gardens," to "Go!" in search of this back-country Eden.[24] But words of encouragement carried ironic seeds of desecration. The more persuasive Schäffer's message, the more compelling her call to the wild, the more often would "great un-lonely silences" be broken, the more often would secret places be exposed. According to Reichwein and McDermott, the challenge of "safeguarding wilderness from overdevelopment" required of Schäffer "a pragmatic compromise between wild nature and gross capitalist exploitation."[25]

A similar balancing act was required of Canada's national parks' personnel by the complex, shifting mandates under which they operated. Canada's "first national park," at Banff, began as a spa and health reserve and was envisaged two years later, in the Rocky Mountain Parks Act of 1887, as a "public park and pleasure ground," within which there would be a commitment to the "preservation and protection of game and fish, and of wild birds generally."[26] Regulations soon prohibited "the shooting, wounding, capturing or killing of any wild animal or bird" in the park, yet wolves and other "noxious" animals and birds, including coyotes, lynx, skunks, weasels, eagles, and cormorants were exempt from protection.[27] At the turn of the twentieth century, a bounty was offered for wolf kills in the park and a few years later, Persian sheep, coyotes, cougars, a timber wolf, a badger, and two golden eagles were caged and displayed alongside a herd of elk in the Banff animal paddock. Just as roads, bridges, and buildings were necessary to "make of the reserve a creditable national park," so the elimination and confinement of local fauna "improved" the park for human visitors.[28] Meanwhile, poachers, aware that there were too few rangers to police the backcountry effectively, preyed on protected species within the park with relative impunity. By 1900, the park was devoid of wapiti (*Cervus canadensis*); once wolves had been eliminated from the Bow Valley, in 1914, several hundred elk were brought to Banff from Yellowstone Park in the United States. National park "nature" was bent, from the first, to human design.

Those who have written about Canadian parks have offered widely different interpretations of their origins and purpose. Four decades ago and more, historian R. Craig Brown argued that Canada's first national parks were established to be "useful" rather than in reflection of lofty preservationist goals. In this view, the early Canadian Parks movement was simply an extension of the Macdonald Government's economic policies, which rested in large part on the use of natural resources to further national development. Parks were set aside to allow business and government to make the fullest possible use of their resources. This interpretation quickly gained traction and was reinforced by Leslie Bella's *Parks for Profit*, published in 1987, which argued forcefully that Canada's parks were foci of economic development rather than places removed from capitalist exploitation. Indeed, the creation of the Parks Branch in the Dominion Forest Reserves and Parks Act of 1911 gave some credence, as parks historian C.J. Taylor has suggested, to the view that parks were "fundamentally resource reserves, allowing for the controlled exploitation of a range of resources such as minerals, timber and water as well as scenery."[29]

For all that, preservation, broadly defined, is widely understood to have become a more important guiding principle in parks management after the appointment of J.B. Harkin as the first commissioner of parks in 1911. Hailed as an ardent conservationist by the author of an institutional history of the park service, Harkin was also celebrated in Janet Foster's book *Working for Wildlife*, published in 1978. This influential study made the bureaucrat a hero by proclaiming his visionary role (fifty years ahead of the Americans and a century in advance of his fellow countryfolk) in articulating a coherent "philosophy of wildlands preservation."[30] A more judicious assessment reveals the commissioner as a more enigmatic figure through his quarter century at the head of the expanding parks branch. Although he claimed that Canada's national parks were places "in which the beauty of the landscape is protected from profanation, the natural wild animals, plants and forests preserved, and the peace and solitude of primeval nature retained," he consistently embraced the secular or "commercial" (as he once had it) alongside the sacred or "humanitarian" purpose of parks.[31] In the latter vein, he often insisted that a return to nature, as demarcated by the boundaries of Canada's parks, offered a magic cure for nervous exhaustion and other afflictions of modern (urban) life. In the former, he famously calculated the yield from Canada's wheat fields at little more than a third of that from its scenery ($4.91 per acre compared with $13.88).[32] Both revenue and rejuvenation were important, and National Parks yielded dividends – in gold and in human well-being – for the country.

Perhaps the best assessment of all of this has been provided by environmental historian Alan MacEachern, who has interrogated the underlying assumptions and political utility of Brown's and Bella's arguments, and analyzed Harkin's career to conclude that "there has never been just one doctrine directing the national park system."[33] Even the National Parks Act of 1930, which separated the administration of parks and forest reserves and prohibited mining and restricted logging in parks, failed to banish the ongoing tension between use and preservation by dedicating the parks to the "benefit, enjoyment and education" of the people of Canada and requiring that they be "maintained and made use of so as to leave them unimpaired for future generations."

Only with the rise of the environmental movement in the 1960s were parks staff enjoined to recognize the preservation of significant natural features as their "most fundamental and important obligation," and it was not until the late 1970s and 1980s that parks policy made use secondary to the maintenance of ecological integrity in the parks. Yet the dilemma continued. The environmental enthusiasm of the 1960s pulled people back to nature. Coupled with rising affluence and increased leisure time, improvements to roads, and ever-increasing automobile ownership, this led to a rapid and sustained rise in park visits. Annual visitor counts at Jasper have increased by approximately 3 percent per year since 1970 and are now near the 2 million mark. In recent years, both the Jasper Environmental Association, a local conservation group that has been monitoring Parks Canada's efforts to manage the ecological health of Jasper National Park since 1989, and the Northern Alberta Branch of the Canadian Parks and Wilderness Society have expressed concerns about park management plans that continue to encourage tourism, envisage alterations to wilderness zone boundaries, and allow expansion of commercial activities in ecologically sensitive areas, while remaining vague about what measures might be taken to protect the ecological integrity of the park.[34]

Far from pristine Edens, Canada's mountain parks have been (and remain) contested, negotiated, real, imagined, manipulated, managed, and malleable places. From Mary Schäffer's day to our own, they have been endowed with many meanings and called upon to serve many purposes. Then as now, these meanings and purposes reflected not only what was there (the biogeophysical landscape of the cordillera – nature) but also the ideas that shaped the ways in which people viewed, imagined, and described what they saw. In much the same way as the desert canyon once known as the *Chasm of the Colorado* became a Grand national monument and a symbol of something unique about the United States of America, so too Rocky Mountain splendour – the "Nature" that defined the essence of Canada's mountain parks – was created rather than revealed.[35] Understanding these places requires more than knowledge of their ecology, more than an appreciation of their political and administrative history, more than awareness of the details of the regulations under which they operate, more than familiarity with the names and personalities of those charged with administering them. To grasp their broader meaning requires a sense of why people came to these places, what they thought they would find there, and how they responded to what they encountered.

These are questions at the very centre of Keri Cronin's *Manufacturing National Park Nature*. Focusing on photographic representations of Jasper National Park, this revealing and richly illustrated study lays bare the gap between what is pictured and what is concealed in tourist images of the park and offers an intriguing commentary on the ways in which visual depictions have shaped both "imaginative" and "actual" landscapes in this region. Working the fertile borderland between cultural production and environmental values, it reveals how government agencies, tourism operators, environmental activists, and tourists themselves have drawn from and given substance to the idea that National Parks encompass pristine Nature.

Considering somewhat similar, albeit generally slightly earlier, developments south of the 49th parallel, historian Mark Barringer has explicitly linked the development of America's western parks to America's frontier mythology. In this account, Yellowstone and other mountain parks were celebrated as the last remnants of a continent once new, "natural and almost magically alive" that inspired generations of Americans to "awe and reverence." They preserved "those things lost to progress elsewhere" and became "repositories of ... [a] national mythology" and symbols of American identity. Here, visitors looking out at "mountains, waterfalls, canyons, glaciers, and geysers," watching bison and elk grazing in meadows, and marvelling at bears alongside the road saw what they expected to see: the nation's past. But they had other expectations too. They wanted comfortable accommodation from which to venture into the wilderness; they wanted roads to carry them to especially scenic or remarkable spots; they hoped to see bison, deer, and elk "on demand"; and they wanted "dance halls, swimming pools and bear-feeding shows to reflect the belief that nature's bounty had created the most affluent society on earth, able to afford such whimsical pursuits." And so, says Barringer, America's national parks were designed "to fit popular beliefs about what they should be," and "both the physical Yellowstone and its image in the collective imagination underwent tremendous change."[36]

Although Cronin's and Barringer's books reveal some broad parallels in the ways in which mountain parks north and south of the border were shaped by visitors' expectations, it is important to recognize the differences between Canadian and American stories here. Different historical and geographical circumstances gave rise to different national mythologies. Early European explorers of the northeastern foreland of the American continent were more often cognizant of its peril than its promise. Thus the northern reaches of the continent were characterized as "the land God gave to Cain" while southerly latitudes entered English literature more propitiously as places "so full of grapes [and with signs of] such plenty" that those who first encountered them after crossing the Atlantic "did thinke in the world were not the like abundance." To put none too fine a point on it, while those who settled Canadian space grappled with what Voltaire described dismissively as "quelques arpents de neige" [a few acres of snow], Americans were awed by what Scott Fitzgerald imagined, in *The Great Gatsby,* as the "fresh green breast of the new world."[37] Similarly, those who occupied the scattered archipelago of habitable islands across the continent's northern limits of agricultural settlement rarely found American historian Frederick Jackson Turner's notion of a continuously unfolding frontier of agrarian opportunity a convincing account of their experience. Barringer may be right to tie perceptions of America's mountain parks to American mythologies (and no doubt American influences have spilled across the border to influence Canadian ideas in these matters as in so many others) but, as Cronin recognizes, more prosaic and immediate considerations bring us closer to understanding the forces at play in shaping Canada's Rocky Mountain parks.[38]

Following those who see photography playing a major role in the naturalization of cultural constructions, Cronin argues that the photographic representations so common in illustrated guidebooks to Jasper National Park, on souvenir postcards of the area, and in "how-to" manuals about nature photography, have encouraged people to see the landscape of the Canadian Rockies in particular ways. Because these images almost invariably portray the "flora, fauna, geological features, and landscapes of the park" (144) in ways that minimize the human effects upon them, and because photography is widely regarded as an "objective" practice – how many times have we heard that "the camera never lies"? – these representations have helped to embed conceptions of the Rocky Mountain region as "wilderness" or "unspoiled Nature" in the popular mind. They have shaped ideas of "what nature is and how humans ought to think and feel about it," and they have mirrored the values of consumer culture in doing so.[39] They have worked, in other words, to persuade people that a carefully manufactured cultural product is "natural."

There are many smaller ironies catalogued in these pages. Among them: the claim of one recent guidebook that 8 million visitors enjoy the "untrammelled" Canadian Rockies each year; the assumption that railcars or automobiles can deliver visitors to places beyond civilization, unaffected by technology; the sense that wilderness can be experienced while hiking carefully maintained trails; the erasure of the past (including that of indigenous peoples) through the belief that wild places are necessarily devoid of human presence; the conception of nature as static; and so on. Noting each of these small absurdities serves, in its own way, to challenge taken-for-granted assumptions and to sharpen reflection about the ways in which the members of modern western societies think about and interact with the natural world. More than this, however, *Manufacturing National Park Nature* speaks to enduring societal convictions about nature and non-human animals. For all the environmental, social, technological, and political changes of the last century, visual representations of Jasper National Park have remained surprisingly constant through the years.

By focusing the tourist gaze (and the attention of those who consume this landscape from afar) upon supposedly "unspoiled" or "untouched" scenes while excluding from the frame of everyday perception the disrupting effects of the python of commercial development, representations of the park have encouraged people to imagine this space much as Mary Schäffer did a hundred years or so ago (and for equally complicated reasons) as a "fairyland," a stunningly beautiful, pure, and undefiled natural h(e)aven. By focusing upon the manner in which these images are produced, Cronin reminds readers that the scenic views and landscape representations that shape our perceptions of the world, within and beyond park boundaries, are less transparent portrayals of reality than they are reflections of both societal understandings of the environment and dominant pictorial conventions. Because we see what we have been conditioned to think we are looking at, Cronin (and others) would argue, we are all too easily persuaded of the pristine quality of beautiful places even as these places are suffused with and changed by "that fatal breath of 'improvement.'" Realizing as much is the first step to unsettling such cultural representations and thinking anew about both dominant understandings of place and the imbalance of power between human and non-human inhabitants of the earth.

Acknowledgments

A project such as this could not come together without the assistance of a great number of people. I must begin by thanking my family, who sparked my interest in the Canadian Rockies by taking me on numerous camping trips to Jasper National Park when I was growing up. As I walked the trails around Maligne Lake with my parents, cousins, sister, aunt, and uncle, I had no idea, of course, that one day I would write a book about the landscape that inspired so many of our family outings, yet those experiences form the heart of this project.

I began to think critically about ideas of nature and place when I was a graduate student at Queen's University. I feel very fortunate to have had the opportunity to work with Lynda Jessup during that time and appreciate her continued guidance and friendship. I would also like to acknowledge the mentorship of the other faculty members whom I worked closely with at Queen's, specifically Allison Goebel, Janice Helland, Vojtěch Jirat-Wasiutyński, and Joan Schwartz.

I would like to thank the staff and volunteers at Jasper Yellowhead Museum and Archives, the Whyte Museum of the Canadian Rockies, and Library and Archives Canada for their kindness, patience, and willingness to share their expertise as I was gathering my research on this topic. In addition, Tom Thurston and Todd Crawshaw of the Royal Alberta Museum (formerly the Provincial Museum of Alberta) were particularly helpful in answering my questions about the Wild Alberta installation, and I would like to thank them for their assistance in that capacity. Kevin Manuel at Brock University's James A. Gibson Library also provided

valuable assistance with tracking down information on legislation per-
taining to Canada's National Parks.

As those who work on visual culture topics are all too aware, working
with images can present extra challenges for a researcher. I would like to
thank Cheryl Williams and Fiona McDonald for cheerfully offering their
advice and assistance on this aspect of the project, especially in the final
few months. Meghan Power at the Jasper Yellowhead Museum and Archives, Marcia Rak at the Canada Science and Technology Museum, and
Lena Goon at the Whyte Museum of the Canadian Rockies were a tremendous help in this area, and I thank them for all their assistance and
advice. Joyce Ennis, Marion Goos, Sheryl McKay, John and Marg Morck,
and Carol Roy generously dug through their closets, cupboards, and stor-
age boxes in search of postcards and tourist brochures of Jasper National
Park, and I am grateful that they saw fit to share their precious collections
with me in the name of research. Likewise, I truly appreciate the tireless
efforts of my mother, Ruthie Morck, in helping me to build my collection
of promotional and historical materials from Jasper National Park.

It would be difficult to complete a project like this one without a strong
network of friends, family, and colleagues. Bill Casey, Nikki Cormier,
Jenny Cronin, Scott Cronin, Stacey Cronin, Fiona McDonald, Ruthie
Morck, Laurie Morrison, Maria Power, Kirsty Robertson, Kim Wahl, and
Anne Whitelaw all contributed to this project in more ways than they
know, and I am truly grateful to each one of them. I would also like to
acknowledge the support of my colleagues at Brock University, especially
Lauren Corman, Catherine Heard, Leah Knight, Duncan MacDonald,
Linda Steer, and Katharine T. von Stackelberg.

It has been a pleasure working with UBC Press on this project, and I
would like to thank, in particular, Laraine Coates, Randy Schmidt, Graeme
Wynn, and the two anonymous reviewers for their helpful and thought-
provoking feedback on earlier versions of this book.

Manufacturing National Park Nature has been published with the help
of a grant from the Canadian Federation for the Humanities and Social
Sciences, through the Aid to Scholarly Publications Programme, using
funds provided by the Social Sciences and Humanities Research Council
of Canada. I would also like to acknowledge the Humanities Research
Institute and the Office of Research Services at Brock University for their
financial assistance with this project.

Manufacturing
National Park Nature

1

Grounding National Park Nature

Jasper National Park is one of Canada's best-known tourist destinations. Nestled in the eastern slopes of the Rocky Mountains and referred to as "the gentle giant of the mountain national parks," this UNESCO world heritage site has captured the imaginations of thousands of visitors each year.[1] Canada's national parks are world famous and are seen as icons of Canadian national identity by visitors and residents alike. For over a century, they have been imaged and imagined as quintessentially Canadian, and this designation seems to ring especially true in the parks located in the Rocky Mountains. Like the Royal Canadian Mounted Police, the Rocky Mountains are a significant and established part of Canadian iconography. The visual culture of Jasper National Park reinforces these sentiments – from collector coins to postcards, from postage stamps to tourist photographs, specific views of this landscape have been consumed and replicated since the park's official establishment in 1907.

Of particular interest for the following discussion are the ways in which the play among visual culture, regional specificity, and national symbolism has influenced environmental perceptions and realities, both in Jasper National Park and in the broader context of the Canadian nation. In this book, I explore how visual imagery shapes conceptions of nature in a variety of complex ways. Photography, in particular, has been a significant means of creating cultural expectations of place, and I am interested in exploring the ways in which the camera has shaped certain ideologies about this landscape.

Of course, photography is not the only visual medium that has been used to represent the area now known as Jasper National Park. Examples of sketches, paintings, poetry, and prose inspired by this mountain land-scape abound, many dating from well before the designation of Jasper as a federally sanctioned forest reserve in 1907. As historian Karen Jones has pointed out, Reverend George Grant, who accompanied an 1872 survey party to the region, "advertised nature's canvas in Jasper as an inspiring panorama for budding artists."[2] Sportsmen and explorers who visited the region in the nineteenth century employed dominant pictorial modes of the day in published accounts of their travels in the Canadian Rockies.[3] The celebrated explorations of Lord Milton and Dr. Cheadle in British North America took them through what we now know as Jasper National Park, and their published accounts of this journey include landscapes that emphasize "the picturesque, despite the desolation of the British North American West."[4] Canonical Canadian artists such as Paul Kane, Lawren Harris, and A.Y. Jackson also produced images of the Jasper landscape.[5] Kane arrived at Jasper House in 1846, and many of the sketches he made during this trip appeared in his well-known publication *Wanderings of an Artist* and served as reference material for his watercolour paintings.[6] Even though paintings of the northern Ontario landscape are usually identified with the Group of Seven, paintings of Jasper by the artists found their way into the rhetoric of the tourism industry, as evidenced by the inclusion of sketches by Harris, Jackson, and Franklin Carmichael in a 1927 promo-tional brochure produced by Canadian National Railways.[7]

Many well-known writers have embraced the romantic mythology of the Canadian Rockies over the past several decades. In 1914, Arthur Conan Doyle visited Jasper, a trip that inspired the famed creator of Sherlock Holmes to write a poem entitled "Jasper National Park on the Athabaska Trail," in which he declared that

The mighty voice of Canada will ever call to me.
I shall hear the roar of rivers where the rapids foam and tear,
I shall smell the virgin upland with its balsam-laden air,
And shall dream that I am riding down the winding woody vale,
With the packer and the packhorse on the Athabaska Trail.[8]

Canadian writers have also been drawn to the imagery and mythology of the Rocky Mountains. For instance, the personal scrapbooks of Lucy Maud Montgomery, author of the *Anne of Green Gables* series, include postcard imagery of one of Jasper's most recognizable geographical features,

Mount Edith Cavell.[9] A more recent example is Thomas Wharton's award-winning 1995 novel *Icefields*, a fictional account of a glacier exped-ition in the Jasper region.[10] That such a diverse group of high-profile producers of cultural capital have shared a sense of fascination with Jasper speaks volumes about the position this specific geographical location holds in dominant cultural constructions of Canada.

This book focuses on Jasper National Park for three main reasons. First, Jasper National Park is one of Canada's best-known vacation destinations, and the image culture of this Rocky Mountain vacation destination has helped to define, in the minds of many, what nature looks like in a Can-adian context. Second, the park's centenary celebrations in 2007 provoked reflections on this particular landscape in the context of twenty-first century environmental concerns. And third, in recent years there has been much debate and public awareness surrounding the ecological health of the Canadian national park system. The Canadian Rockies are a significant location for biodiversity – a recent count indicated that there were "277 species of birds, 1,300 species of plants, 20,000 species of insects and spiders, 15 species of amphibians and reptiles and 69 species of mammals" in this region – and, at a time when concerns about ecological sustainabil-ity are becoming increasingly urgent, it is important to re-examine our connections and cultural ideals about these types of spaces.[11] As one of the famed Rocky Mountain parks, Jasper National Park has been at the centre of many of these discussions and serves as a good case study for the current inquiry. In addition, I hope that this book will add to the growing body of critical analysis on Jasper National Park, a landscape that has been, until recently, relatively neglected in comparison with neighbouring Banff National Park.[12]

PHOTOGRAPHY, TOURISM, AND NATIONAL PARK NATURE

Jasper National Park has had a long and complex photographic history and has been the subject of countless photographs since it was first set aside as a federal forest reserve in the early twentieth century. Although photography has been used in numerous ways in the park – among them in wildlife management, scientific studies, geological mapping, law en-forcement, and as an aid to exploration and natural resource extraction – photographic images of Jasper have been, and continue to be, predomin-antly related to the tourism industry. Photography has been an active component of the commodification of the Canadian wilderness, what

Patricia Jasen has described as "the process by which meaning [has been] encoded, saleable imagery ... identified, and tourist sights ... made to speak to consumers on an imaginative level, through the language of signs."[13] Photographic imagery has thus had a significant impact on how the supposedly natural region of the Canadian Rocky Mountains has been understood, a process that has been the result of sophisticated and carefully rehearsed representational techniques. It is this *understanding* of place – what I refer to as "National Park Nature" – and how this understanding has been mediated and manifested through photographic imagery that comprise the focus of the following chapters.[14]

National Park Nature is a way of seeing that shifts according to the landscape under consideration. It is not a static or easily identifiable entity but a system of visual organization predicated on dominant cultural values regarding nature, non-human animals, and "the environment."[15] National Park Nature is mediated by technologies of vision, such as photography, and differs from other modes of engaging with the landscape due to its relationship with contemporary notions of environmentalism.

In Jasper, National Park Nature has been shaped predominantly by the cultural constructs of "wilderness," "recreation," and "wildlife," key components of both the visual identity of the region and the promotion of Jasper as a popular vacation destination. Throughout the park's history, photographic imagery has played a key role in creating and sustaining these specific conceptions of what it means to engage with nature in the Jasper region. Photographic representations of National Park Nature have reinforced assumptions about what constitutes acceptable activity and behaviour in this culturally defined space, while at the same time often masking local environmental and cultural tensions. Photographic images of National Park Nature provide the illusion of imparting objective and unmediated visual information when in actuality they are thoroughly shaped by the dynamics of consumer culture, of which tourism is a significant part.

National Park Nature in Jasper has been characterized by a complex dynamic between a desire for "pristine" and "unspoiled" wilderness and the development of amenities such as recreation facilities and luxury accommodations. The gap between what is pictured and what is concealed in tourist photography relating to Jasper National Park is of central concern in the following discussion. The "erasure of locality" from dominant discourses surrounding National Park Nature has led to specific forms of environmental knowledge in this context, including the notion that Nature is a static entity that needs to be preserved from human use and abuse.[16]

As ecologist Daniel Botkin has argued, "We have tended to view nature as a Kodachrome still-life, much like a tourist-guide illustration ... but nature is a moving picture show."[17] Botkin's analogy is significant here since it underscores the sense of interconnectedness between tourist imagery and dominant ideologies of Nature.

National Park Nature informs the representational politics of Jasper National Park and figures prominently in illustrated tourist brochures and photographic postcards. As the examples I draw on in this book demonstrate, National Park Nature is often pictured in ways that serve to reinforce the mythological construction of a Nature/Culture divide that many scholars argue is at the root of the current ecological crisis in North America.[18] In a variety of ways, photography has been used as a means to perpetuate this myth, in particular because of the persistent assumptions about the capacity of the camera to record "the truth." On the basis of studies in British Columbia, geographer Bruce Braun has pointed out that most photographs made in the context of Nature (or "adventure") tourism mask the process of image production. The photographer and, by extension, the technological trappings that placed him or her in that specific locale and facilitated the production of the image are excluded from the frame, thus allowing the landscape in the picture to be conceived of as unmediated by human presence or, simply, as a record of Nature. Further, as Braun argues, pictorial conventions reinforce the notion that Nature and Culture are two distinct realms: "By situating the viewing subject behind the (absent) camera, looking out into the wilds, the image firmly situates the viewer *in* modern society and asks him or her to ponder the yawning gap between culture and nature, city and country, modernity and its premodern antecedents."[19] Much of the tourist photography that defined Jasper National Park during the twentieth century and into the twenty-first century has had the effect of constructing borders around the park, setting it in opposition to other, more urbanized, parts of Canada.

Although I focus on camera-based imagery in this study because it has dominated the history of visual culture in Jasper National Park, my analysis relates to the broader history of European and North American landscape art in a number of ways. The visual legacy of the European aesthetic traditions of the "sublime" and the "picturesque" is found in the images of the Canadian Rockies, though they are modified to suit early-twentieth-century sensibilities. In previous historical eras, paintings of mountains by well-known landscape artists such as Salvator Rosa conformed to a visual rendering of the sublime intended to raise in the viewer an emotional response just shy of fear. Dark crags, shadowy caves, and impossible jagged peaks formed the cornerstones of these types of images. In the twentieth century, representations of mountains were still intended to evoke a sense of awe, but this was a tamer, safer sense of awe, more congruent with contemporary efforts to promote tourism in the region. Likewise, elements of the picturesque – literally meaning "like a picture" – found in Jasper National Park imagery are compositionally different from the rolling hills and quaint farmlands of eighteenth- and nineteenth-century British landscape art. Yet the notion that Jasper National Park is a space that is at once aesthetically pleasing to look at and "tamed" by human society remains a significant part of this body of imagery.

The many connections between visual representations of a landscape and the social, political, and environmental issues shaping it are of particular significance. Scholars such as John Barrell have described how landscape imagery can be understood as a site of power relations among various social classes.[20] In his classic text, *The Dark Side of the Landscape: The Rural Poor in English Painting, 1730-1840,* Barrell offers an analysis of well-known paintings by canonical British landscape painters such as John Constable, George Morland, and Thomas Gainsborough to demonstrate the ways in which these images corresponded to the needs of the dominant social classes of the time. What happens when we place a similar analytical framework over the visual culture of a landscape such as Jasper National Park? What kinds of power relationships – both between different groups of human actors and between different species – are created, challenged, and sustained when we think about representations of this mountainous landscape? If, as British cultural historian Malcolm Andrews has asserted, "landscape is a political text," then it is no longer sufficient to consider representations of beloved "natural" spaces such as Jasper National Park as existing outside political, social, and environmental tensions.[21]

Yet a sense of leaving behind such tensions has characterized cultural understandings of spaces such as Jasper National Park. Today we continue to look wistfully at tranquil scenes from the Canadian Rockies, daydreaming about a relaxing vacation away from the demands, pressures, and stresses of "real" life at home. In many ways, we are no different from the generations of tourists who have sought out this landscape in previous decades. National Park Nature has historically been informed by the notion that so-called wilderness destinations, like Jasper, are an escape from the effects of modernity. Yet, as historian T.J. Jackson Lears reminds us, "anti-modernism was not simply escapism; it was ambivalent, often coexisting with enthusiasm for material progress."[22] The seemingly dichotomous positions of "escape to nature" and "enthusiasm for material progress" are intimately related.

The history of Jasper National Park teems with examples of this relationship; as tourists, we have arrived by automobile to a destination purportedly untouched by industry, technology, and innovation, we have hiked on carefully maintained trails in search of the timeless, spiritual qualities we have come to associate with Nature. These ways of enjoying landscapes such as Jasper National Park are not, in and of themselves, negative. In fact, the pleasure, enjoyment, and sense of wonder we experience in these spaces can result in many positive benefits, among them a deeper sense of appreciation of the species we share the planet with. What is essential, however, is the recognition that these spaces are part of – and not separate from – the industrial and technological forces driving life in the twentieth and twenty-first centuries. This is not, of course, a new revelation. Scholars such as William Cronon have been arguing this point eloquently for years.[23] For all that, however, dominant representations of landscapes such as Jasper National Park continue to reinforce notions of the pristine, the unspoiled, and the untouched. Even as tourist publications boast about the number of visitors to the Rocky Mountains each year, they continue to emphasize these ideals: "more than eight million people visit the Canadian Rockies every year," the 2008 issue of *Our Alberta* claims, before assuring potential visitors that this region is "untrammelled."[24]

Representations of recreation and wildlife in Jasper National Park also play upon the notion that Nature and Culture are separate and distinct entities. It is within these thematic and pictorial frameworks, perhaps, that this dynamic becomes especially pronounced. Whereas scenes of wilderness landscapes mark the distinction between Nature and Culture through the erasure of human presence, the ideologies informing scenes of recreation and wildlife perpetuate the notion that Jasper National Park is a space where the two realms can intersect and harmoniously coexist, yet remain distinct and different from one another, each being defined by what it is not and, thus, revealing their mutually constitutive aspects.

Building on arguments made by Braun, this volume takes the position that the type of Nature tourism that has historically defined spaces such as Jasper National Park "reorders nature through a *visual* logic, not an *ecological* one."[25] In other words, dominant ideologies of National Park Nature have more to do with the ways in which this landscape has been pictured than with environmental actualities, which themselves are subject to cultural interpretations and political influences. In her book *On the Beaten Track: Tourism, Art, and Place,* art historian Lucy Lippard has discussed how park spaces need to be understood as examples of visual culture. "The most famous National Parks," she writes, "have come to resemble television shows or photography books – controlled or static sequences of scenery and sights."[26] As a key aspect of this transformation, the representation of National Park Nature through photography sets up a dichotomous relationship between what is seen and experienced while on holiday and the broader ecological picture of the region. In this way, the environmental actualities of a place can become masked through dominant forms of visual representation.

National Park Nature, then, is a specific way of seeing that has been replicated in large part through photography and, by extension, the intertextual relations that arise when photographs are circulated in the context of tourism. National Park Nature is dependent on both the medium of photography and the tourism industry, and, not coincidentally, all three of these entities can be traced to the same historical phenomenon, the intensification of modernity during the nineteenth century.

TOURIST PHOTOGRAPHY AS VISUAL ECOLOGY

Jasper's position as a national park, and thus a "protected" landscape, came about as a result of dominant cultural ideas regarding Nature and modernity reproduced largely through photographic imagery. In this way, photography has been used to draw boundaries between areas to be "conserved" and the rest of North America.

Of particular interest here are the ways in which national parks became equated with the idea of the environment over the course of the twentieth century as "green" values became increasingly part of mainstream society in North America. One result of this process is that National Park Nature has become a dominant mode of understanding and engaging with nature, even though this is, by definition, a very select perspective. Contemporary understandings of national parks as a means to achieve a sense of ecological balance for the country as a whole are a relatively recent development; the nineteenth-century and early-twentieth-century origins of Canada's national parks had more to do with the promotion of tourism and revenue generation than the preservation of the environment on an intrinsic level.[27] In recent years, however, the establishment of new national parks in Canada is usually celebrated as a victory for the environmental movement. This dominant way of understanding the role of national parks has had the result of obscuring some significant environmental concerns. As David

Suzuki has pointed out, "It's a common misconception that environmental salvation can be had by simply putting dotted lines around tiny areas on a map where humans aren't allowed to run amok."[28] This sentiment is echoed by Parks Canada biologist Kevin Van Tighem, who takes the position that "if Canadians fail to sustain Canada, no amount of protection will sustain our parks."[29] Marc Bekoff, renowned scholar of evolutionary biology and one of the world's leading experts on the emotions of non-human animals, goes so far as to argue that "whenever humans seek to 'manage' nature, creating parks and artificial boundaries, it is always only for the benefit of humans."[30] What these activists stress is that while parks such as Jasper may indeed have a certain level of ecological value, their inherent sense of segregation creates a difficult situation in terms of twenty-first-century environmental concerns. This sense of geographical segregation has resulted, in large part, from the ways in which these types of spaces have been imaged and imagined over the past several decades.

National parks are cultural artifacts, and within their borders National Park Nature is manufactured in both a physical and a psychological sense. As with any other cultural artifact, there are social and symbolic arguments to be made in terms of value and preservation in places such as Jasper National Park. Conceptual problems begin to arise, however, when it is assumed that these culturally created spaces can be sealed off and "saved" in a manner beneficial to broader planetary systems. But as environmental concerns increasingly become part of everyday parlance, the identification of these socially designated spaces as "the environment" (in general) becomes, paradoxically, further solidified.

From politicians and policy makers looking to benefit from a rising environmental awareness among their electorate to concerned citizens trying to reconnect with Nature and "save the planet," Canadian national parks are increasingly being promoted as a means to restore Earth to a state of ecological harmony, while at the same time playing upon long-standing ideologies regarding the position of Nature in discourses of Canadian national identity. To this end, Stéphane Castonguay has argued that, even though most contemporary environmental issues have global implications, it is important to look at the role of nation building and the role of the nation-state in environmental ideologies since, for the most part, federal powers have "created and managed institutions for the exploitation, conservation, and preservation of natural resources."[31]

Even as landscapes such as Jasper National Park are celebrated as unspoiled and untouched, the cumulative environmental effects of building highways, hotels, and recreational amenities in this region continue to add up. These kinds of developments have been known to interrupt migration patterns and result in habitat fragmentation, and the long-term effects of such disruptions are still being discovered. We do know, however, that the movement patterns of large carnivores (e.g., grizzly bears and wolves) have shifted due to increased human presence and activity in certain regions of Jasper National Park.[32] As these carnivores moved farther away from areas dominated by human activity and infrastructure, their prey (notably elk and deer) began to thrive in these areas. Without predators to keep these populations in check, a number of problems began to arise. Concerns over biological diversity, the spread of disease, and the impact that an ever-growing population of ungulates can have on vegetation became the focus of both scientific research and parks management. Further, instances of human-elk confrontations began to reach an unprecedented level, and concerns about property damage and human safety could no longer be ignored. During the 1990s, for example, there were several hundred re-ported instances of humans being chased or injured by elk in Jasper National Park.[33] The strategies for dealing with large numbers of elk populations have ranged from relocating animals deemed to be problem-atic to the establishment of an abattoir, a controversial development that allowed "population management" to be undertaken out of the view of tourists until the facility was shut down in 1970.[34]

The management of garbage and of human waste generated by the throngs of visitors constitutes another serious concern for those overseeing the day-to-day operations of Jasper National Park. Such concerns led to the establishment of the "solar pooper" – a $200,000 restroom facility built on the shore of Maligne Lake.[35] This "total biological system" runs on solar power, and the sewage and waste water from the facility are broken down using anaerobic bacteria, a process that results in "swimming-pool clean" water.[36] The treated water is then used to water the trees in the vicinity. Given that "sewage effluent" has presented prior ecological prob-lems in this landscape, the solar pooper is a significant development in terms of tourist infrastructure in the park.[37]

One of the central questions underlying these kinds of development and management decisions is the ability to maintain "ecological integrity." This phrase is vague and has been interpreted in many different ways by different stakeholders, but the definition of this concept that guides the management strategies of Jasper National Park is that a landscape is con-sidered to have ecological integrity "if all the plants and animals that should be in the park still thrive there, and people use the park and its surroundings in ways that respect the needs of those plants and animals and allow fires, floods, weather and other natural processes to create natural habitat."[38] As the examples discussed above indicate, achieving ecological integrity in space marketed as a tourist destination is an extremely complex undertaking.

Environmental activists often lament the fact that many Canadians are simply not aware of the many environmental threats facing their national parks. As Rick Searle writes, "Tragically, the ecological deterioration of the National Parks is going largely unnoticed by most Canadians. To many eyes, everything appears fine." Searle argues that, in spite of appearances, "Canada's National Parks are dying," largely due to a widespread "domestication of the wild" in these spaces. This has created, Searle insists, "Phantom Parks" – "places that still look beautiful, but where the essential quality of wildness is largely absent."[39] Searle is correct in his conclusion that wildness is missing from Canada's national parks; however, the assumption that this quality can somehow be reobtained is a misleading one that has come about largely through the ways in which these spaces have been depicted. The paradoxical situation is that people generally are not aware of environmental problems in national parks because what they see corresponds with what they have been conditioned to think Nature should look like. Nature looks this way, however, because this is how dominant cultural forces have decided it should look. Further, as I discuss throughout this book, very little about these spaces can be said to be free from human intervention.

This is not to discount the passionate pleas made by committed environmentalists such as Searle; indeed, this landscape is being changed at a rapid rate in ways that many would agree are not socially or environmentally responsible. However, this dynamic cannot be structured in a humans versus nature framework because it would oversimplify the situation to a point at which sustainable solutions cannot be found. As Searle and others have argued, Canada's national parks are indeed at an ecological crossroads. Solutions such as teaching people to "genuinely love the wild," however, run the risk of replicating the situation that brought us to this point in the first place. Parks are as domesticated and as human manipulated as the rest of the Canadian landscape; they only *appear* to be wild to a public that has been conditioned to equate National Park Nature with unmediated nature. Searle argues that a change in "heart and mind" regarding Canada's national parks is required; what I am arguing in this book is that this shift of perception needs to begin with a shift in representation.[40]

NATURE AND NATION

The history of Canada's national parks is characterized by the association between scenery and state, a connection that has, in essence, legitimized the designation and development of park space under the guise of nation building. Cultural constructions of Canadian identity have hinged on wilderness ideals, including those perpetuated by Group of Seven imagery and Margaret Atwood novels. In recent years, this dynamic has been further complicated by the mainstreaming of environmental values; there is little doubt that the rhetoric of environmental stewardship has made inroads in the consciousness – if not always in the actions – of Canadians from coast to coast, as evidenced by social shifts such as the implementation of curbside recycling programs and the introduction of environmentally friendly products in grocery stores. In this context, the long-standing link between Nature and nation in Canada has necessarily been recontextualized.

As debates over the Kyoto Accord, "mad cow disease," and clear-cut logging began to reach the nightly news in recent years, many Canadian public figures and policy makers attempted to appear sensitive to environmental issues. This sense of environmental stewardship has also been played out on a global stage, in no small part through the promotion of the Canadian national park system. It was no accident, for instance, that former prime minister Jean Chrétien's announcement that his government was committed to funding and developing ten new Canadian national parks took place during the 2002 World Summit on Sustainable Development in Johannesburg, South Africa.[41] In his announcement, Chrétien stated that "Canada is blessed with exceptional natural treasures ... We owe it to Canadians, and to the world, to be wise stewards of these lands and waters."[42] Following this announcement, however, leaders of the environmental movement in Canada were cautiously optimistic about what this plan meant for the national park system as a whole. For instance, Jim Fulton of the David Suzuki Society applauded the funding announcement but drew attention to the needs of the currently existing parks: "I tip my hat to him, but an awful lot of it is 'buns.' An awful lot of us who know the national park system – and particularly the national park system that still needs to be done – are asking, 'Where's the beef?'"[43] This point was made previously by other advocates for the national park system who pointed to a lack of funds to maintain existing sites managed by Parks Canada.[44]

This idea of national parks as spaces of ecological purity and sources of national environmental pride relates to the nostalgic search for an authentic, unspoiled land that has been a defining characteristic of tourism in this region. Photography has played an important part both in this search, which is often enacted in photographs that tourists take on their vacations, and in the perpetuation of the myth that the object of this search – an Edenic, unspoiled landscape – exists, as is suggested by photographs that appear in brochures and advertisements for these destinations. Within this framework, representational strategies have set Jasper National Park up as "a landscape of mourning," to use Braun's terminology. As Braun points out, "Paradoxically, it is in the continuous *failure* to locate the not yet destroyed that we sustain our sense of ourselves as modern, for it provides the very evidence of modernity's destructive force (look, it's already happened here!) and leads to additional rounds of nostalgic yearnings."[45] The location of spaces such as Jasper in this cycle of "nostalgic yearning" has resulted in specific ways of seeing and engaging with nature.

Many environmental educators and activists have argued that the federal designation of landscapes as national parks is environmentally beneficial for several reasons, not the least of which is that industrial development is stopped or at least restricted.[46] Canadian national parks do give people an opportunity to interact with and learn about nature through direct experience, something that many see as essential for establishing a sense of environmental stewardship. Further, many scientists claim that parks act as "natural laboratories," allowing the concentrated study of ecosystems, species interaction, geology, and anthropology.[47] These are significant points, and there is indeed environmental value in the establishment and maintenance of a park system. However, as Suzuki and Taylor note, this is "only the start of conservation."[48]

Canadian national parks face many of the same stresses as other regions of the Canadian landscape, stresses that are masked through the rhetoric of pristine wilderness so dominant in National Park Nature. Environmental concerns such as pollution, habitat fragmentation, and competition among native and introduced species of plants and animals affect the parks as much as they do areas outside park boundaries, and, as such, representations of these landscapes as uninfluenced by human activity, wild, and environmentally pristine are at best well-intentioned visual myths. For instance, aquatic ecosystems in Jasper National Park have been significantly altered by human activity during the twentieth century and into the twenty-first century, and research conducted by Parks Canada has determined that a significant proportion of fish species – four of eighteen – in this landscape are non-native.[49] The biodiversity of plant species has also been affected by human presence in the landscape. As a result of fire suppression policies throughout the twentieth century, there has been a change in the plants that dominate this landscape. As the recent Jasper National Park management plan acknowledges, montane grasslands in this region have shrunk considerably, and there is a "decline in biodiversity, specifically in aspen, open conifer, riparian willow, and young pine stands."[50]

Moreover, as sociologist John Urry has argued, preserving a particular area for its "special environmental quality" often has the effect of drawing large crowds to the region, a process that creates a new set of environmental concerns. As Urry writes, "To designate somewhere as a national park is to generate a kind of magnet, sucking in potential visitors who otherwise might visit many different places."[51] The concentration of millions of visitors each year to Canada's national parks virtually ensures that the pristine and untouched qualities for which they are so often celebrated will not be found.

In the following discussion, I explore how diverse groups such as government agencies, tourism operators, and environmental activists have drawn on and promoted this mythology of pristine National Park Nature through visual means over the course of Jasper's history. The repetition of these images and ideologies has constructed the sense of authenticity that shapes tourist encounters and expectations in Jasper National Park. Visual technologies have set up specific ideas of what Nature means in a Canadian context; as Timothy Luke argues, the "green gaze" of landscape photography "becomes the normalizing framework for imagining what Nature really is."[52] This has often masked the results of human activity within the park and does not address fundamental questions regarding consumption and human activity outside national park borders. Moreover, this point of view does not easily accommodate introspective questions regarding the status quo values that have created the cultural demand for these spaces.

One of the key arguments informing my discussion is the assertion that visual imagery has played a key role in sustaining power relationships between *homo sapiens* and the species with which they share the planet. My research has investigated some of the cultural and corporate powers that have shaped this dynamic and how photography has been a recurring feature in this process. An important assumption underlying the following discussion is that so-called wilderness spaces are never free from human intervention. This discussion, then, builds upon arguments made by writers such as William Cronon and Simon Schama, who have argued that notions of Nature and wilderness are deeply dependent on human values.[53]

This does not mean, however, that they exist *only* in human values, perceptions, and discourses. As Cronon writes, "Yosemite is a real place in nature
– but its venerated status as a sacred landscape and national symbol is very
much a human invention."[54] In this example, and in all other examples of
spaces designated as wilderness, the cultural and the natural merge and
are necessarily intertwined. All human conceptions of and interactions
with what has come to be known simply as Nature are a negotiation between these tensions and as such are continually being contested. It is this
dynamic that is the focus of the following discussion. The central question
of this book is: How has the visual history of Jasper National Park shaped
both the imaginative and the actual landscapes of that region?

An Ecocritical Approach to Visual Culture

There are several ways to approach the intersection of cultural production
and environmental values. From my position as a historian of visual culture,
I am interested in investigating the complex relations between imagery and
ecology. How, for instance, does the way in which a specific landscape is
pictured influence human interactions with and attitudes toward that place?
    Much has been written about environmental, or "earthwork," artists
such as Robert Smithson, Walter de Maria, Michael Heizer, and Andy
Goldsworthy.[55] However, an ecocritical approach to the study of visual
culture is not limited to a certain genre, time period, or select group of
artists. It has a much broader scope and questions the role of a diverse
range of images and cultural practices in shaping how societies interact
with and impact the physical environment. In other words, those concerned
with taking an ecocritical approach to the study of visual culture need to
focus on how imagery has complicated, constructed, and sustained relationships between humans and their environments in a variety of contexts,
geographical locales, and historical periods.[56] In addition, the environmental impacts of systems of image production and distribution must be
taken into account. The consumption of images is linked to the consumption of landscapes and natural resources in a number of complex ways,
and these relationships and connections will inform the direction of
ecocritical studies of visual culture in the coming years.
    An ecocritical approach to visual culture is an interdisciplinary under-
taking. My research is informed by a number of different scholarly traditions, but two academic fields shape the following discussion: visual
culture and environmental studies. Put simply, visual culture studies are

concerned with imagery, and environmental studies focus on the physical environment of Earth and how human societies interact with it. These
two elements come together in the following discussion to form a new
object of inquiry. The chapters that follow investigate the production of
environmental knowledge by considering how images shape understandings of and interactions with nature. Here, as W.J.T. Mitchell has argued,
"the point is to let the terms interrogate each other, to negotiate the
boundaries between them"[57] to understand how the production of environmental knowledge through visual means is dependent on both
dominant understandings of the environment and dominant pictorial
conventions.

PHOTOGRAPHY AND THE ENVIRONMENT

The role of photography in shaping dominant ecological ideologies and
environmental knowledge is a central focus in this book, for, as Joan
Schwartz and James Ryan have noted, "from daguerreotypes to digital
images, from picture postcards to magazine illustrations, photographic
images have been an integral part of our engagement with the physical
and human world."[58] From the earliest days of photography, the camera
was used to make landscape images, and this process remains deeply in-
grained in representational practices.

Australian scholar Tim Bonyhady has charted something of photography's always ambiguous relationship with the conservation movement.
In his view, many well-known nineteenth-century landscape photographers actively altered elements of the physical environment in order to obtain
a photographic image that corresponded to what scenic views were expected
to look like.[59] Well-known photographers such as Carleton Watkins and
Eadweard Muybridge routinely chopped down trees, rearranged tree
stumps, boulders, and other such "scenic elements," and "replanted"
vegetation in foreground areas that were found to be lacking elements of
visual interest.[60] In this respect, photographic images further perpetuated
cultural notions of how Nature was supposed to appear. The ideals of
National Park Nature that linger into the twenty-first century owe much
to these processes.

In his recent publication *Natural Visions: The Power of Images in American Environmental Reform,* Finis Dunaway argues that the environmental movement gained momentum in the United States not only
because of changes in legislation but also because of the role of visual

culture. As Dunaway argues, "The history of environmental reforms is more than the passage of a series of laws; it is also the story of images representing and defining the natural world, of the camera shaping politics and public attitudes."[61] Photography, in particular, has played an instrumental role in how North Americans think about and interact with the physical environment.

Since the nineteenth century, photographs of culturally specific landscapes, wilderness areas, and exotic-looking flora and fauna have been found in innumerable contexts in our day-to-day lives. Although the use of this type of imagery has a long history, it is only in recent years that a handful of scholars, among them Bonyhady and Dunaway, have begun to analyze the cultural history of Nature photography from an ecocritical perspective. An impressive body of critical scholarship has convincingly unravelled the myth of photography's objectivity with regard to the complex ways in which the medium has been used to reinforce hierarchies of gender, class, and race; however, ecocritical analysis of photographic imagery remains a developing category of scholarly inquiry.[62]

It is my contention that photographic imagery, in particular, is directly related to the conditions of the physical environment, precisely because of its ever-persistent ability to convince people that it records the truth. As Bonyhady has demonstrated, however, these images often obscure the conditions of their production. Photographic images play a significant role in the perpetuation of dominant values when it comes to ideas about Nature and the environment. This aspect of photography, coupled with the "naturalization" of cultural constructions such as National Park Nature, have resulted in the double layer of masking that is my focus here.

Photography and the Environmental Movement

The 1960s and 1970s saw the emergence of environmentalism as a widespread social movement. During these decades, environmental issues were brought forcefully to public attention through the publication of influential books, such as Rachel Carson's *Silent Spring* and Paul Ehrlich's *The Population Bomb*, as well as through events such as the "energy crisis" of 1973 and the first Earth Day, held on 22 April 1970. The relationship between photography and the environmental movement has revolved around use of the camera as a form of eyewitness. From photographs exposing perceived environmental atrocities and injustices to use of the camera in attempts to illustrate the intrinsic value of Nature and, thus, its need for protection and preservation, photography has been a dominant weapon in the arsenal of environmental activists for the past several decades. Campaigns such as the now famous Preserve and Protect calendar, which featured women from British Columbia's Salt Spring Island posing nude in the landscape they sought to protect from logging, have become increasingly sophisticated in their use of photography as a means to gain support for environmental causes.[63]

Perhaps one of the most famous photographs associated with the environmental movement is the so-called whole Earth image – a photograph taken of Earth from space in 1972 during the Apollo 17 mission. As Denis Cosgrove notes, this photograph – officially titled AS17-148-22727 by NASA – is "a favored icon for environmental and human-rights campaigners and those challenging Western humanism's long-held assumption of superiority in a hierarchy of life."[64] Although this image continues to be celebrated by environmental groups as demonstrating both the fragility of nature and the interconnectedness of all life systems on Earth, some cultural analysts have argued that this photograph has also perpetuated unsustainable environmental messages. Yaakov Jerome Garb argues, for instance, that it has encouraged a sense of psychological distance in landscape imagery that has perpetuated the notion that humans are separate from Nature instead of an integral part of the global ecosystem.[65]

During the 1970s, activist groups began to recognize how public opinion could be shaped through exposure to photographic and filmic imagery.[66] Photography quickly became an integral part of "visual lobbying" by environmental groups.[67] Greenpeace, for instance, used the camera to create "mindbombs" – shocking film and still footage of environmental exploitation – in the hopes of angering people into action and bolstering support for their various environmental campaigns.[68]

This type of approach has also been adopted by individual photographers who have attempted to use their photography as a means of making visible the ways in which human activity alters the global landscape. W. Eugene Smith's 1972 photographs exposing the environmental damage and human suffering resulting from widespread industrial-related mercury poisoning in Minamata, Japan, are a well-known example of this practice. More recently, photographers such as David T. Hanson, Peter Goin, and Edward Burtynsky have attempted to reframe understandings of the relationships between human society and the physical world through their photographic practices. These photographers use their cameras in ways that ask viewers to consider the impacts that human activities have had on the physical environment and, in doing so, disrupt a particular way of seeing that has become deeply entrenched in dominant ideologies of Nature.

A more familiar form of Nature photography follows in the tradition of Ansel Adam's work with the Sierra Club in the United States and uses photography to present views of Nature as Edenic and unspoiled. As Deborah Bright notes, the work of Edward Weston, Eliot Porter, and Adams in the early decades of the twentieth century typified a landscape aesthetic "premised on an identification between a mythical Eden and the American landscape."[69] These photographers – and, by extension, the conservation movements of which they were a part – were confident that such photographs would be effective in persuading anyone who saw them "of the inherent worthiness of wilderness preservation."[70] Not surprisingly, North American national parks were photographed with this goal in mind. In both 1946 and 1948, for instance, Adams photographed the American national parks in the hope that the resulting images would "restore a lost experience of nature that had become corrupted by the postwar burgeoning of family tourism."[71] Although the majority of his photographs focus on American monuments and landscapes, examples of photographs taken in Canada exist; in 1928, several years prior to embarking on his American national parks project, Adams photographed the mountains of Jasper National Park.

At times, as in the case of Adams, the work of these photographers is elevated to the status of fine art and is found hanging on the walls of art galleries or reproduced within the pages of art history textbooks. However, this type of image is reproduced and circulated in a wide variety of forums, thus shaping and framing the ways in which dominant understandings of nature are manufactured in a number of different contexts. Photographs by Adams, in particular, currently occupy a place within the realms of both fine art and popular culture, having been frequently reproduced on greeting cards, decorative posters, and wall calendars.

As Cosgrove notes, "The making, circulation, and consumption of pictorial images cannot be divorced from an embodied engagement with the world."[72] In other words, images of nature are always already bound up in political, social, cultural, and environmental processes. The job of the ecocritically minded historian of visual culture is to continue to unravel the ways in which these dynamics shape and inform one another. In the case of photography, this becomes a particularly urgent task because of the ways in which camera-based images continue to be pressed into service as pictorial evidence of "what really happened" or as a way to demonstrate what something "really looked like" even though the very act of using imagery in this way necessarily selects certain points of view over others.[73]

TOURIST PHOTOGRAPHY IN JASPER NATIONAL PARK

As is the case with the environmental movement, photographic images used in tourism frame nature and non-human animals in culturally specific ways. Photographic representations of Jasper National Park can be understood as indicators of deeply entrenched, dominant cultural values regarding Nature and the commodification of so-called wilderness spaces. Specifically, tourist photography in the Canadian Rocky Mountains has helped create and sustain the belief that destinations such as Banff and Jasper National Parks are pristine wilderness areas where one can enjoy a fun-filled vacation complete with luxury accommodations and a wide array of recreational pursuits set against a backdrop of spectacular scenery and adorable animals. This set of ideals informs the production of a manufactured wilderness experience that is rarely questioned.

In the years since Jasper Forest Park was first established, there have been many social, political, cultural, and environmental changes in North America, but for the most part the representations of this landscape have changed very little. Amid far-reaching phenomena such as the world wars, the Great Depression, and the rise of 1960s counter-culture, the landscape of Jasper National Park continued to be depicted as a safe and tranquil place, one that represented the antithesis of social and political change and in which Nature existed as a timeless entity. Within the park itself, changes in management, boundaries, and government policies have done little to unsettle the ideals of National Park Nature that continue to define this landscape for so many. Even as roads, ski lifts, and hotels were constructed, these dominant ideals remained firmly entrenched. Research conducted by botanists, biologists, and geologists continues to add to our knowledge of nature and non-human animals, and this research, in turn, often shapes changes in national park legislation. Yet in the midst of all these changes, there is a sense of continuity in how this landscape is imagined. For instance, in 1981 the National Historic Parks Wildlife and Domestic Animals Regulations became part of the legislation governing Canadian national parks. With the introduction of these regulations, it became illegal to "touch or feed wildlife in a Park or entice wildlife to approach by holding out food-stuffs or bait of any kind."[74] Thus, a once popular activity became outlawed, and the feeding of wildlife in Jasper

National Park today is both illegal and a social taboo. However, while the specific behaviour has been modified, the cultural ideals that drove that behaviour remain intact. In other words, the practice of feeding wildlife in the park was not driven from a sense that the animals were particularly hungry. Rather, this behaviour stemmed from the desire to experience a direct connection with the megafauna that have become so symbolic of National Park Nature. This desire did not vanish with the introduction of the 1981 National Historic Parks Wildlife and Domestic Animals Regulations. As anyone who has visited the Rocky Mountain national parks in recent years knows, a bear or elk along the side of the road virtually ensures a line-up of parked cars full of tourists hoping to get a closer look, a snapshot, or video footage of the encounter. Paul Kopas's recent study of national parks policies in Canada underscores the shifts that have taken place with respect to management and legislation of these spaces, for "the meanings of parks are not static but varied and complex."[75] Yet the patterns of representation that have come to visually define landscapes such as Jasper National Park have remained relatively constant throughout the twentieth century and into the twenty-first century, and these sets of images, in turn, continue to inform expectations of and experiences for visitors to this region.

Tourist photography has been a key feature in the formation of what we now know as Jasper National Park and draws on accepted images and dominant ideas of Nature in an attempt to frame the tourist experience in a way that is both culturally specific and financially lucrative for those with a stake in the tourism industry of the region. Photographically illustrated publications have become one of the most common means of "manufacturing nature." Potential visitors have been enticed by images of mountains, lakes, rivers, and forests and are encouraged to visit "Canada's Playground," "See Alberta First," and take "A Real Vacation" in the heart of the Canadian Rockies (see Figure 1).[76] In 1944, for instance, the *Traveller's Digest* used photography to illustrate "Pleasurable Places in the Wide Open Spaces," while other publications promised "A Vacationtime Superb" in which travellers could see firsthand the geographical features and wildlife pictured in the brochure (see Figures 2 and 3).[77] The covers of these three brochures prominently feature a photograph of a car winding its way through the mountain landscape and, as such, point to just how crucial cultural inventions and technologies are to dominant understandings of Nature. In each example, however, there are only one or two cars on the road, a not-so-subtle suggestion that this is still a landscape predominantly unchanged by these very inventions and technologies.

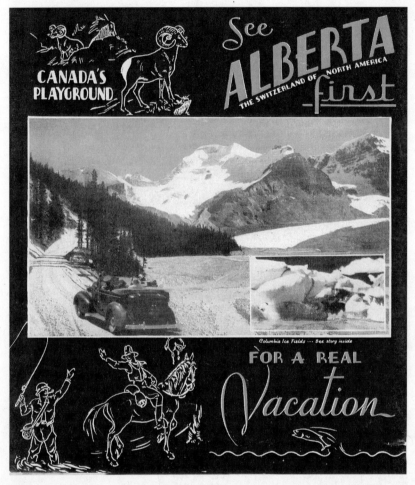

FIGURE I   Cover of a 1938 tourist brochure enticing visitors to vacation in Alberta. *Alberta Provincial Tourist and Publicity Bureau, See Alberta First, 1938. Jasper-Yellowhead Museum and Archives, Accn#994.45.1.1, Doris Kensit Fonds.*

As Jasper's tourist infrastructure became increasingly developed, these publications often juxtaposed images of wilderness scenes with photographs of modern conveniences such as luxury accommodations and facilities for automobiles available in the park. Through the use of these types of framing devices, this particular section of the Canadian Rocky Mountains was transformed into a cultural landscape, even though that transformation was entirely dependent on the process of transformation itself being

FIGURE 2 Cover of a 1944 tourist brochure. The Traveller's Digest, Pleasurable Places in the Wide Open Spaces, *1944. Jasper-Yellowhead Museum and Archives, Accn#84.161.72, Jasper-Yellowhead Museum and Archives Book.*

Icefield Peaks from a Highway Lookout

FIGURE 3   Cover of an early tourist brochure for Jasper National Park. Jasper in June: A Vacationtime Superb in the Canadian Rockies, *n.d. Jasper-Yellowhead Museum and Archives, Accn#2005.44.13a, Jasper National Park Travel Brochure and Memorabilia Collection.*

masked. To put it another way, for the wilderness industry of Jasper National Park to succeed, it required the illusion that these were not cultural landscapes but natural spaces unspoiled by human intervention. Tourist photography of Jasper National Park has continually offered up scenes of seemingly pristine mountain landscapes that at once encouraged travel to Canada's mountain parks and served to spark campaigns focused on the preservation of these landscapes from further human encroachment. Developments such as the Jasper Park Lodge and the Marmot Basin ski resort, and the establishment of fish hatcheries in the park, were unproblematically factored into this equation because these amenities and facilities were understood as complements to the wilderness experience and therefore essential parts of National Park Nature. Photography has been an integral part of this process and, as such, has played a key role in this transformation of "land into landscape."[78] As Steven Hoelscher has noted, in the context of tourist spaces, "nature's scenic transformation was succinctly accomplished by photography – a superb vehicle of cultural mythology."[79]

From the early days of Jasper National Park, photographic images have been used in advertisements, postcards, and other assorted promotional materials. In this way, commercially produced images of wilderness destinations such as Jasper can be considered part of what historian Tina Loo has termed "commodity environmentalism" or "knowledge about the natural world circulated by mass-marketed products."[80] Tourists, too, have been encouraged to record their experiences in the park photographically. As a 1948 publication entitled *Photographing the Canadian Rockies* points out, "Most tourists are photographers, and vice versa, but all who are confronted with the magnificence and splendour of the Canadian Rockies will wish to take back with them vivid memories of the scenic grandeur they have beheld."[81] As tourist photographs are placed in albums, framed, and shared with friends, the process of commodification continues.

Photography has become so deeply entrenched in the tourist experience that it has been described as "one of the most usual things to do while on vacation."[82] John Urry argues that photography "gives shape to the very processes of travel so that one's journey consists of being taken from one 'good view' to capture on film to another good view. It has also helped to construct a twentieth-century sense of what is appropriately aesthetic and what is not worth 'sightseeing'; excluding as much as it includes."[83] The "good views" that Urry refers to are shaped, in large part, by scenes presented to visitors and potential visitors in publications and souvenir items produced by the tourism industry. Tourism in Jasper National Park, like many similar destinations in North America, is dependent on the production and sale of specific types of imagery, a significant component of what may be conceived of as a "wilderness industry." Although the idea of such an industry runs counter to values traditionally associated with these types of spaces, I characterize Jasper National Park in this way because, like other industries, a specific product – in this case the wilderness experience – is assembled, marketed, and sold. As is the case in other industries, the use of visual material plays an important role in this process.

The success of the wilderness industry depends on the level of perceived authenticity that a tourist experiences when visiting locales such as Jasper. As Christopher Steiner has argued, in the context of tourism this sense of authenticity is created through repetition: "Tourists are not looking for the new but for the obvious and the familiar."[84] Certain types of images have come to be associated with the socially defined spaces of national parks in North America and have been repeated in various media over the past several decades. For instance, in her discussion on the representation of Canada in *National Geographic* magazine, Sylvie Beaudreau points out that the Rocky Mountains, "it seems, [are] Canada at its eternal best, and the images found in the 1960s were repeated almost exactly in the 1990s[,] suggesting their enduring appeal to a worldwide audience."[85] This "iconographic redundancy" plays a key role in defining what constitutes an authentic experience for the thousands of people who visit the region each year.[86]

Repetition of specific iconography and notions of authenticity in tourist discourse have ensured that Jasper National Park continues to be conceptualized as a pristine wilderness playground. Signifiers of regional specificity become subsumed in a national mythology through representational strategies that have changed very little over the past century. The continued appropriation of the regional landscape in these contexts has served to construct and sustain the notion that this is a land devoid of environmental tensions. Explorations of negotiations between various groups of human actors, as well as inter-species relationships, in a consideration of this landscape on a local level, however, reveal a much different story. That these tensions are minimized and most often completely disregarded in dominant representations of Jasper speaks volumes about the highly constructed and select view of the region that characterizes National Park Nature.

Representations of an untouched wilderness, for example, disregard human presence in this region prior to 1907, the year Jasper Forest Park was established. Research into how Aboriginal cultures used this land is ongoing, but the evidence collected so far suggests that the area we now know as Jasper National Park was not traditionally a location in which large permanent settlements were established, especially when compared with the archaeological evidence found in other nearby regions.[87] However, in 1909 those Aboriginal families who did settle on the lands that would eventually be part of the park found themselves suddenly characterized as squatters and were subsequently evicted from their homes.[88] These evictions paved the way for a mythology of untouched wilderness that could be conveniently marketed and sold. Although themes of Aboriginality are occasionally evoked in the promotion and marketing of Jasper National Park (see, for instance, Figures 8 and 12), this has not been done to the same extent as in neighbouring Banff National Park, where events such as Indian Days remain an important part of the tourist experience. This erasure of Aboriginal presence and history from the dominant narrative of Jasper National Park was acknowledged by Parks Canada in its 2008 *Jasper National Park of Canada: State of the Park Report*. The document acknowledged that "Aboriginal perspectives are not well represented in the current management plan and decision-making processes; opportunities to learn about and experience Aboriginal culture are not well represented in the suite of park visitor experiences."[89] In response to this situation, the Council of Elders of the Descendents of Jasper (formed in 2004) and an Aboriginal Forum (formed in 2006) were established to look at ways to ensure more Aboriginal involvement in the park and better recognition of the Métis history in this region.[90] In the 2010 management plan for Jasper National Park, Parks Canada stated that "it is committed to building strong and mutually beneficial working relationships with Aboriginal people" and that "the perspectives, cultural ties, and stories of Aboriginal people are an important part of the park's historic fabric and its future."[91]

The Rocky Mountains have become symbols of Canadian culture, history, and wilderness ideals, and there exists a rich and complex photographic history from which to draw when undertaking an analysis such as this. Collectively, this photographic history has fostered the notion that Nature – in particular Nature found within the borders of national parks – is primarily scenic. This view sees destinations such as Jasper National Park as unspoiled, virgin, and pristine, even in light of recent studies indicating that the ecological integrity of Canada's national parks is "under threat."[92] In fact, concerns about the ecological integrity of the Rocky Mountain national parks have reached the point where UNESCO, the UN branch monitoring World Heritage Sites, has expressed concern about

ongoing development near parks such as Jasper.[93] One of the central goals
of this project, then, is to explore the gulf that exists between how this
landscape has been pictured and some of the environmental factors that
tend to be excluded from the frame.

MANUFACTURING NATIONAL PARK NATURE

Jasper National Park provides an ideal vantage point from which to exam-
ine the issues raised here, though the decision to focus a discussion of the
ecological implications of visual imagery on such a site may seem il-
logical initially. After all, in comparison to urban centres, the environmental problems facing national parks appear minimal. However, it is
precisely there that an investigation into the ways in which imagery and
ecology are intertwined must begin. Wilderness areas such as Jasper National Park are most often defined by what they are perceived not to be,
namely, urban, crowded, polluted, and industrial. The "imaginative geographies" of these seemingly separate realms, however, are necessarily
intertwined and, as such, shape and inform one another.[94] It is no accident
that Jasper National Park was established precisely at the moment Canada
was undergoing a transition toward a predominantly urban nation.[95] As
Richard Tresidder argues, "sacred landscapes" such as Jasper National Park
provide an "apparatus to escape from the very society that has created it."[96]
It is necessary, therefore, to unravel the deeply entrenched cultural and
economic processes that have created a cultural desire for places such as
Jasper National Park in order to arrive at a more complete understanding
of how human society acts on and interacts with nature. This process of
manufacturing a wilderness experience, as this book demonstrates, is intimately linked with the photographic history of the region.

As will become immediately evident, this book does not attempt to
present a linear narrative of the photographic history of Jasper National
Park. Rather, it is a thematic exploration of how National Park Nature is
created and sustained through camera-based imagery of this landscape.
Throughout the following discussion, I explore connections between images and ideologies and consider some of the ways in which the physical
and photographic environments have shaped and informed one another
throughout the history of Jasper National Park. One of the central arguments of this book is that visual imagery plays a significant role in how
we think about and interact with our physical environments; a second yet

equally important concern addresses some of the environmental consequences of tourist photographic practices. A number of questions have
guided my research. In what ways do photographs serve to promote certain
values and conceptions of Nature at the expense of others? How does this
affect tourism, and in turn how does the promotion of tourism through
photographic means affect the ecological health of destinations such as
Jasper National Park? How does photography shape visitor perceptions of
and interactions with such wilderness destinations? In what ways do these
images contribute to cultural constructions of Nature in a broader context,
and what are the ecological implications of these practices? How are shifts
in dominant forms of environmental knowledge registered in tourist
photography of Jasper National Park?

The following chapters draw on established methodological frameworks
and theoretical positions used in other disciplines in an attempt to stimu-
late dialogue about how imagery and ecology are necessarily intercon-
nected. Visual material under consideration in this analysis ranges from
photographically illustrated tourist brochures and postcards to government documents and promotional films produced by institutions such
as Parks Canada and the Canadian Government Motion Picture Bureau.
Photographs accompanying newspaper and magazine articles, as well as
corporate links between the photographic industry and business entities
operating within park borders, are also considered in this project. This
link between imagery, ecology, and industry is fundamental to my study,
and the following discussion explores these connections as they have been
mediated through visual representations of National Park Nature in the
context of Jasper National Park.

The construction of National Park Nature in Jasper has been achieved
through the use of photographic imagery to promote this space as a vacation destination where one can escape to the wilderness and enjoy an
abundance of leisure activities set against a scenic backdrop of forests,
mountains, lakes, streams, and of course the non-human animals who live
there. These three often competing and overlapping themes – wilderness,
recreation, and wildlife – form the central structure of National Park
Nature, and the following discussion considers each in a separate chapter.
In these chapters, I discuss how these ideals have been played out through
familiar forms such as picture postcards, illustrated brochures, and tourist
guidebooks – standard fare for any vacation in the Canadian Rockies.
Rather than simply providing information about what to do, where to
stay, and what to eat, these popular tourist items also shape how visitors

think about and experience nature. National Park Nature is constructed, in part, on the glossy pages of these souvenir items; nature is mediated according to hegemonic values.

In Chapter 2, I focus on images that have promoted the idea of wilderness in Jasper National Park. Wilderness, in this context, refers to a landscape that is aesthetically pleasing and has minimal (if any) overt visual reference to human-designed technologies or structures. Images from Jasper National Park that fit into this category tend to focus on geological features (mountains, bodies of water, towers of ice) and/or scenic vistas. In many of these images, human figures are absent. When humans are present in these wilderness scenes, they are either solitary or in very small groups symbolic of an intimate family unit. The primary exception to these representational patterns relates to the depiction of Aboriginal cultures. Although the visual representation of Aboriginal cultures in tourist imagery of Jasper National Park is nowhere near as dominant as in neighbouring Banff National Park, examples do exist. In these examples, Aboriginal cultures tend to be represented in a generalized and simplified manner, often a single figure or cultural object symbolizing European and Euro-Canadian mythologies about the lives and histories of First Nations peoples (see, e.g., Figures 8 and 12).

In Chapter 3, I focus on images of recreation and leisure in Jasper National Park. The visual culture of this region contains many examples of images showing visitors enjoying activities such as golfing, skiing, canoeing, and fishing. These images are characterized by an overarching sense of harmony as the recreational activities depicted do not disrupt the aesthetic pleasures of the wilderness landscape. Whether it is a round of golf set against the backdrop of snow-peaked mountains, canoes gliding effortlessly along the glassy waters of Lac Beauvert, or the professional landscaping around the swimming pool at Jasper Park Lodge, these images collectively imply that recreational pursuits need not disrupt enjoyment of the wilderness and, in fact, are an important part of experiencing Nature in the park.

Chapter 4 explores some of the dominant ways in which non-human animals have been represented in the context of Jasper National Park. Not surprisingly, the majority of these images have been produced for and consumed by tourists in the park. Representations of bears – perhaps the classic example of megafauna in the Canadian Rockies – dominate the visual culture of this region. In many of these examples, the viewer is confronted with a deliberate and at times jarring juxtaposition of non-human animals with human-built technologies. This chapter explores this representational pattern and discusses how the context in which these images are viewed can shift them from simple souvenir items to visual agents of activism and education. For example, a snapshot depicting a tourist eagerly extending his or her hand to feed non-human animals encountered in the park can easily shift from being a personal visual reminder of a trip to the Rockies to being part of a widespread campaign to stop the illegal practice of feeding wildlife in Canadian national parks (see, e.g., Figure 35). Such examples underscore the fluidity of visual culture and demonstrate the potential of images to disrupt ideals of National Park Nature.

To further underscore the idea of National Park Nature as a way of seeing, Chapter 5 compares this perspective with both "fake nature" and the "museological gaze." The museum has long been regarded as a temple of knowledge, and natural history museums in particular have been a means since the nineteenth century for people to learn about nature. These are spaces revered for their intellectual rigour and educational value. The phenomenon of fake nature theme parks, in contrast, is often derided as cheap entertainment that further separates humans from their natural surroundings. By situating national parks in a discussion bracketed by these two extreme ways of viewing Nature, I aim to unsettle assumptions about all three.

As I was researching this topic, the debate over a proposed mine near Jasper National Park loomed large. The proposal of a natural resource extraction site so near a supposedly protected area has raised concerns over the environmental impact of this industrial endeavour. Concern over what constitutes proper use of the region has often positioned humans against nature in a most simplistic yet deeply troubling way. Indeed, the ideals of National Park Nature are threatened by these types of industrial development, but what has been excluded from these discussions thus far are considerations of the cultural systems and values that shaped this understanding of the landscape in the first place. The social values and human activities that have resulted in the construction of National Park Nature in this location are not addressed; this particular way of relating to this landscape is taken as a given. The adversarial frames used to describe the Cheviot mine debate replicate assumptions that Nature and culture are necessarily separate spheres.[97] As Neil Evernden has argued, when environmental issues are presented in this way, it is unlikely that appropriate solutions can be reached.[98] Part of the process of negotiation over land use will need to consider questions such as: Where did this specific way of understanding this region come from, and why has it remained so dominant?

Who benefits from maintaining National Park Nature as *the* dominant mode of understanding this landscape?

My motivation for undertaking this study was not to present a discussion of the pros and cons of development in or near Jasper National Park. Rather, I am interested in taking a step back and trying to piece together how this dominant cultural understanding of Jasper has been created, specifically through the medium of photography. How has the photographic history of this region served to naturalize complex power dynamics? Like many Canadians, I enjoy and value Jasper National Park. Contrary to popular assumptions, critical analysis of such landscapes should not be equated with systemic condemnation of their simple existence. In discussing Jasper in these terms, I am not seeking to find fault or lay blame. Instead, I am hoping to contribute to developing dialogues surrounding the cultural values that have created this space, the ways in which visual images have participated in this process, and how both, in turn, are situated in relation to twenty-first-century notions of environmental protection. To have meaningful dialogues regarding the future of the park and indeed of ecosystems across Canada, it is crucial to begin to understand how these spaces have been shaped and informed through visual culture.

2

"Jasper Wonderful by Nature": The Wilderness Industry of Jasper National Park

The notion of wilderness is a cultural construct artfully employed by those with corporate and economic interests and underscores the interconnectedness of economic and environmental factors in the Canadian Rockies. Through the widespread circulation of images confirming what wilderness is expected to look like, a cyclic process of production and consumption of National Park Nature occurs in the landscape of the Canadian Rockies.

Wilderness is most often conceived of as a space where humans are not. By extension, such spaces are perceived as landscapes protected from the environmental stresses facing other locations. When this definition is applied to popular tourist destinations, such as North American national parks, contradictions and complexities begin to surface. Jasper National Park is neither an uninhabited space nor a pristine landscape, even though this is how it is often presented in tourist imagery.

The wilderness gaze that characterizes most expectations of and interactions with the landscape of Jasper National Park can be understood as a way of seeing and engaging with a particular landscape that focuses on the perceived "wildness" and "untouched" aesthetic qualities of the region at the expense of all else. The camera has a long history of being used to perpetuate these ideals. There are countless photographs offering views of what a wilderness area is supposed to look like in the Canadian Rocky Mountain parks. These images, however, are the result of careful manipulation undertaken to reflect dominant cultural expectations and corporate investments. Canadian parks historian Leslie Bella noted years ago how the earliest postcards sold in Banff National Park had to be touched up because a large forest fire had occurred a year prior to establishment of that park; the inclusion of green pigment on the surface of the photographic cards, it was hoped, would mask the "unattractive" appearance of the charred tree branches.[1]

In places such as Jasper National Park, wilderness is commodified; a wilderness industry dependent on manufacturing ideals and experiences consistent with what wilderness is thought to look like is a driving force in the production of these culturally defined spaces. As Richard White has argued, in parks such as Jasper, "wilderness is not so much preserved as created."[2] Much effort has been expended by those with a stake in the tourism industry of the Canadian Rockies to ensure that the landscape of Jasper National Park fits within a framework of wilderness aesthetics that has largely been replicated through the circulation of photographic imagery. Wilderness restoration projects in Jasper have kept up the appearance that this is a pristine and untouched space. During the 1970s, Parks Canada staff attempted to restore vegetation to high-traffic areas in the park to mask physical evidence of the thousands of visitors to Jasper each year. The pathways around Athabasca Falls underwent restoration because tourists hiking through the area had caused the elimination of all vegetation except tall trees. Even the trees that remained showed signs of wear and tear; heavy foot traffic had exposed their roots, demonstrating "what 175,000 well-meaning people can do, inadvertently."[3] The replanting project reduced the extent of trampled vegetation, and the area once again seemed to be an untouched wilderness space. Such practices ensure that the physical landscape of the park matches what tourist photography has led visitors to expect.

The process of manufacturing wilderness aesthetics through photography is related to contemporary notions of environmentalism. As sociologist John Urry argues in his groundbreaking book *Consuming Places,* "larger numbers of people seek, in their visual consumption, solitude, privacy, and a personal, semi-spiritual relationship with their environment ... The romantic tourist gaze thus feeds into and supports attempts to protect the environment."[4] Visual consumption of the landscape through the mediating agents of tourism and photography can have environmental benefits. But the relationship between photography, ideals of wilderness, and environmentalism is much more complex than it first appears. The production of wilderness is a highly complex endeavour, and its relationship to the physical environment is far from straightforward.

Within the rhetoric of wilderness, human presence is occasionally acknowledged, in a controlled and limited form. Many of the guidebooks produced by Canadian National Railways (CNR) discuss the "discovery" of Jasper by explorers such as David Thompson and Jasper Hawes. A 1927 souvenir booklet put together by the CNR describes Jasper's early human history: "Great names linger among its mountains and passes, names of those intrepid pathfinders who, with incredible hardship and suffering, hewed the first trails through the chaotic wilderness of the mountains."[5] First Nations peoples are also often presented in these early histories of the region; tales are told of their roles in either helping or hindering explorers and fur traders in what we now know as the Canadian Rocky Mountain parks. The people involved in these stories – the rugged explorer and the "savage tribes" – are presented as being less civilized and close to Nature, and thus their presence in these heroic and historical narratives does little to unsettle tourist perceptions of the wild qualities of this space.[6] Fishing and golfing in the wilderness also go unchallenged for the most part as these recreational activities are framed to perpetuate the notion that they exist in harmony with the ideals of National Park Nature and thus do not disturb dominant wilderness ideologies.

Scenic views have dominated tourist photography throughout the history of Jasper National Park. This type of imagery, with its emphases on landscape, vegetation, and geological formations, has a long association with North American national parks. In these representations, human presence in the landscape invariably exists in harmony with nature. From the early work of photographers such as Charles Horetzky and Mary Schäffer to current advertisements for vacation getaway packages, these dominant ideals of wilderness are firmly embedded in Jasper's photographic history.

Horetzky's nineteenth-century survey photographs of the region focus on the geographical and aesthetic features that would have been of interest to his employer, Canadian Pacific Railway (CPR). In his 1872 photograph "Canadian Pacific Railway Survey at Jasper House with Roche Ronde to the Northwest" (see Figure 4), visual emphasis is placed on the snow-capped peaks in the centre of the composition. The three figures in the foreground, while dwarfed by the mountain landscape, do not appear to be threatened or overwhelmed by it. The inclusion of Jasper House, a site that served as a supply depot for the North West Company in the early decades of the nineteenth century, further underscores the sense of humans as coexisting peacefully with nature.[7] By referencing both the railway and

FIGURE 4   A 1872 photograph of the landscape that would eventually become Jasper National Park. *Charles Horetzky, "Canadian Pacific Railway Survey at Jasper House with Roche Ronde to the Northwest," 15 January 1872. Library and Archives Canada, PA-009173.*

the North West Company, the image suggests the potential for industrial and capital ventures in this landscape. Even though the CPR eventually located its main rail route through the Rockies elsewhere, the elements characteristic of Horetzky's early survey photographs of the region continue to be a dominant aspect of representations of Jasper National Park. The repetition of this photograph in various aspects of the park's visual culture – for instance, on the cover of a 1960 issue of *Jasper Tourist News* – further solidifies this relationship between image and landscape.[8]

Mary Schäffer's 1911 photograph "Mount Athabaska" (see Figure 5) also emphasizes the scenic qualities of the region.[9] The camera positions the viewer at the edge of a glacial vista and visually orders the landscape into a framework familiar to early-twentieth-century viewers of this image.

FIGURE 5   Mary Schäffer's early-twentieth-century photographs of Jasper National Park continue to be popular images of this region. *Mary Schäffer, "Mount Athabaska," 1911. Whyte Museum of the Canadian Rockies, V527/PS-58.*

Three distinct pictorial planes give a sense of depth and dimension to the scene. This sense of aesthetic familiarity is significant, as it tames an un-familiar landscape in ways that would eventually help to foster a successful tourist industry in the region. These early representations of the Jasper landscape continue to influence dominant conceptions of this region. The photographic history of Jasper National Park, then, owes much to long-standing pictorial conventions regarding landscape imagery.

EMPTY LANDSCAPES

Much of the tourist photography produced in Jasper National Park em-phasizes "empty landscapes," scenic views appearing to be devoid of human presence or influence. An undated photographic postcard by G. Morris Taylor entitled "Mt. Edith Cavell from Lac Beauvert, Jasper Park," is typical of this type of image (see Figure 6). The scene is framed by trees and shows a snow-capped mountain reflected in the calm lake. Not a ripple, a canoe, or even a vacationing swimmer disturbs this tranquil scene. The only overt sign of human life is the footpath that runs along the foreground of the image. This type of imagery has played a key role in the perpetuation of what J.G. Nelson has termed a "wilderness ideal" or "a sense of pristine environment largely undisturbed by human actions."[10] As scholars such as Eric Higgs and Ian MacLaren have demonstrated, however, Jasper is very much a "cultured wilderness" and has been shaped by the presence of humans for centuries.[11]

The human history of Jasper National Park dates back several thousand years; archaeological evidence suggests that First Nations peoples in-habited the region at least 12,000 years ago.[12] The first flurry of European and Euro-Canadian interest in the area did not occur until the early nine-teenth century, when the region served as an important route for explor-ers and fur traders heading toward the Pacific coast.[13] In September 1907, the dominion government officially converted a 12,950 square kilometre parcel of land into the Jasper Forest Park of Canada, setting the course for the establishment of one of Canada's most visited tourist destinations. This development was closely linked to the western expansion of the Grand Trunk Railway (now CNR).[14] The development of automobile tourism also had a significant impact on the development of the park. Highways linking Jasper to Edmonton and Banff were established in 1931 and 1940, respectively, and allowed even more visitors to experience the park.[15] These corridors of transportation are a significant part of the human history of

FIGURE 6   An example of a tourist postcard emphasizing an "empty landscape" view of the park. *G. Morris Taylor, "Mt Edith Cavell from Lac Beauvert, Jasper Park," n.d. Collection of the author.*

this region as they have brought more and more tourists to Jasper. It is now estimated that approximately 2 million tourists visit Jasper National Park each year.[16] In November 2009, the *Edmonton Journal* reported that park management would like to see the number of visitors to Jasper increase, a goal that has alarmed many environmentalists in Alberta.[17]

Despite the persistent presence of human activity in this space, images of empty landscapes remain a dominant means of identifying wilderness areas such as Jasper National Park. This type of tourist photography can be seen as part of a broader trend in imagery used to promote vacation destinations in Canada.[18] Certain scenes have been photographed repeatedly since Jasper was first designated as a park in 1907. The type of empty landscape images that dominate the photographic history of Jasper National Park have environmental consequences because they mask human intervention and perpetuate the notion that this is an environmentally pristine landscape when there is much evidence to the contrary. In the 2008 *State of the Park Report* for Jasper, Parks Canada listed a number of areas of "ecological concern" in the park and rated the level of overall ecological integrity as "fair."[19] Most of the areas of highest concern were places where grizzly bear and woodland caribou habitats had been disrupted. Although much of Jasper National Park has "good habitat security" for grizzlies, there are still areas in which this habitat could be improved.[20] The woodland caribou population in the Jasper region is in decline, a concern that is heightened because this species is considered to be "at risk" by the Committee on the Status of Endangered Wildlife in Canada (COSEWIC) and is protected under the Species at Risk Act (SARA).[21] There are also concerns about the prevalence of non-native species in the park and the killing of wildlife by trains and automobiles. To be sure, conservation efforts have addressed and begun to remedy earlier identified areas of concern. The ecological integrity of the aquatic ecosystems in the park is improving thanks in large part to improvements made to sewage treatment facilities.[22] But resource extraction industries operating near park borders have far-reaching ecological effects, and roads built to serve these industries have markedly increased habitat fragmentation in the region.[23]

Further, the use of an empty landscape motif in visual constructions of this space ignores human history and presence in this region. First Nations peoples have been present in the area now known as Jasper National Park for several thousand years, though archaeological evidence suggests that early Aboriginal societies had only sporadic settlement in this region and tended to limit activities in this landscape to "seasonal hunting and gathering."[24] In her history of the "people, places, and events" of Jasper National Park, Cyndi Smith lists a number of First Nations societies that have occupied this area in various capacities, including the Shuswap, Stoney, Iroquois, Sekani, Beaver, Sarcee, Cree, and Métis peoples.[25] Eric Higgs has drawn attention to the difficulty of asserting the exact nature of the relationships between these early societies and the non-human species in the region, but he points to ongoing ethnolinguistic, paleo-ecological, and archaeological studies attempting to piece together this aspect of the region's environmental history.[26] Ongoing research indicates that Aboriginal families – including Iroquois who had come from eastern Canada – began to settle in this region in the late eighteenth century.[27] Eviction of the Métis who had settled in the upper Athabasca Valley occurred just a few years after with the establishment of Jasper Forest Park, and the federal government paid out cash settlements to these families as part of the process of creating wilderness in this space.[28] This was part of a widespread North American movement to transform designated landscapes into wilderness areas for the purposes of tourism and, as such, has played a significant part in the construction of National Park Nature.[29]

In spite of these actions, tourist photography in the Rocky Mountain parks has frequently referenced Canada's indigenous populations by including iconic features such as teepees and totem poles in wilderness landscapes. This dynamic is also played out in the souvenir items for sale in the Rocky Mountain parks. Items such as miniature totem poles, plastic tomahawks, and replica "tom-tom" drums have been sold in tourist shops in this region alongside postcards with this type of imagery.[30] First Nations peoples in the Rocky Mountains did not carve totem poles, and any reference to them in Jasper National Park is, therefore, explicitly designed to appeal to the imaginations and fantasies of tourists (see, e.g., Figure 12).

The ways in which First Nations peoples are represented in the pictorial landscape of Jasper National Park reduce complex cultural histories to visual advertisements for a tourist industry looking to profit from an increasing fascination with wilderness in the early twentieth century. So a teepee echoes the form of the mountain behind it in a colour-tinted postcard postmarked July 1934 (see Figure 7), creating an aesthetically pleasing view that was undoubtedly assembled for tourist consumption. Even though teepees were used by non-Native wilderness guides and explorers during the 1930s, the symbolism of this image appealed to tourist fascination with First Nations peoples. The inscription on the front of the card – "Photo by Courtesy Can. Nat'l Rys" – indicates that this type of scene was actively promoted by those involved with the tourism industry of Jasper National Park. This is very similar to the prominent place the famous Jasper totem pole has held in the marketing and visual promotion of the park (see Figure 12). Brought to the Rockies from northern British Columbia to promote tourism in western Canada and planted outside the rail station in Jasper, this pole became part of a tourist fantasy of the west in which specific details about Aboriginal cultures (including regional variances) were glossed over.

The nineteenth-century encroachment of European settlement in western North America was frequently documented by the camera.[31] Photographic expeditions to document Canada's Native peoples, for instance, were often justified for scientific reasons, and it was not uncommon for anthropologists to accompany survey expeditions on trips to western Canada to ensure that Canada's original inhabitants were studied, documented, and classified in much the same way – and for many of the same reasons – as the surrounding geographical formations.[32] Images of Aboriginal peoples became subsumed in the marketing of certain destinations, particularly in the Canadian and American west. In places such as Jasper and

FIGURE 7   Hand-coloured photographic postcard of Mount Erebus with a teepee in the foreground. *Canadian National Railways, "Mt Erebus, Jasper National Park," c. 1934. Collection of the author.*

Maligne Lake, Jasper National Park, Alberta.

FIGURE 8   This undated postcard shows two figures – one whose head is adorned with a feather – paddling in a canoe on Maligne Lake. *Novelty Manufacturing and Art Company, "Maligne Lake, Jasper National Park, Alberta," n.d. Collection of the author.*

Banff National Parks, this body of imagery was often blended with wilderness scenes as part of National Park Nature. The undated tourist postcard reproduced here as Figure 8 provides a particularly illustrative example of this sentiment. It shows two figures in a canoe paddling away from the viewer on the calm waters of Maligne Lake. The size of the figures in the image makes it difficult to discern specific details of their clothing, but one of the figures appears to be wearing a feather headdress. Inclusion of this aspect can be read as an allusion to the symbolic presence of Native peoples in this landscape, even though the processes that gave rise to this form of representation did much to mask the actual history of Aboriginal cultures in this region.

Pictorial representations of the Canadian Rockies have generally framed Jasper National Park as a pristine wilderness destination, a space offering an escape from the pressures and perceived environmental atrocities of urban existence. This characterization has been played out in large part through tourist photography. The "wish you were here" sentiment of photographic postcards underscores Jasper's position as geographic other; this is a space that is physically and psychologically separated from the everyday and the ordinary through both pictorial and textual devices. A postcard of Maligne Lake mailed during the summer of 1949 illustrates this form of tourist photography (see Figure 9). It features a photograph taken by the Jasper-based photographer Tom H. Johnson and presents a typical soothing scene. The tranquil waters of Maligne Lake, the seemingly undisturbed landscape, and the towering mountain peaks render this landscape the antimodern antithesis of urban-industrial society. The message scrawled on the back of this card, "Having a wonderful time in this most beautiful spot," further emphasizes that this is an extraordinary landscape that differs from what both the sender and the recipient of this card experience on a daily basis. Although most of us do not have mountain vistas in our backyards, in examples like this, word and image work together to set up the region of Jasper National Park as a wilderness landscape that is different and distant from the rest of North America. The sense of separation not only removes tourists from the hustle and bustle of their day-to-day lives but also compartmentalizes Nature into easily digestible segments. In this framework, there is no room for environmental tensions, interspecies discord, or activities that disrupt the fantasy of a peaceful experience in an untouched wilderness.

A recent Travel Alberta promotional photograph entitled "Maligne Lake, Jasper National Park," is typical of this form of visual promotion. In this image, a solitary figure in a red shirt sits on an overturned rowboat balanced on the end of a pier jutting out into the lake. The sky above the lake includes a rainbow arcing over the snow-capped mountains, and the lake itself has only the smallest of ripples in it. This is, in short, a scene of tranquility. Travel Alberta has used this photograph in numerous campaigns advertising Jasper National Park and tourism in Alberta.[33] Even though this stock photograph is the result of a carefully planned professional photo shoot, we are encouraged to believe that the person in the image is just returning from, or about to embark on, a leisurely boating excursion and has taken a moment to contemplate the scenic wonders stretched out before him. This seemingly simple image is, in fact, carefully contrived. It relies on familiar visual codes to replicate a sense of tranquility and solitary meditation that has come to be expected in this landscape. The same ideals were utilized in earlier promotional materials employed by

FIGURE 9 Front and back of a postcard sent in the 1940s from Jasper National Park. Here Maligne Lake is described as a "most beautiful spot," a sentiment that many visitors would still agree with today. This type of tranquil scene quickly became a standard aesthetic for postcards set in the Canadian Rockies. *Tom H. Johnston, "Maligne Lake, Jasper National Park, Canada," 1949. Collection of the author.*

Canadian National Railways. A 1938 advertisement, for instance, relies on textual and visual cues to entice visitors to "enjoy a vacation of a lifetime at Jasper National Park."[34] The ad, which describes Jasper as the "gem of the Canadian Rockies," also features a photograph in which visitors to the park (this time in an automobile) are free to contemplate the scenic wonders of the landscape without the complications of other tourists.[35]

How these types of images and advertisements are interpreted has much to do with pre-existing expectations of place. In the foregoing examples, the absence of other visitors is significant and indicates that this is a landscape primarily defined by ideologies of wilderness. This dominant understanding is a result of the "perceptual carrying capacity" of this particular tourist destination.[36] The Travel Alberta promotional image discussed above would be read very differently if the waterfront pier were chock-a-block with vacationing merrymakers. As Urry notes, "Perceptual capacity is immensely variable and depends upon particular conceptions of nature and of the circumstances in which people expect to gaze upon it."[37] He emphasizes the point by discussing how popular seaside resorts such as Brighton Beach, Blackpool, and Coney Island would "look strange if they were empty."[38] Jasper National Park, on the other hand, would appear strange to most people's sensibilities if it appeared crowded.

Perceptions of tourist spaces are invariably coloured by socio-economic issues. Today the Rocky Mountain national parks attract a range of visitors to both high-end spa-type resorts and hostels catering to backpackers. Since the rise of automobile tourism in places such as Banff and Jasper, opportunities for affordable holidaying have sprung up.[39] Reflecting on the 2009 decision to freeze National Park fees for two years, federal environment minister Jim Prentice said, "In this time of global economic recession, our government is doing what it can to encourage Canadians to enjoy these places ... For many families, every dollar counts."[40] However, Canadian national parks have not always been affordable destinations. In the early days of Banff National Park, guests arrived by train for lengthy stays in the luxurious Banff Springs Hotel, and corporate entities such as the Canadian Pacific Railway courted wealthy travellers through their early advertising campaigns. Places such as Coney Island and Brighton Beach, in contrast, are largely remembered for their histories as working-class holiday destinations, even though current conditions have shaped these famed landscapes in much different ways than they often exist in the collective cultural imagination.[41]

In essence, photographs of wilderness scenes in Jasper National Park have masked corporate and cultural biases present in these representations and have normalized a particular way of visually ordering the landscape. The sophistication of this wilderness industry has resulted in specific ideas of Nature and nation promoted in a seamless and environmentally harmonious manner through the authority of the camera lens. As Neil Evernden has argued, these types of representations lead to a myth of Nature as an object unmediated by human intervention. This is significant. As Evernden states, "When we are able to remove the impression of human agency from our description of the world and insinuate a natural reality, we will appear to be dealing with indisputable facts."[42] These "indisputable facts" have significant implications for how this landscape is conceived of and treated.

That those with corporate and cultural interests in the Canadian Rocky Mountain parks actively promoted the region through visual material is not a revelation.[43] However, I am interested in exploring the longevity of representational codes and conventions used in this type of imagery, in particular after the rise of the popular environmental movement of the 1970s. Further, as the rest of this chapter reveals, I am interested in relationships among this body of imagery, the ways in which these representations are produced, circulated, and consumed, and the ecological integrity of the region. What, in other words, can be said of the discrepancies that exist between how wilderness areas such as Jasper National Park are pictured and the actual environmental conditions of the region?

AN UNTOUCHED NORTHERN WILDERNESS?

A recent advertising campaign proclaims "Jasper Wonderful by Nature" (see Figure 10). This tagline has been included in advertisements for park amenities such as ski lodges, restaurants, and hotels. Full-page ads with this heading, accompanied by colour photographs and descriptive text celebrating the "untouched northern wilderness" of the park, offered up a much different view of Jasper than that presented by environmental activists and advocacy groups. Ian Urquhart's introduction to a collection of writings on environmental concerns facing the Rocky Mountain region of Alberta is typical in contrasting the portrayal of this space as pristine with a discussion of increased human development in the region. As Urquhart notes, "Our century-long search for economic growth in Alberta has left very few corners of these ecosystems untouched by development."[44] A recent "report card" issued by the Jasper Environmental Association (JEA), a non-profit society that acts as an "independent environmental

FIGURE 10   Advertisement for Jasper National Park from the winter 2002-3 issue of *Jasper Visitor's Choice* magazine. *Edi Klopfenstein, Stan Sakic, and* Visitor's Choice Magazine, *"Jasper Wonderful by Nature,"* 2002.

monitor in Jasper National Park," commended Parks Canada on a number of initiatives, including banning motorboats on Pyramid Lake and reducing public access to certain areas of the park at specific times of the year in order to minimize disturbance to wildlife activities (e.g., protecting elk during calving season). But it also expressed concern about developments such as the installation of a snow-making system at Marmot Basin and the introduction of guided mountain biking in the park, developments that, the JEA fears, will lead to more visitors to the region and increase the stress on its natural environment.[45]

The 2002-3 *Jasper Visitor's Guide* devotes no fewer than four glossy, full-page spreads to the "Jasper Wonderful by Nature" campaign; the pictures and text combine to give the impression that this is indeed unspoiled wilderness that faces no environmental stresses whatsoever. Photographs of the world-famous Spirit Island in Maligne Lake, picturesque waterfalls, and majestic mammals invite the viewer to "step back in time" and explore the "wonder of nature" in Jasper National Park. The advertisements boast that "Jasper's exquisite natural beauty is a testament to the power of the sublime over encroaching human settlement. Even the millions of visitors passing through Jasper's gates each year leave little impact on the glimmering glaciers, bountiful wildlife, serene lakes, crashing waterfalls, cavernous canyons, lush forest, and overwhelming rugged mountains."[46]

As demonstrated by a 1927 promotional piece attempting to attract American tourists to Jasper National Park, advertisements for tourist destinations in the Canadian Rockies have long played on ideas of unspoiled beauty: "See the towering snow-capped peaks, ghost-like glaciers, yawning canyons, rumbling rivers and primeval forests of this mountain wonderland," the ad proclaims. "Visit this vacation paradise" (see Figure 11).[47] Douglas Nord's study of the imagery used to advertise Canadian tourist destinations to potential travellers from the United States explains how the promotion of Canada in this context plays on existing stereotypes. His study demonstrates that, "from the tourism promoter's perspective, it is the physical qualities and resources of the land that are central to the portrait of the Canadian Nation."[48] Nord argues that such promotion presents a skewed version of Canada, one that has continually overemphasized wilderness and rural areas. "What is clearly missing from this type of presentation of Canada," he writes, "is any substantial effort to discuss the urban and industrial character of the country."[49] Although this is no doubt a valid concern, the question I find most significant is this: What are the ecological consequences of this "artfully packaged" view of Canada?[50]

FIGURE II   A 1927 advertisement encouraging tourists to "Vacation at Jasper National Park." *Canadian National Railways, "Choose a Canadian National Vacation This Year," April 1927. Advertisement in* World's Work Magazine. *Collection of the author.*

As the JEA raises concerns about wildlife mortality and increased development in Jasper National Park, the rhetoric of tourist literature promoting the region continues to draw on notions of unspoiled wilderness lands. The wilderness ideal has, in fact, become so deeply entrenched in the way that the park is pictured that this frame of reference has been naturalized, making it difficult to conceive of the region as anything but a scenic paradise. A recent advertising brochure for resort accommodations in Jasper pairs photographs of the mountain landscape with bold text encouraging visitors to "relax in unspoiled beauty." The pamphlet goes on to proclaim that Jasper is "a place that stirs the soul and quenches a natural thirst for escape from the everyday. Surrounded by incredible mountain ranges, pristine lakes and rare, untamed wildlife, Jasper is the best nature has to offer."[51] These sentiments, expressed through a combination of images and text, have become standard fare in the promotion of the Jasper National Park wilderness experience.

As enticing as these advertisements are, it is important to interrogate their message, in particular in light of reports claiming that "the loss of ecological integrity" is a significant threat in Canada's national parks.[52] In fact, the 2000 report of the Panel on the Ecological Integrity of Canada's National Parks stated that Jasper National Park is currently experiencing a "major" level of ecological impairment related in many ways to human activity within park borders.[53] Further, statistics kept by the JEA indicate that budget cutbacks and management decisions continue to threaten the ecological integrity of the park.[54] What are we to make of this discrepancy?

A Succession of Picture Postcard Scenes

Like most national parks in North America, Jasper has been imaged and imagined according to specific wilderness and cultural ideals that have only recently become the subject of critical analysis. Picture postcards, for instance, have repeated certain themes and views of Jasper since the park was first promoted as a vacation destination in the early twentieth century.[55] Writing in 1913, photographer I.C. Adams linked this type of repetition with the creation of a profitable postcard business: "I sincerely believe that the more a certain beauty spot is photographed and the greater the number of photographs that are distributed, the larger will be the sale of easily available, good view cards showing the same scene."[56] This principle seems to have guided postcard production in Jasper National Park. For instance, Maligne Lake – described as the "scenic showpiece of the

Canadian Rockies" – has adorned thousands of postcards sold in the many gift shops of Jasper over the past several decades.[57] The repetition of certain landscape views on mass-produced items such as picture postcards has helped to define what an authentic wilderness experience in the Canadian Rockies should be.

The postcard remains a popular souvenir item for visitors to destinations such as Jasper National Park and has influenced dominant conceptions of this space. In fact, the landscape of the park is often described in terms of postcard aesthetics, as this excerpt from a recent brochure demonstrates: "Drive through the Rockies and you'll enjoy a Canadian vacation classic. While relaxing in the comfort of your car or touring coach, a succession of picture postcard scenes rolls past like your own personal travelogue."[58]

Postcards define the tourist experience and allow visitors to situate themselves within National Park Nature. Further, postcard imagery becomes iconic in that it reduces a landscape to a series of familiar visual symbols. A photographic postcard dating from 1944 (see Figure 12) provides an example of this process. It features a photograph by the Jasper-based photographer Joe Weiss and has the following message written on the back: "We are sitting in the Pyramid Hotel just a step from this scene on this card, looking at the Great Rocky Mountains. I would give most any thing if you could be with us for this must be the most Beautiful sight in the World."[59] The elements of this text – awe-filled admiration for the scenery, a desire that the recipient of the card also be part of the vacation adventure, and the use of language directly linking the sender's experience to the picture on the front – have been echoed on countless postcards mailed from Jasper National Park through the years. This postcard also focuses on the lone totem pole in the park, a tourist attraction until 2009.[60] The pole was made by a Haida carver in the late nineteenth century and brought to Jasper from northern British Columbia in the early decades of the twentieth century as part of a campaign to promote railway tourism in western Canada. The pole appears on a number of postcards and in other forms of tourism imagery in the park and has become a symbol of Aboriginality in a general sense. That the pole did not originate in the Rocky Mountains did not seem to matter to the countless visitors who collected images of it as evidence of their vacation experience. As anthropologist Aldona Jonaitis has demonstrated, "tourism-related businesses have also long recognized the commercial potential of totem poles."[61] So the Canadian government collaborated with CNR to place northwest coast poles along the rail lines in western Canada to attract tourists to this region. The famed pole that so many visitors to Jasper National Park photographed

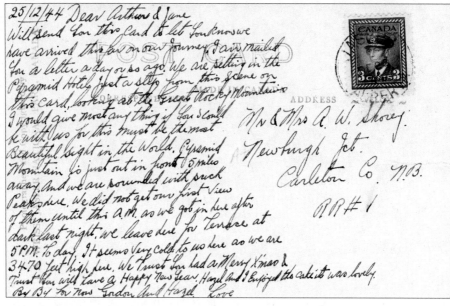

FIGURE 12   Front and back of a postcard sent in the 1940s. This card features the totem pole that was once a major tourist attraction in Jasper National Park. *Joe Weiss, "Totem Pole," c. 1944. Collection of the author.*

(or collected photographic postcards of) during the twentieth century was part of this process, even though, as Graeme Wynn notes, the pole's placement in the park "speaks of cultural loss, the denial of memory, the hubris of the colonizer and a striking disregard for the environment in its broadest sense."[62]

Art historian Lucy Lippard has described postcards as "photographic clichés" and argues that they are "at best ... a consensus of what viewers hope to see."[63] This is true in many ways, as postcards draw on iconic imagery and shape what visitors see and experience during wilderness vacations. However, purchasing and sending postcards also situates tourists as "subjects of their own performance" of travel.[64] By participating in the cyclical process of postcard consumption, tourists to Jasper National Park are able not only to claim a piece of the mountain landscape for pocket change but also to use these popular souvenir items to stake their presence in this culturally privileged landscape. Whether mailed to family and friends as evidence of individual experiences in this space, or added to photo albums on the visitor's return home, the images and textual messages on these cards personalize the tourist experience through a mass-marketed vehicle. As historian Marguerite Shaffer has argued, the memorialization of a vacation experience through the production of albums, scrapbooks, or collections of visual souvenirs creates a tangible, material product marking individual participation in the commodity culture of tourism.[65]

You Should Be Here

A recent advertisement for hotel accommodations in Jasper also demonstrates the interplay between individual experience and mass-produced vacation adventure that defines the wilderness industry in places such as Jasper National Park. Potential visitors to the park are invited to imagine themselves as wilderness tourists as they gaze on a photograph of one of the most recognizable geographical features of Jasper – Spirit Island in Maligne Lake. From the summer 2003 pages of *Travel Alberta* magazine, this advertisement declared that "there is no place on earth" quite like Jasper National Park and offered yet another example of representational rhetoric advancing the notion that Jasper is geographically and conceptually separate from other regions of the country and, indeed, the rest of the planet.[66]

The top of the advertisement was dominated by the text "you should be here," which in turn was linked to the photographic image by the arrows that locate the viewer in a canoe gliding lazily along the calm waters in front of Spirit Island. Not content to rely on subtle suggestion or casual coercion, the producers of this advertisement combined text and image to offer an irresistible wilderness scene in marked contrast to the daily experiences of the mostly urban readers of *Travel Alberta*. Use of the phrase "you should be here" implies that the reader of the advertisement is not in Jasper but in some concrete jungle that serves as a counterpoint to the park space. Such representational techniques play on a desire for isolated, individual wilderness experiences – a key component of what sociologist John Urry calls the "romantic tourist gaze" – even as they use a mass-produced, visual media vehicle to offer the same "individual" experience to the thousands of readers of the magazine.

Tourism in Alberta, as in most other regions of the country, is big business. In 2002, residents of Alberta spent $2.9 billion on tourism within their home province, and this is but one target market for the *Travel Alberta* campaigns.[67] Alberta Economic Development, a ministry of the provincial government, spends vast amounts of money each year promoting tourism in Alberta; $18.1 million was budgeted for the 2003-4 tourism season, with $13.2 million of that amount allocated for tourism marketing.[68] The marketing schemes designed to promote the Rocky Mountain Tourism Destination Region (TDR) attempt to convey to potential visitors that this particular part of Alberta is a "must-see experience."[69] The emphasis, almost exclusively, is on sight, as indicated by the language of description used in these types of promotions. In regions such as Jasper, one does not simply explore the landscape but also becomes immersed in a "pleasureland of scenic splendour in the heart of the Canadian Rockies."[70] Photography, then, is an essential tool in this type of promotion; camera-based images repeatedly serve to underscore the primacy of the visual in the construction and experience of National Park Nature.

THE CN WILDERNESS

In both Canada and the United States, railway companies were responsible for much of the early promotional material encouraging tourists to visit national parks. When the Grand Trunk Railway and the Canadian Northern Railway merged in 1923, Jasper National Park was promoted by a single railway company, Canadian National Railways. In much the same way as its rival, Canadian Pacific Railway, CNR advertised and promoted tourist destinations along its line and produced brochures, travel guides, postcards, and illustrated timetables to entice visitors from eastern Canada, the United States, and Europe to visit the "Rocky Mountain playgrounds."[71] The photographic history of the region reveals that wilderness scenes quickly became part of the CNR's visual identity. During the 1920s and 1930s, the railway produced a series of postcards of Maligne Canyon that underscored the unique geological features of this aspect of the park. In F.A. Jackman's 1930 photograph "Maligne Canyon" (see Figure 13), for instance, the juxtaposition of a tiny human figure with a massive wall of ice found in the wintry canyon offers a sense of sublimity attractive to both the producers and the consumers of postcard images.

CNR published photographically illustrated guidebooks on a regular basis throughout the park's history. These books provided visitors with information about the history, amenities, and activities of the region, with special emphasis on facilities owned and operated by the railway company. The CNR guidebooks of the Jasper region presented visitors with sample itineraries to suit any travel plans; "suggestions for one-day guests" were listed alongside suggested activities for visitors who planned to stay in the region for several days. The use of imagery in these publications, much like the use of imagery in more traditional single-page print advertisements, ensured that the landscape was understood in specific ways by those contemplating a visit to the park.

CNR brochures used photographic imagery to highlight the landscape and tourist facilities in the park. These brochures typically followed the same general format, though specific content varied from year to year. Most discussed the history of the region, listed recreational opportunities, and included detailed descriptions and plenty of photographs of the Jasper Park Lodge. Wilderness shadowed all. Whether on its own or as a backdrop to recreation, wilderness imagery reinforced a sense of the timelessness and symbolic significance of the region. A caption accompanying a photograph of three tourists playing golf on the CNR-owned course found in

FIGURE 13   Photographs of spectacular formations in the landscape were often used for tourism promotions. Such images offered a balance between showcasing something that a visitor to the park would be unlikely to see in other landscapes and visually assuring potential visitors that this was a "safe" and "tamed" landscape. *F.A. Jackman, "Maligne Canyon," c. 1930. Jasper-Yellowhead Museum and Archives, PA 7-130, Major Frederick Archibald Brewster Fonds.* ▶

the 1953 version of the brochure, for instance, stated, "The colourful face of Pyramid Mountain provides a backdrop for the ninth tee of the famous Jasper Park Lodge Golf course."[72] The railway companies in Canada's Rocky Mountain parks often worked closely with local photographers such as W.H. "Billy" Robinson, Frank Slark, Joe Weiss, G. Morris Taylor, Harry Rowed, and F.A. Jackman in the production of postcards, illustrated guidebooks, and other promotional materials.

Photographs taken by Byron Harmon, one of the most famous and prolific photographers in the history of the Canadian Rocky Mountain parks, perhaps comprised the quintessential tourist photography in the early decades of the twentieth century.[73] In the spring of 1925, several British newspapers, including the *Sphere,* the *Daily Mail,* the *Birmingham Post,* and the *Liverpool Courier,* published engravings based on Harmon's mountain photographs, much to the delight of the Canadian press, which enthusiastically declared that "this is indeed one kind of advertising that really assists Canadian tourist trade, and will probably enthuse many old country people to visit our mountain parks this summer."[74] Harmon moved to Banff in 1906 with the intention of setting up a commercial photography business. His attention quickly turned to the mountain landscape, and he produced a vast number of photographic images of the Canadian Rockies, many of which were turned into souvenir postcards and collectible stereograph cards.[75] This was a highly successful venture for Harmon, and many of the photographs he marketed and sold conformed to ideals of what wilderness was expected to look like in the Canadian Rockies: serene and devoid of any overt signs of human presence. Images such as his 1924 image of Maligne Lake, originally produced as a stereograph (see Figure 14), went a long way toward confirming National Park Nature in the minds of many. The reflections in the foreground and the snow-capped peaks in the distance would have made this an especially popular choice for the stereo format, as these compositional elements would have enhanced the sense of three dimensionality when this pair of images was viewed through a stereoscope. Harmon's photographs continue to be a key component of tourist photography in Banff and Jasper and are found on postcards and within the pages of tourist brochures to this day.[76]

The History of a Nation

Illustrated publications produced by the government of Canada have followed a similar format, though, not surprisingly, they have also emphasized

FIGURE 14   Maligne Lake is one of the most photographed landscapes in Jasper
National Park. Byron Harmon originally produced this image as a stereograph, an
indication of how commercially lucrative this type of image could be. *Byron Harmon,
"Maligne Lake," 1924. Whyte Museum of the Canadian Rockies, WMCR-V263/NA-5896.*

links between scenery and state, in essence legitimizing the designation and development of park space under the guise of nation building. The government of Canada has been involved in the production of tourist literature and advertising for both the national parks system as a whole and individual parks such as Jasper. One of the earliest and most success-ful illustrated guides to Jasper was *Description of and Guide to Jasper Park,* published by the Department of the Interior in 1917. This book was pro-duced by M.P. Bridgland, E. Deville, and R. Douglass and has been de-scribed as influencing the design and style of subsequent guidebooks to the region.[77]

As with the railway publications, photographs showcasing spectacular scenery, recreational opportunities, and visitor amenities were a main feature of this body of promotional material. In addition, these publica-tions emphasized ideas of nationhood, and in this respect visual imagery has gone a long way in promoting now standardized views of wilderness scenery to the status of national icons. A publication produced by the Department of Mines and Resources in the late 1940s, entitled *Jasper National Park in the Canadian Rockies,* contains both descriptions and images of the park that demonstrate the blend of history, culture, wilder-ness, and ideas of nation that is a key feature of government rhetoric re-garding national parks in Canada. This publication goes to great lengths to describe and illustrate the ways in which Jasper has "contributed to Canada's greatness": "With the history of a nation etched on her mountain walls, and the ghost of the explorer and fur trader still haunting her wooded valleys, Jasper Park links the lusty traditions of Canada with the recreations of the modern world."[78]

Much like CNR tourist brochures, the federal government publications have followed a standard format and included many photographic images. Scenic attractions such as Sunwapta Falls, Tonquin Valley, Maligne Lake, and Mount Edith Cavell share pages with pictures of visitors hiking, fish-ing, boating, and above all enjoying a leisurely vacation in the park. These publications also provide ample discussion and photographic evidence of the first-class amenities and the beauty offered along "magic trails" such as the Banff-Jasper highway, which motorists could tour at their leisure, both aspects of a vacation that tourists understood as a means to engage with wilderness in a way that was at once individualized and authentic.[79]

All of these publications rely on descriptive images and text to empha-size the wilderness of Jasper National Park as both an attraction in itself and a scenic setting for facilities such as the golf course and swimming pool at Jasper Park Lodge. Landscape imagery showcasing the scenic wonders of the Rocky Mountain wilderness has done more than simply attract tourists and generate revenue for local businesses and government agencies; this body of imagery has also been significant in defining what Canada is and means for both domestic and foreign tourists. Sentimental links between nature and culture run through federally produced publications showcasing Canada's national parks. One publication, produced by the Government of Canada in the 1930s, praises the mountain parks and declares that

> no one can spend even a few hours among their natural wonders without gaining a new conception of the greatness of the Dominion ... The mountains yield their riches only to those who come and live among them; from their beauty and endurance come strength, health and restoration of spirit against the stress and cares of a restless world.[80]

This type of promotion remains with us. A Parks Canada publication from the late 1980s proclaims, simply, "You haven't seen Canada until you have visited its National Parks," and a more recent example declares that Canada's national parks "characterize our country and define who we are as Canadians."[81] Both publications follow earlier conventions in using photographs to present parks as perfect blends of wilderness experience and outdoor recreational pursuits, and in doing so they further solidify the link between nature and nation in the minds of visitors and Canadian citizens alike.

Photographers such as William J. Oliver, who worked for Parks Canada on a contract basis for thirty years, played a significant role in shaping a specific image of the Canadian wilderness. "His pictures," as one commentator has observed, "made Canada's wilderness beauty world famous."[82] Oliver, who lived in Calgary, spent considerable time photographing in the Rocky Mountain parks and is well known for his still and moving pictures of this region.[83] Perhaps his most famous photograph is "The Narrows, Maligne Lake, Jasper Park," one of a series taken in Jasper during the autumn of 1929 (see Figure 15).[84] It shows three figures in the mountain landscape, and a canoe and a teepee-like shelter allude to both the qualities of recreation and rejuvenation often emphasized in visual promotions of this region and to the history of Aboriginal presence in the Canadian west. These factors, coupled with the aesthetic beauty and tranquility of the scene, have made this image a particularly popular example of Jasper tourist photography. It has been reproduced many times in government promotions of Jasper National Park, the Rocky Mountain

FIGURE 15   William J. Oliver's photograph of Maligne Lake was reproduced in many different tourism publications. *William J. Oliver, "The Narrows, Maligne Lake, Jasper National Park," September 1929. Library and Archives Canada, PA-116694.*

region, and the wilderness aspects of the Canadian nation. A promotional pamphlet produced by the Department of Mines and Resources during the 1940s featured a copy of this photograph (see Figure 16) accompanied by the following description:

> For sheer magnificence, no scene in Jasper Park – or indeed in all the mountains of the West – can surpass that from The Narrows of Maligne Lake. Here Nature appears to have drawn upon the Alps, the Trossachs and the Norwegian fiords for this symphony of wonder, and have bound together the whole with that aura of wild beauty that only the Rockies possess.[85]

FIGURE 16   Example of a publication using Oliver's famous 1929 photograph of Maligne Lake. *Government of Canada, Department of Mines and Resources, Cover of* Jasper National Park in the Canadian Rockies, *1940s. Jasper-Yellowhead Museum and Archives, Accn#994.45.1.2, Doris Kensit Fonds.*

Likewise, in a brochure entitled *Canada's Mountain Playgrounds,* Oliver's iconic photograph appears with the following caption: "Maligne is one of the largest and most beautiful glacial-fed bodies of water in the Canadian Rockies."[86] As these examples demonstrate, image and text work together and over and over again to solidify dominant cultural ideals of wilderness that define National Park Nature in Jasper.

Such materials function as visual advertisements for the region, and they play into an ever-growing fascination with the wilderness ideals thought to be embodied by destinations such as Jasper National Park. Correspondence between Oliver and the Department of the Interior, for instance, indicates that there was a big demand for photographs of Jasper National Park, and the role of government agencies in controlling how this landscape was represented ensured that the link between nature and nation remained firm.[87] Oliver worked closely with those responsible for the visual promotion of Canadian national parks, and both his still and his moving images were used in a wide variety of formats, including newspapers, travel books, print advertisements, and as decorative elements in hotel lobbies and university offices.[88] Oliver has been rightly described as "one of the most important cogs in the work of publicizing Canada."[89] Yet, as one journalist noted, the government policy not to publish individual credit lines for images (which may have added authority to them) meant that many people were unaware they were looking at Oliver's work in tourism promotional materials. As Harper Cory put it in 1937, "Few newspapers or magazines of note exist in Britain or North America which have not published prints by W.J. Oliver at some time or another ... Millions of people in many countries have applauded his films – and yet few editors or audiences have heard of the photographer's name or seen it in print."[90]

FAÇADE MANAGEMENT IN JASPER NATIONAL PARK

In much the same way that complex cultural histories have been erased through dominant wilderness representations, tourist photography has obscured and negated environmental realities in the Canadian Rockies. Tourist photography has presented Jasper National Park as a place where one can relax and enjoy an abundance of leisure pursuits in the most scenic of settings, qualities that undoubtedly draw thousands of visitors to the area each year. This in itself is not a problem. What is cause for concern, however, are the various ways in which this aesthetic view of nature is permitted to dominate all other environmental aspects of the area. Historian of North American national parks Richard West Sellars has termed this process "façade management" and defined it as the practice of "managing scenic parks for the public's enjoyment, but with little understanding of the biological consequences."[91] Perhaps the best example of façade management in Jasper National Park was the implementation of fire suppression policies mandated by the 1930 National Parks Act. Historian Ian MacLaren points out that as a result of this policy Jasper "now wears a nearly uniform green demeanour, agreeable to most tourists. The sight of a burnt hillside saddens if it does not disgust and repel us because it appears to preclude the restorative wilderness experience that enables our spiritual union with nature."[92]

Tourists hold specific expectations about what they will see and do in locations such as Jasper National Park. Part of this is a sense that the view in front of them should match what they have seen in guidebooks, promotional pamphlets, and postcards prior to their visit. Much has been done in the way of park management to make certain that this is the case. Even though Parks Canada is now realizing the ecological effects of policies such as fire suppression, the legacy of such decisions will linger as both natural processes and biodiversity in the region have been severely impacted as a result.[93]

Yet tourist photography has also had positive impacts on the environment in and around Canada's national parks. As the recent 2010 management plan for Jasper National Park points out, "Protecting healthy ecosystems is also critical to ensuring that visitors continue to have outstanding opportunities to experience, enjoy, and learn about the unique natural heritage of Jasper National Park."[94] A key environmental aspect of tourist photography relates to expectations of tourists that they will encounter scenes on their journeys that have some resemblance to the photographically illustrated promotional brochures that attracted them to destinations such as Jasper National Park in the first place. As Carol Crawshaw and John Urry have argued, "Photographic images provide a kind of 'mirror' on the society within which they are located ... Within the last decade the increased reflexivity about the environment has partly come about because of still and live photographic images of the visual and other effects upon nature of unrestrained economic development."[95] It makes economic sense for tourist destinations to maintain at least the appearance of ecological integrity. Urry points out, for instance, that "one effect of more tourists may be to improve the campaiging for an improved environment ... It is because of tourism that many National Parks have been created and without them many animal and plant species would have disappeared."[96] What tends not to be adequately addressed in these analyses is that these tourism-inspired campaigns for environmental preservation seem to focus only on the aspects of the landscape that correspond with dominant visual paradigms that have defined destination spaces. Many environmental threats are not easily visible or photographable. Reduction in biodiversity, habitat fragmentation, and competition between native and non-native flora and fauna are not readily evident in representations of the landscape and, as a result, are rarely the focus of conservation campaigns. Development and construction projects that alter the familiarity of the Rocky Mountain landscape, on the other hand, are both evident and frequently adopted as part of the visual language of environmental advocacy in this region.

Advocacy groups also often rely on the same visual codes that inform corporate constructions of National Park Nature. Writing about environmental discourses, geographers Lisa M. Benton and John Rennie Short have pointed out that environmental organizations such as the Sierra Club increasingly employ the power of consumerism as an activist tool.[97] This does not automatically result in negative environmental impacts on the landscape, but it does return to questions raised previously about influences shaping dominant representations of the landscape. In particular, who benefits from ensuring that these representations remain the status quo? In this context, both the tourist industry and environmental advocacy groups have continually drawn on a specific version of wilderness to further their sometimes divergent agendas. In these representations, the environment invariably takes the form of a wilderness landscape unmodified by human presence and is marked by the images of vast, empty tracks of unspoiled Nature.

This dominant view of wilderness has had the effect of setting Nature apart from human existence, a place to visit and enjoy on weekends but not an important part of daily life. The problem with perpetuating this notion, as William Cronon has famously pointed out, is that, until we are able to conceive of nature as including all aspects of human society and not just select areas that conform to what we think nature should be, it will be impossible to find ways of solving the environmental issues facing North American society both within and well beyond park borders.[98] As Cronon writes, "To protect the nature that is all around us, we must think long and hard about the nature we carry inside our heads."[99]

Photographic images of Jasper National Park often encompass competing values. Dominant notions of wilderness are sustained and reinforced through visual material and in this way serve to construct the authentic wilderness experience as characterized by a sense of harmony between humans and the rest of nature. However, at the same time, these images contribute to alteration of the physical landscape of the park by advertising its attributes and encouraging potential tourists to vacation there. Photographs featuring breathtaking vistas and pristine-looking landscapes are cornerstone images associated with the wilderness industry of Jasper National Park. Yet the continual influx of visitors to the region greatly reduces the chance that the sublime, solitary mountain experience promised in the brochures will be found. Further, the facilities and infrastructure needed to accommodate visitors result in environmental realities not typically depicted on souvenir postcards. From wastewater management policies to legislation dictating that environmental assessments must be carried out on new building projects in Canadian national parks, the environmental impacts of tourism drive much of the administrative activity in places such as Banff and Jasper National Parks.[100] These dialogues, however, remain largely absent in the visual vocabulary of National Park Nature.

CONCLUSION

Scenic photographs have dominated representations of Jasper National Park over the past several decades. Photographs of streams, forests, mountains, and waterfalls have been especially prominent in the pictorial history of the park. These images emphasize a sense of environmental difference in that they focus on elements of nature that would not, for the most part, be directly experienced in an urban setting. John T. Faris's illustrated account of travels in Canada during the 1920s is but one example of this process.[101] Alongside text marvelling at the Nature found in spaces such as the Canadian Rockies, images such as "Athabasca Falls, Jasper Park, Alberta," emphasize the wilderness qualities of the region above all else (see Figure 17). In this photograph, the slow shutter speed of the camera has blurred the powerful, rushing waters of the falls, underscoring the awe-inspiring sublimity that this landscape scene was undoubtedly intended to evoke. The composition of this image positions the viewer at a clearing in the treed vista surrounding the falls. This vantage point frames the viewer's experience of this image as a privileged one. The photograph not only offers the familiar sense of solitary meditation so characteristic of wilderness photography but also suggests that this is available only to a select number of people. By suggesting that to reach this vista one would have to traverse a wild landscape, the photograph implies that strong will, physical ability, and perseverance are necessary to see this sight. The transportation technologies that facilitate relatively easy access to popular tourist sites such as Athabasca Falls are most often excluded from such photographs. Inclusion of this image in a book intended for commercial

Figure 17   A view of Athabasca Falls included in John T. Faris's 1924 illustrated book *Seeing Canada. James A. Gibson Library, Brock University.*

sale further democratizes the experience of this landscape, for even armchair travellers are able to take in this view of Athabasca Falls.

Illustrated travel accounts, postcards, and guidebooks have transformed the landscape of Jasper National Park into an easily consumable tourist commodity through continued reliance on a wilderness aesthetic. The use of this landscape as a background for Hollywood films and television commercials has further solidified this position. In 1993, for instance, the Phillip Morris corporation shot some of its (in)famous Marlboro Man advertisements in Jasper National Park.[102] This process has not been limited to multinational corporations using the mountainous landscape of Jasper as a backdrop to sell their products. The commodification of the landscape according to a wilderness aesthetic has been ongoing throughout the park's history.

The processes of picturing, visiting, and engaging with a landscape cannot be separated. Each element is dependent on the other and necessarily has some level of impact on the environment of the region. Automobile tourism, for example, was one of the most significant developments affecting Canada's national parks during the twentieth century and became an important factor in shaping both the experiences of visitors to destinations such as Jasper and the physical characteristics of the region. In this context, the automobile facilitates new forms of engagement with the wilderness, as the view of National Park Nature from the car window offers a new way of visually organizing this landscape. As Cronon has argued, however, roads also expedited the process of transforming wilderness into "just another consumer good."[103] In other words, the sense of therapeutic escape promised by wilderness destinations such as Jasper became even further entwined with the politics of commodity culture once automobile tourism became a dominant feature of Canadian national parks.

In much the same way as the landscape of Jasper National Park has been transformed into a "windshield wilderness," nature has been conceptually transformed by the camera lens.[104] The introduction of new technologies has continually resulted in new ways of picturing Jasper National Park. Construction of the Jasper Sky Tram in 1962, for instance, gave tourists the opportunity to get a bird's-eye view of the park landscape. Within this framework, however, dominant cultural ideologies regarding the perceived wilderness qualities of this region remain firmly entrenched in how this space is imaged and imagined.

New technologies have enabled tourists to seek views they previously encountered on picture postcards and within the pages of illustrated guidebooks. But these developments are not environmentally neutral. For instance, the obvious physical changes that automobile tourism brought to the Jasper region include the development of roads and related facilities such as service stations and parking lots. As David Schindler has pointed out, transportation corridors have also had significant impacts on wildlife habitats. These human-built structures, as Schindler argues, have altered the physical characteristics of rivers in the Rocky Mountain parks and, as a result, have severely impacted aquatic species in the area.[105]

This is not to suggest that the landscape of Jasper National Park needs to be restored to some authentic, pre-technological wilderness state, even if such a task were possible. So-called wilderness spaces, such as Jasper, are never static or natural; rather, they are the products of decades of human activity and, as such, are constantly in flux. As David Nye has argued, "Human beings have repeatedly shaped the land to new uses and pleasures, and what appears to be natural to one generation often is the end result of a previous intervention."[106] Human societies have lived in, explored, and enjoyed this space for many years. This is not something that could, or even should, be changed. It will be increasingly important, however, to unpack the complex interrelationships between the way a landscape is pictured and the way a society chooses to treat it if we are to arrive at the most environmentally sustainable means of negotiating the inevitable interspecies relationships that exist in places such as Jasper National Park.

3

An Invitation to Leisure:
Picturing Canada's Wilderness
Playground

Photographs of people canoeing, horseback riding, mountain climbing, and participating in high-profile (and, not coincidentally, high-cost) leisure pursuits such as golfing and skiing have formed a significant part of the representational rhetoric surrounding Jasper National Park. Illustrated guidebooks, advertisements, and promotional brochures have offered potential tourists vivid descriptions and eye-catching images of a wide range of activities awaiting them in Jasper. A 1934 advertisement in *Maclean's* magazine was typical in encouraging readers to visit the "magnificent Jasper Park in the heart of the Canadian Rockies" and describing both the scenery and the experiences one would have on arrival as nothing short of miraculous: "One deep breath of the tonic mountain air and you're ready for anything. To scale peaks that rival the Alps themselves. To ride. To swim. To golf on a championship course at Jasper Park Lodge. To motor through country of unimaginable splendour."[1] This type of description is often accompanied by visual culture offering evidence of the extraordinary sights and opportunities to be found in the park.

The transformation of this mountain region into a series of culturally tailored "sportscapes" has depended heavily on visual representations.[2] At the same time, this transformation has reordered how the space is used and conceived of, and it has initiated physical processes that have markedly altered the environment.

A Landscape of Leisure

Recreation has long been seen as an integral component of National Park Nature in Canada. From the early days of the Dominion Parks Branch, as parks historian C.J. Taylor has pointed out, Commissioner James Harkin drew links between physical fitness, mental well-being, and outdoor recreation areas in the promotion of Canada's national parks. In 1914, he stated that "the most important service which the parks render is in the matter of helping to make the Canadian people physically fit, mentally efficient, and morally elevated."[3] The Rocky Mountains have come to be recognized as one of the key symbols of Canada for both domestic and foreign tourism markets, and Jasper's location in the midst of this world-famous region has further solidified associations between sports and symbolic notions of Canada as leisure pursuits such as downhill skiing and canoeing have become associated with Canadian national identity.[4]

The conceptualization of the Canadian Rockies as a unique wilderness playground continues to be dominant in promotional literature on Jasper National Park. A recent publication describes the mountains as being

> all about edge. Scraping the sky and framing the prairies – the legendary Canadian Rocky Mountains zig-zag up the entire western border of Alberta, creating diverse eco-systems along the way. Climb them. Hike around them. Raft or kayak right on them. Or wing your way over them in a helicopter or hang-glider. But you have to see them – to believe in their breathtaking beauty.[5]

Such descriptions and their accompanying photographs construct an idea of the Canadian Rocky Mountain parks as scenic playgrounds – a significant aspect of National Park Nature.

In this chapter, I explore intersections among recreation, imagery, and environmental ideologies in the park and present examples of how certain types of leisure activities, including amateur photography, have been represented in the context of Jasper National Park tourism. Underpinning this discussion is an ecocritical re-examination of Thorstein Veblen's concepts of "conspicuous leisure" and "conspicuous consumption."[6] Veblen, an American economist, was writing about the consumption of material goods and leisure time in the late nineteenth century, the same historical moment that gave rise to the national park system in North America. In re-examining the function of these spaces from an ecocritical point of view, a return to Veblen's writings is useful.[7]

Veblen's writings rest on a keen awareness of class and economic divisions in western society. This is important in a critical analysis of Jasper National Park and in considerations of the history of how this space has been represented and consumed. Since its creation, the park has been clearly demarcated as a landscape of leisure and, in this respect, has been situated as the antithesis of urban and industrial landscapes of labour. This is another cultural construction defining the park as a place where work is not done; rather, it is where one goes to escape from work through the pursuit of leisure activities such as golfing and skiing. To maintain the mythology of National Park Nature, the labour necessary to create and maintain park spaces is erased in dominant representations of Jasper National Park.[8]

The delineation of separate spheres of work and play created through the establishment of parks such as Jasper has also masked environmental impacts of leisure on these spaces. The sense of denial that accompanies popular conceptions of national parks as landscapes where work is not done also factors into modern notions of environmentalism. As Richard White has argued, "Mainstream environmentalism creates a popular imagery that often harshly condemns all work in nature."[9] This sense of condemnation sets up a false cycle of ideas. Since this landscape is understood to be a space where work is not done, it follows that this environment has yet to be destroyed by human industry. In popular thinking, then, the landscape remains pristine and free of the harmful effects of human work that abound in less protected landscapes, a notion both created and reaffirmed through photographic imagery used by the tourism industry.

SELLING EXPERIENCES

The idea that spaces such as Jasper National Park are landscapes of leisure is propagated by the tourism industry, which is focused on "selling experiences." In the representational rhetoric of Canadian national parks, activities such as skiing, canoeing, and mountain climbing are promoted as healthy ways to pass the time with family and friends. This, however, is only part of the story; these pursuits are also necessarily bound up with dominant socio-economic assumptions regarding nature and nation. Indeed, environmental activist Hal Clifford has noted in a discussion of the ski industry in North America that "snow is a commodity, just like timber or oil or gas," and needs to be conceived of in these terms.[10] The consumption of images, leisure activities, and natural resources are necessarily interrelated in the context of National Park Nature. Tourist photography

FIGURE 18   A swimming pool along the shores of Lac Beauvert is among the many amenities visitors to the Jasper Park Lodge can enjoy. *Canadian National Railways, "Jasper Park Lodge, Jasper, Alberta, Canada," n.d. Collection of the author.*

depicting landscapes and recreational activities in this space has been instrumental in shaping leisure experiences into a commodity for tourists to enjoy.

John Bale, a researcher whose work focuses on the geography of sport, insists that such sportscapes are "forms of power or domination ... [that] do not necessarily result from a hatred of nature but, rather, a desire to civilise it." He discusses how framing sportscapes as natural, despite high levels of human manipulation, has been a key component of marketing and promoting these spaces in recent years.[11] In this way, the juxtaposition of human-built and naturally occurring recreational facilities – for instance, the construction of a swimming pool on the shore of Lac Beauvert at Jasper Park Lodge – is not given a second thought (see Figure 18). The employment of "aestheticizing techniques" such as the inclusion of specific species of plants, as well as the construction of associated architectural forms that correspond to antimodern ideals, are also significant aspects of this type of landscape transformation.

In recent decades, statistics have shown a slight decline in the annual number of visitors to Canada's national parks. In 2001-2, approximately 12.6 million people vacationed in these parks. In 2005-6, the figure was 12.2 million.[12] Marc Gregoire, director of Parks Canada's visitor experience branch, attributes this modest decline to visitors' growing desire to be comfortable. In a recent interview, he stated that visitors "want to cycle in the day or canoe, but at night – a nice glass of Beaujolais and a fondue. We have to offer that or we're going to lose them."[13] There is also a desire to attract more visitors from younger generations to the national parks of Canada. Although activities such as skiing and snowboarding remain popular, Gregoire also points to the need to keep up with new trends in adventure and entertainment. Geocaching, for instance, has recently begun to be pursued in national parks, reflecting a change in policy in order to accommodate new interests and activities. Of this switch, Gregoire stated, "When they came to us the first time, we said if it is not hiking, it's not allowed. We don't say that anymore. They're young, they're on the web, they're techies. They come, they sign in to participate. It's fantastic."[14] What is interesting about these shifts is that the base idea of the marketing for these experiences remains rooted in traditional notions of antimodern wilderness experience while promising urban comforts and activities.

JASPER PARK LODGE

Perhaps the views in and around the world-famous Jasper Park Lodge have done the most to solidify Jasper National Park's reputation as a wilderness playground; as one CNR publication put it, "To speak of Jasper is to speak of Jasper Park Lodge."[15] The lodge, which opened for business in 1922, is one of the best known and most photographed features of the park (see Figures 19 and 20). It consists of a series of low wooden cabins clustered around a main building that serves as the hub of social activity at the lodge. In comparison to the imposing, castle-like structure of the Banff Springs Hotel in Banff National Park, Jasper Park Lodge was built to blend in with its surrounding landscape. CNR brochures described this resort as

THE BUNGALOWS. JASPER PARK LODGE.

FIGURE 19   In contrast to the castle-like structure of the Banff Springs Hotel, Jasper Park Lodge is comprised of a series of bungalow-style cabins. *Canadian National Railways, "The Bungalows, Jasper Park Lodge," n.d. Collection of the author.*

a miniature village of rustic bungalows grouped around a main lodge on the shores of Lac Beauvert, whose emerald waters mirror the encircling mountains. Built of huge white boulders and logs brought down from the mountain slopes its architecture blends so perfectly with the surroundings, that it seems as much part of the scenery as the mountains themselves.[16]

The building materials and the understated architectural style of the individual bungalows convey the notion that these accommodations are an extension of the trees and geological formations of the park. As Gabrielle Zezulka-Mailloux notes in her study of promotional materials used in this region, "Jasper Park Lodge was consistently marketed as a hotel that, unlike the grandiose Banff Springs and Chateau Lake Louise, does not try to compete with the sublimity of the mountains."[17] In this way, the lodge projects the illusion that it offers an antimodern escape into Nature, despite the highly manicured grounds and the wealth of facilities existing entirely for the comfort and convenience of its guests.[18]

FIGURE 20   A 1929 postcard featuring the Bungalows at Jasper Park Lodge. *Folkard Company of Canada, "Bungalows, Jasper Park Lodge Alta. Canada," 1929. Collection of the author.*

CNR owned and operated Jasper Park Lodge until 1988 and laid visual claim to this landscape through the use of tourist photography.[19] Not only did the company regularly publish illustrated brochures and guidebooks showcasing this location, but it was also involved in the production of

FIGURE 21   Canoeing on Lac Beauvert in Jasper National Park has always been a
popular tourist activity. *Canadian National Railways, "Lac Beauvert-Jasper National
Park," 1930s. Jasper-Yellowhead Museum and Archives, PA 12-12, Hartley Family Fonds.*

photographic postcards that routinely used text and image to solidify the
association between CNR and the leisured landscape surrounding the
lodge. A postcard produced by the company during the 1940s (see Figure 21) features a photograph of tourists canoeing in front of the world-
famous resort and is accompanied by the following inscription: "Lac
Beauvert-Jasper National Park. Can.Nat.Rlys."

Lac Beauvert is a popular spot for canoeing enthusiasts. The canoe has
long been seen as emblematic of the quintessential Canadian wilderness
experience.[20] Scenes of paddlers enjoying the tranquility of Lac Beauvert
have been among the most consistently reproduced views associated with
Jasper National Park (see Figure 22), and the longevity of this pictorial
formula has helped to position these types of images as expected elements
of National Park Nature.

The golf course at Jasper Park Lodge has also become a destination
within a destination and is recognized as one of the most famous attractions of Jasper National Park. In fact, as a recent publication enthused, in
the Canadian Rockies "golf has become so popular that it seems more of
an attraction than the mountain scenery!"[21] Alan MacEachern has noted

FIGURE 22   A postcard from the 1950s showing visitors to Jasper National Park canoeing on Lac Beauvert. *The Gowen, Sutton Company, "Bungalows, Jasper Park Lodge, Alberta," c. 1951. Collection of the author.*

that golf courses have been "seen as absolutely essential to National Parks ever since James Harkin, himself an ardent golfer, ... commissioned Canadian golf architect Stanley Thompson to build courses at Jasper and Banff in the late 1920s."[22] The golf course at Jasper, much like the lodge itself, can be understood as a means of mediating tourist encounters with nature. From the mountain scenery surrounding the course to frequent encounters with bears and other non-human animals on the links, a game of golf at Jasper promises visitors an apparently authentic wilderness experience in this leisured landscape (see Figures 23 and 24).

   The creation of this celebrated sportscape required considerable restructuring of the landscape around Lac Beauvert, since the golf course was carved right out of the mountain landscape. Although the greens and fairways appear to blend seamlessly with the rest of the landscape in the park, the creation of this course was anything but an effortless procedure. After much deliberation and discussion over where the course would be situated, the current location was selected by Thompson in 1924. As golf historian James Barclay notes, the transformation of this space into the

FIGURE 23   The golf course at Jasper Park Lodge is set right into the mountain land-scape. *Photographer Unknown, "Golfer at the 17th Tee, Jasper Park Lodge Golf Course," c. 1946. Canada Science and Technology Museum, CN006175, CSTMC/CN Collection.*

FIGURE 24   The location of the Jasper Park Lodge golf course has sometimes resulted in "uninvited" guests appearing on the greens. *Photographer Unknown, "Bears on the Jasper Park Lodge Golf Course with Roche Bonhomme in the Distance," n.d. Canada Science and Technology Museum, CN003294, CSTMC/CN Collection.*

FIGURE 25   Construction of the golf course at Jasper Park Lodge – like the construction of all golf courses – required major modifications to the existing landscape. *Photographer Unknown, "Course Construction, Jasper National Park," 1920s. Jasper-Yellowhead Museum and Archives, Accn#992.31.09, Dora Doyle Fonds.*

famous golf course we know today required "fifty teams of horses and five hundred men" to clear away "timber and boulders" from the site.[23] In other words, much political debate and physical labour went into the creation of a course that has been frequently celebrated as "a stunning natural setting" and as "existing in harmony with nature."[24] As photographs taken during construction of Jasper National Park illustrate (see Figure 25), this undertaking required a significant restructuring of the physical landscape.

The participation of famous figures such as Bing Crosby (see Figure 26) in the annual Totem Pole golf tournament added cultural cachet to Jasper Park Lodge; a combination of celebrity and scenery has shaped how this park attraction has been imaged and imagined over the past several decades.[25] Since the 1920s, promotional material has celebrated the "rugged majesty of this national treasure," the golf course, and described

FIGURE 26   Photographs of celebrities enjoying Jasper National Park and its amenities were ready-made promotional opportunities. *Canadian National Railways, "Bing and the Bruin," 1947. Canadian Science and Technology Museum, CN000583, CSTMC/CN Collection.*

the "isolated splendour" and "unspoiled beauty" of its mountain surround-ings.[26] The seemingly dichotomous existence of affluence and celebrity in a space represented as scenic and unspoiled is an important component of National Park Nature.

In his discussion of the development of the Adirondack region as a "wilderness playground" for the urban elite of New York City, Alec Brownlow demonstrates how certain activities carry ideological implications that serve to reinforce both existing class hierarchies and popular environmental perceptions.[27] Simply put, those with the economic means to afford long-term stays in the Adirondacks have also historically determined which activities are deemed acceptable in this environment, including what is classified as "environmentally acceptable." This dynamic, as Brownlow argues, has ensured that the Adirondack landscape has been characterized by recreational activities that most often benefit (or at least do not disturb) the preferred way of life of these wealthy vacationers.[28]

This sentiment has also shaped the history of the golf course at Jasper Park Lodge. Golf is not an environmentally benign sport, and the simple existence of this popular course makes the claims of isolated splendour and unspoiled beauty ring hollow. That construction of a golf course involves considerable alteration of the landscape, a massive expenditure of energy and resources, the disruption of faunal habitats, and regular applications of herbicides, pesticides, and fertilizers does not enter into dominant ways of understanding these spaces.[29] In the twenty-first century, a number of Canadian golf courses have recognized the need to improve their image when it comes to environmental issues, and many courses are being designed (or redesigned) to have a low impact in terms of their ecological footprint.[30] For example, the Jasper Park Lodge Golf course has recently received certification as an Audubon Cooperative Sanctuary for efforts such as reducing pesticide use and protecting the nearby bodies of water.[31] However, many environmental activists continue to believe that golf courses are jarringly out of place in a national park. About a major golf tournament in Banff National Park in 2010, Jim Pissot of the conservation group Defenders of Wildlife stated, "Forty-five hundred people watching a golf star slice a drive into grizzly bear habitat is not a legitimate or beneficial national park experience."[32]

FILMING THE MOUNTAIN LANDSCAPE

If pictorial imagery has been crucial to the transformation of landscapes into sportscapes, the production of promotional films focusing on leisure activities in Jasper offered a key means of visualizing the experience of vacationing in the region. William J. Oliver, a Calgary-based photographer and filmmaker who produced numerous still and moving pictures for both Fox News and the parks branch of the Canadian government, was commissioned to produce films of activities such as canoeing and fishing in Jasper. In the 1930s, the publicity director of Canadian national parks, J.C. Campbell, began to screen films made by Oliver to audiences in the United States as part of ongoing publicity campaigns aimed at bringing more tourists to the region. Among the most popular of Oliver's films showcasing recreational opportunities in the Canadian Rockies was *She Climbs to Conquer* (1931), made in conjunction with the Canadian Government Motion Picture Bureau. This was a two-reel production featuring scenes of an unidentified young woman and a guide climbing Abbott Pass in Jasper National Park,[33] described by the director of the Canadian Government Motion Picture Bureau, F.C. Badgley, as "quite the finest picture of its type that I have ever seen."[34]

A year earlier Oliver had produced two films focusing on trail riding and pack trips in the Jasper region. Both *Trails to the Wilderness,* a film focusing on a pack trip made from Jasper to Tonquin Valley and Amherst Lakes, and *Goodbye to All That,* which showcased a similar ride from Jasper to Mount Robson, were completed for the parks branch.[35] Sport fishing, an extremely popular leisure pursuit in Jasper, was also the focus of a pair of parks branch films. *With Line and Lure in Jasper* (1932) and *Sky Fishing* (c. 1933) showcased not only the fish that one could catch in Jasper's rivers and streams but also the program of fish stocking that aimed to ensure that every angler's trip to the region would be successful and enjoyable.[36]

These films were popular among audiences, and Campbell's plans to promote the region by screening them to recreational clubs in the United States seemed to pay off. In 1932, a reviewer for the *Cleveland Plain Dealer* remarked on the films shown to the Cleveland Travel Club, emphasizing the favourable impressions the fishing films left on audiences. The Minneapolis chapter of the Alpine Club also had an opportunity to view these films, which were enthusiastically received. One member in attendance stated simply that he had "never seen mountain films as good as those which Mr. Campbell showed."[37] They were praised for offering "new views, beautiful scenes, travels through wonderlands which would excite all of us ... in the proper way."[38] Scenes showcasing both the abundance and the size of fish caught in Jasper were of particular interest to American recreational enthusiasts. Reviews of these films by well-known film critics such as W. Ward Marsh lamented that they were being shown only to specialty groups and not wider audiences in movie houses.[39]

AT JASPER PARK.

Nip + Tuck with a Bass.

Copyright Canada 1911 by Canadian Post Card Co. Toronto.

FIGURE 27   A tall-tale postcard alluding to the abundance of fish to be found in the lakes and rivers of Jasper National Park. *W.H. Martin/Canadian Post Card Company, "Nip and Tuck with a Bass," 1911. Jasper-Yellowhead Museum and Archives, Accn#2006.20. 03.01.06, Historical Postcard Collection, Otto Brothers' Photograph Postcard Series.*

NIP AND TUCK WITH A BASS

Sport fishing clearly has been a significant attraction of Jasper National Park and featured in countless examples of tourist photography. On a recent visit to Jasper, for instance, I discovered an intriguing fishing-themed postcard (see Figure 27) dated 1911, the same year that Jasper was officially designated a dominion park. Entitled *Nip and Tuck with a Bass,* this comical depiction of a man struggling to reel in an absurdly large fish uses a photographically based image created by the American photographer W.H. Martin. Martin's tall-tale postcards were extremely popular and distributed in Canada by the Toronto-based Canadian Post Card Company.[40] The phrase "nip and tuck with a bass" was part of Martin's design and has been found on examples of this card that are not associated in any way with Jasper National Park. The words *At Jasper Park* were added after the fact, stamped on the front of the card before it was sold as a tourist souvenir in western Canada. This card contains iconic and admittedly

humorous symbols of the wilderness experience. It was obviously intended to be a visual gag, but in many ways it is precisely such exagger-
ated elements that pave the way for a revisitation of more conventional
photographic representations of recreation in Jasper National Park.

This is not Jasper. It is a fictitious collage created in Martin's Kansas
darkroom.[41] Yet this mass-produced card was sold to and collected by
tourists in the Canadian Rocky Mountains. The specific locale of the image has little to do with the meaning of the postcard; rather, the *idea* of
that locale and the wilderness experience manufactured there are being
promoted and consumed.

Sport fishing was one of the most popular activities among visitors to
the Canadian Rocky Mountains during the twentieth century. Popular
sentiments echoed the text found on a 1929 Folkard photographic postcard
proudly claiming that "Jasper National Park is a paradise for the fisherman.
One of the world's best pastimes, the art of the angler may be enjoyed
there in the midst of green forests and shining mountains" (see Figure 28).
Described as an activity that provides one with "a great host of beautiful
memories to illumine the grey of life's toils," fishing in the Canadian
Rockies has been contextualized as one of the most direct ways to escape
the perceived alienation of modernity.[42] Historian Tina Loo has discussed
how this type of recreational pursuit has functioned in the construction
of a "modern wilderness" by playing into a "bourgeois dissatisfaction with
modern life."[43] The irony, of course, is that this nostalgic, back-to-the-land
sentiment is thoroughly mediated by the trappings of modern society,
among them both roads and railways leading to the park and the photographic images used to promote the recreational activities they made accessible. Further, as Lynda Jessup has argued, it is "the very circuit of
exchange values and commodity relations" typical of modernity that makes
antimodern wilderness escape possible.[44]

Sport fishing was actively promoted through CNR publications and
guidebooks on Jasper National Park published by the Jasper Chamber of
Commerce. Year after year, these booklets described the sport-fishing
conditions in the park for the many "piscatorial enthusiasts" who visited
the area.[45] As an article from the 1965 issue of *Jasper Tourist News* boasts,
"Jasper fishing improves each year; so do the fishermen who visit here ...
Each year the catch increases. Each year brings more adherents to this
wonderful means of enjoying the outdoors and deriving respite from
workaday chores."[46] These descriptions are often accompanied by photographs of a solitary fisherman engaged in this popular recreational pursuit.
Both the absence of other vacationers and the gender of the angler are

(429)   FISHING IN THE ROCKY MOUNTAINS, CANADA.

FIGURE 28   This 1929 postcard is one of many forms of visual imagery that emphasized sport fishing in the Canadian Rockies. *Folkard Company of Canada, "Fishing in the Rocky Mountains, Canada," 1929. Collection of the author.*

highly significant in this context; fantasies of antimodern escape to Nature depended on a sense of solitary communion with nature as well as with the maintenance of "manhood through sport."[47]

Much like Martin's tall-tale postcard, the pursuit of sport fishing can be understood as a means of mediating the gap between Nature and Culture that is characteristic of National Park Nature. In his thought-provoking environmental history of the Columbia River in the United States, Richard White describes how the celebrated writer Rudyard Kipling was drawn to both the river and rod and reel fishing as a means of reconnecting to Nature. Yet, as White describes, Kipling "returned to nature at a hatchery. He caught fish whose destiny was as tied to the new industrial order as was the fate of those that entered the cannery."[48] A similar phenomenon is played out in the waters of Jasper National Park. Throughout most of Jasper's history, fish pursued by sportsmen have been artificially cultivated, but this did not seem to diminish the sense that one could have a real fishing holiday in Jasper National Park.[49]

Beginning in 1917, with the introduction of 8,000 cutthroat trout into Lac Beauvert, the culture of fishing in Jasper was mediated through artificially propagated fish stocks.[50] These stocking programs were implemented entirely for the benefit and enjoyment of tourists since they dealt only with varieties of fish that were the most popular among sportsmen.[51] The parks branch, therefore, capitalized on antimodern desires for these types of activities, and scenes of fishing formed a significant part of promotional material. At no point was there any attempt to hide the fact that the fish found in these bodies of water were not native to the region. Rather, the stocking programs were celebrated, and visitors were encouraged to include a stop at the Jasper hatchery on their holiday itineraries. A 1965 publication produced by the Jasper Chamber of Commerce, for instance, praised the hatchery programs and facilities: "You must visit this hatchery, one of the most modern and interesting in Canada. The courteous and knowledgeable staff members are always happy to explain its function, and to show you trout from three weeks old to the real granddads. Kids, especially, enjoy the antics in the fish ponds."[52] In this context, the fish found in the lakes and rivers of the Canadian Rockies served as a mediating vehicle that enabled tourists to commune with Nature.

Sport fishing began as an elite activity, linked to the rise of a wider conservation movement in nineteenth-century North America through the regulation and management of fish stocks.[53] This "modernization" of wilderness through regulation also became part of the middle-class tourist experience in Jasper National Park in the early twentieth century. There the focus by tourism promoters on fish hatcheries in the park can be understood as a means of reinscribing conservation values for a new, largely middle-class, audience by demonstrating how Nature can be preserved through such management techniques. Scenes of the fish hatcheries (which, of course, ensured fully stocked lakes and rivers) dominated the representational rhetoric of this aspect of the park until the 1970s, when these programs began to be re-evaluated.

During the early decades of the park's history, widely circulated newspapers such as the *Calgary Herald* ran stories praising the success of fish-stocking programs in Jasper, a sentiment echoed by the various commercially produced tourist guidebooks at this time.[54] As a government of Canada publication from the 1930s attests, the hatcheries and the programs of stocking Jasper's rivers and lakes with artificially harvested fish were actually perceived to be an improvement on Nature:

> Many of the lakes and streams of the park contain fish, and during recent years the restocking operations which have been widely carried out have greatly improved the conditions for sport fishing. Lakes formerly barren of fish of any kind, including the Amethyst lakes and the Maligne-Medicine lake system, have been successfully stocked with suitable varieties.[55]

In these publications, fishing is always described in terms of the enjoyment of human participants. Rarely is mention made of the non-human animals so central to this sport. Instead, emphasis is placed on "the successful fisherman" who, as Ernest Voorhis described in 1928,

> is the philosophic sportsman in whom the sight of blue waters, of forest-clad shores and islands, and even of grey skies and lowering clouds, will awaken responsive harmonious thoughts. He who can attune himself in harmony with surrounding nature, whatever be her mood, is the best type of fisherman, for the spirit of the busy office has no place in the peace of nature.[56]

As this example demonstrates, in Jasper fish have long been conceived of as cultural (and cultured) objects and understood as a vehicle for experiencing Nature, where Nature is represented by glacial streams and mountain scenery. Simply put, in the context of sport fishing in Jasper, fish are seen as a form neither of Nature nor of wildlife; they simply exist as an aid to experiencing the park through recreational pursuits. This is underscored by the fact that guidebooks and other such tourist publications have historically represented piscine species very differently from other animals found in the park.

Without exception, the dozens of historic guidebooks of the region that I consulted for my research have a section on wildlife in which certain species (chief among them bears, deer, and squirrels) are presented as tourist attractions in their own right. Fish, on the other hand, are not included in these discussions and are mentioned only in the context of sport fishing. To focus on this difference is not a mere exercise in semantics but strikes at the heart of how representations relate to dominant ideologies of nature.[57] To put it bluntly, a black bear and a Dolly Varden trout are both sentient, non-human animals, yet in the context of National Park Nature and wilderness tourism these species are treated and represented very differently. This separation continues, as evidenced by the fact that in Jasper fishing is legal, whereas hunting is not, even though both sports involve the killing of non-human species.

As Eric Higgs has pointed out, the introduction of fish hatchery programs did more than encourage sport fishing in Jasper. These programs also "led in many cases to a radical transformation of the structure of aquatic ecosystems."[58] The Jasper fish hatchery closed in 1972, coinciding with the adoption of more ecologically aware management policies.[59] In recent years, concerns regarding the sizes and types of fish that Jasper's lakes and rivers can sustain began to receive as much attention as concerns regarding the benefit and enjoyment of the anglers. As a recent government-sponsored travel brochure states, "The practice of catch and release angling is encouraged; our cold waters cannot support large fish populations."[60] However, representations of fishing as a popular pastime remain a standard part of the tourism promotion of the region, even as it is reframed in rhetoric more in line with twenty-first-century ecological concerns.

Because of its proximity to Jasper Park Lodge, Lac Beauvert in particular has been the subject of fish-stocking programs aimed at generating revenue for CNR-owned property. Lac Beauvert is one of the most photographed locations in Jasper National Park, and its shimmering waters have long stood as an icon of National Park Nature. However, as journalist Ed Struzik notes, "this postcard gem ... is also one of the most manipulated water bodies in the country ... Today, there are no non-native species left."[61] Even as the lake is dramatically altered, it continues to be celebrated for its aesthetic beauty. This pattern continues to shape representations of other recreational pursuits in Jasper as well.

"SNOW ... FROM HEAVEN"

The internationally renowned Rocky Mountains have established Canada as one of the most famous destinations for downhill ski enthusiasts, a designation firmly solidified for a global audience after the 1988 Winter Olympic Games. The mountain parks offer visitors world-class skiing in resorts such as Mount Norquay, Sunshine Village, and Lake Louise. As can be expected, skiing in Jasper has also been advertised as a key tourist attraction over the past several decades. A 1939 brochure produced by the government of Alberta, for instance, boasted that "Jasper National Park will offer ski-ing conditions of such a nature as to attract visitors from all parts of the world. A start has just been made, and members of the local ski-ing club are bubbling over with enthusiasm regarding the prospects."[62] Canadian National Railways aimed to capitalize on this sense of enthusiasm and in 1939 planned, albeit unsuccessfully, to commission William J. Oliver to produce a film about the skiing opportunities awaiting visitors to Jasper.[63]

The Marmot Basin ski resort became particularly popular after 1964, when the parks branch developed good road access and the facilities necessary to run a mechanized T-bar lift up the mountainside.[64] That season saw the rapid commercialization of the resort, and over 17,000 skiers flocked to the area between December 1964 and May 1965 to enjoy the "perfect snow conditions" offered by the newly established tourist attraction.[65] Marmot Basin continues to attract much publicity and is a mainstay of Alberta tourism promotions. In the winter 2008-9 issue of *Where* magazine, for instance, a richly illustrated advertisement for Jasper's famed ski resort proclaims that one can find both a "vast skiable terrain" and "spectacular views that fade into infinity."[66] The nine colour photographs in this ad alternate between close-up shots of toque-clad skiers smiling and having fun and more traditional, scenic-type images showing the snowy mountain landscape from a distance.

In much the same way as the image of Bing Crosby popularized the Jasper Park Lodge golf course, ski resorts in the Canadian Rockies also have a history of relying on celebrity imagery in the commodification of these sportscapes. A brochure produced in conjunction with Marmot Basin's twenty-fifth anniversary, for instance, featured a photograph of actress Brooke Shields, skis in hand, presumably about to take on the slopes of Marmot Basin.[67] This type of imagery further underscores the notion that this is a landscape of leisure and privilege.

Marmot Basin has also been celebrated in promotional material as a place to connect with the landscape and scenery of the Jasper region. "Imagine," the ski resort's website entreats, "a place where snow comes from heaven, not from Earth. A place where you spend more time on your favorite run than in lift lines. A place where the wildlife is not limited to party animals but includes deer, elk and other creatures."[68] In this context, the representational rhetoric of skiing as an essential component of National Park Nature plays on dominant cultural associations of wilderness ideals in the construction of this space in both physical and descriptive terms. The emphasis on "snow ... from heaven" and the presence of "deer, elk and other creatures" present this activity as harmonious with the ideals espoused by National Park Nature.

A photograph used in a recent promotion for Marmot Basin is typical of how this sportscape has been visually represented. The two skiers in this photograph are shown effortlessly descending a steep mountain run; in spite of the huge mountain peaks, this is not presented as a threatening landscape. Rather, it exists to be enjoyed and consumed. The absence of other skiers coupled with the exclusion of the infrastructure necessary to ensure commercial success of this sportscape alludes to the perception that skiing in the Rockies offers a means to escape to a wild, unmediated Nature.

In contrast to this type of promotion, scholars such as Hal Clifford have focused on the "extraordinarily destructive set of environmental practices" that characterizes contemporary commercialized ski resorts such as those found at Banff, Lake Louise, and Jasper.[69] "Whether they're bunny slopes or double-black-diamonds, ski runs are permanent clearcuts," Clifford argues.[70] His point is evidenced by aerial photographs of the ski areas in Jasper National Park (see, e.g., Figure 29); in such images, the ski runs that cut an abstract pattern through the mountain landscape can clearly be identified by their lack of forest vegetation. Annie Gilbert Coleman has also explored this aspect of alpine skiing and describes the "powerful ways skiers and snowboarders affect mountain landscapes through consumption."[71] Arguments made by Clifford and Coleman stand in marked contrast to the ways in which skiing has been depicted in the context of tourism over the past several decades.

Although the tourism industry continues to promote alpine skiing as a "fun, friendly, and natural"[72] way to experience the outdoors, evidence is mounting that this popular recreational activity has significant environmental impacts. In recent years, it has become increasingly clear that the maintenance of commercial ski resorts is an environmentally unsustainable

FIGURE 29   This 1955 photograph shows how trees were cleared to make way for ski runs at Whistlers Mountain. Marmot Basin eventually replaced Whistlers Mountain as the ski resort of choice in the park. *Fred Brewster, "Whistlers Mountain, Jasper National Park, Showing Ski Runs," March 1955. Jasper-Yellowhead Museum and Archives, PA 7-140, Major Frederick Archibald Brewster Fonds.*

venture, a situation that has led to campaigns to halt development of new runs and resorts.[73] Environmental activists claim that the tourism industry uses campaigns of "brilliant misinformation" as a means to downplay the ecological impacts of this type of development.[74] A standard tool in this process, activists claim, is the use of selective framing in photographic images showcasing the natural beauty of the regions in question. By cropping out evidence of human impacts on these landscapes, those with stakes in the tourism industry can continue to perpetuate the myth that alpine skiing is a form of antimodern wilderness escape, even though anyone who has visited such resorts knows that they often contain many of the same amenities found in city landscapes. In addition, it is becoming increasingly hard to accept the claim that commercialized ski resorts are environmentally benign. From the disruption of faunal habitats to the construction of large hotels and related tourist infrastructure, and the massive amounts of energy and resources consumed during the operation and maintenance of the resorts, these types of recreational sites are increasingly becoming cause for concern from an ecological point of view.[75]

Activist groups such as the Jasper Environmental Association (JEA) have argued that ski hills should be removed from Canada's national parks because they "don't fit in with the national parks mandate."[76] On the other side of the equation, spokespeople for the ski resorts in the Canadian Rocky Mountain parks argue that they should be given the opportunity to grow their businesses but agree that this must be done in an environmentally sensitive manner. Green initiatives such as eco-friendly ski wax and encouraging skiers to car pool or take public transit are becoming common in North American ski resorts.[77] This debate, of course, goes beyond the sport of skiing and is underscored by differing visions of what this landscape should look like and what its primary purpose should be. Is this to be a landscape that is left as untouched as possible, or is it to be a landscape in which one can enjoy recreational pursuits while drinking in the mountain scenery? The bifurcated advertising campaigns for places such as Marmot Basin – impossibly promising both at once – further confuse the issue.

The popularity of downhill skiing in Alberta has led to tensions between federal and provincial powers over development and tourism.[78] During parliamentary talks surrounding Bill C-30, a 1988 revisitation of the Canadian National Parks Act, the Alberta government sought more control over development in the parks to facilitate the building of more ski resorts in the Canadian Rockies and to expand the existing ones in places such as Banff and Jasper.[79] Environmental lobby groups such as the Canadian Parks and Wilderness Society applauded the federal government's decision not to permit this but have also repeatedly argued that tourism and environment do not necessarily have to be mutually exclusive entities.[80]

In 2006, new guidelines for the operation of ski resorts in national parks were introduced by the Canadian government. These new guidelines allowed for expansion – which the 2000 Panel on Ecological Integrity had recommended not be done – providing that "substantial environmental gain" was part of the plan. In theory, this meant that a ski resort could expand and reconfigure its borders to exchange lands deemed "environmentally sensitive" for parcels lacking that designation.[81] In practice, however, these guidelines have resulted in ongoing controversy. According to the JEA, the changes that Marmot Basin is making under these new guidelines do not result in substantial environmental gain. The lobby group argues that new development plans not only increase the footprint of the ski resort but also threaten wildlife in Whistlers Creek Valley, situated next to the site of a proposed expansion to Marmot Basin.[82]

About this development, the JEA asks, "How can the surrender of already protected important wildlife habitat in exchange for major development right next to it possibly constitute a 'substantial environmental gain'?"[83] Further, the expansion at Marmot Basin is designed to increase the number of skiers on the site by 60 percent. This increase would bring with it an increase in "power consumption, sewage, water use, staff numbers, highway traffic," all factors that the JEA has expressed concern about.[84]

ENVIRONMENTAL IMPACTS OF WILDERNESS PLAYGROUNDS

Throughout the twentieth century, the seemingly opposite yet fundamentally intertwined notions of Canada's national parks as both nature preserves and wilderness playgrounds have influenced everything from park management to holiday itineraries. The National Parks Act of 1930 codified this awkward position by legislating that parks such as Jasper were "dedicated to the people of Canada for their benefit, education and enjoyment ... and such parks shall be maintained and made use of so as to leave them unimpaired for future generations."[85] A publication entitled *Canada's Mountain Playgrounds,* published just after the establishment of this federal legislation, underscored this: "National Parks are now also serving as national recreational areas, where beautiful surroundings are enjoyed each year by thousands of Canadians and their guests from other lands."[86] Government publications encouraged the use of park space for both nature study and recreation as they were thought to be able to coexist harmoniously, a position perpetuated through the uncomplicated alignment of wilderness and recreation in the tourism industry.[87]

Visual representations embedded in promotional materials and items of popular culture have been especially influential in propagating the notion that this is a seamless and ecologically sustainable relationship even though this has not always been the case. There are many examples in the history of Jasper National Park of significant environmental impacts caused by leisure activities. During the summer of 1999, the Sierra Legal Defence Fund and Parks Canada celebrated a federal court ruling to uphold a ban on commercial rafting on the Maligne River in Jasper National Park.[88] Rafting has been a popular activity in the park, with an estimated 15,000 tourists participating in rafting tours on the Maligne River between June and September 1998. However, this activity has also had a significant environmental impact. Groups such as the JEA studied the effects of this popular vacation pastime on the river and concluded that it was threatening the habitat and numbers of harlequin ducks in the park.[89] Although the rafting ban had been challenged by several river rafting companies operating in the region, evidence that the harlequin duck population had increased considerably since the ban weighed heavily in favour of the most recent court ruling.[90]

Use of sections of the Tonquin Valley for trail riding offers another instance of recreational pursuits having severe environmental impacts in the park.[91] Recent studies have indicated that this is an ecologically sensitive area, and over $1 million have been spent in attempts to repair damage caused by equestrian-related activities there. Yet conceptions of environmental problems tend to shift over time. Current patterns of thought see trail riding as causing ecological damage; however, in 1988 Alberta's environment minister praised construction of the Tonquin trails as an environmental solution because it concentrated tourist traffic in one controlled corridor, a plan, it was hoped, that would leave the rest of the region "untrampled."[92]

In the late 1970s, the environmental effects of large numbers of people in these spaces became the focus of management strategies. Policies such as restrictions on the numbers of people who were allowed access to Jasper's back-country trails were implemented, and under this system access to the trails became governed by a system of advanced registration.[93] Another action was the deliberate reduction of advertising during the peak months in an attempt to stop overcrowding. Reduction in the number of tourists arriving in Jasper during the peak months in subsequent years was seen as a direct result of this action and underscores the close connections between commercial representations of the park and the physical environment.[94]

When spaces such as Jasper National Park receive large numbers of tourists, it becomes increasingly difficult for visitors to find the solitary mountain experience that likely drew many of them to the park in the first place. When landscapes become filled with tourists, they are no longer "the pristine wilderness upon which the visitor had expected to gaze."[95] Overcrowding often relates to physical concerns such as the erosion of hiking trails, but more often than not the complaints of overcrowding in these spaces stem from perceptions that an authentic wilderness experience has been ruined by the presence of other tourists. These expectations stem from the dominant ways in which this region has been visually represented throughout its history.

The Canadian National Parks Act of 2000 aims to "make the protection of ecological integrity the first priority for all aspects of national park management."[96] This can be seen as an extension of the mainstreaming of environmental values in contemporary Canadian society. Growing debate about ecological issues and the introduction of green products and lifestyle choices have brought the environment front and centre in Canadian culture, even if opinions differ about the benefits of this development. As an extension of these shifts, the most recent parks legislation has placed more emphasis on ecology; however, as a quick survey of promotional material relating to Jasper National Park shows, leisure and recreation maintain a dominant position in this particular wilderness industry. Moreover, the Canadian Parks and Wilderness Society, a non-profit organization dedicated to the conservation of Canada's national parks, has argued that the new legislation appears to be applied inconsistently and points to ongoing development projects in Jasper National Park. For instance, permission has been granted for projects such as expansion of the Jasper Park Lodge as well as construction of a new ski lift at Marmot Basin.[97] In spite of changes in legislation, Jasper National Park – in fact the entire Alberta Rocky Mountain region – continues to be described and promoted as a "Rocky Mountain playground."

"Shutterbug Guides"

In light of recent environmental concerns in national parks, tourists are often told to "take only pictures, leave only footprints." The pursuit of photography by recreational enthusiasts has a long history in Canada's national parks. "Bring your camera!" the brochures have boldly exclaimed for the past several decades.

> When you are happy, time passes all too quickly and your vacation at Jasper seems to go in the twinkling of an eye. What can you do to carry some of

it back with you to the workaday world? You can take the health you have
stored up and you have your memories. There's something else though ...
Trap the shadows of those delightful hours on the film of your camera! Take
Jasper home in movies or stills, in black and white or color.[98]

Through the years, most tourist publications about Jasper National Park
included a section devoted to amateur photography and often featured
tips for getting that postcard-perfect snapshot alongside information about
where to buy photographic supplies.

The links between photography and recreational activities in the region
were reinforced by direct alignment of the photographic industry with
visual promotion of such activities in the park. A ski brochure produced
in the late 1980s included an advertisement for Kodak boasting that this
particular brand of film was the official film of Marmot Basin, Jasper's
world-famous ski resort.[99] Here the act of skiing at Marmot Basin becomes
an extension of the corporate brand; Kodak is not merely selling photographic products but also positioning its products and services as an essential element of National Park Nature. Similarly, the summer 2001 issue
of *Jasper* (a free publication given to tourists entering the park) contained
an advertisement featuring a digitally altered image of a bear standing atop
an impossibly large box of Kodak film. The accompanying caption proclaimed that "wild life looks best with Kodak film and paper." Such advertisements underscore the idea that taking pictures is an important part
of the tourist experience in Jasper National Park.

Snapshots allow tourists to reinforce the notion that spaces are uninhabited; pictorial conventions lead most people to frame their snapshots
to exclude other tourists from the scene (apart, perhaps, from one's immediate family or travelling companions). When these pictures are developed,
put into albums, and circulated among family and friends, the visual mythology that defines wilderness as tracts of uninhabited (and therefore untouched and pristine) land is repeated and further solidified. This type of
tourist photography allows what John Urry calls the "romantic tourist gaze"
to be "endlessly reproduced and recaptured."[100] In this way, tourist photography plays a significant role in the construction of National Park Nature.

The landscape of Jasper National Park is visually ordered in a specific
way. Through various representational means, tourists are told what to see
and what to take pictures of; roads carry travellers to designated scenic
attractions, and certain features are marked on maps and named in brochures. These framing devices, by extension, also dictate which aspects of

nature are valued and inform the production of environmental knowledge for many park visitors. The development of automobile tourism in North American national parks played a significant part in this process as tourists no longer had to rely on public forms of transportation to visit these spaces. As part of these new transportation developments, roadside pullouts that encourage tourists to stop at designated spots to take photographs have become a popular feature in parks such as Jasper. Although the automobile freed tourists from the rigidity of train schedules, visual engagement with the landscape remained highly structured, and tourists were encouraged to see and photograph the same sights that countless other tourists saw and photographed. Far more than visual souvenirs, these holiday snaps add another layer of naturalization to the ideals of National Park Nature.

The photogenic qualities of the region were praised in much of the tourist literature, and, as the following excerpt from a 1942 CNR publication demonstrates, tourist photography quickly became a favourite activity for many visitors to the park:

> To camera fans – and their number is legion, Jasper National Park offers opportunities unexcelled on the Continent. The clear atmosphere of the Canadian Rockies, and the brilliant light make it possible to secure photographic gems in black and white, and natural color, that serve as the finest mementos of a visit to this unmatched scenic region.[101]

Similarly, a 1948 publication by Bill Gibbons, entitled *Photographing the Canadian Rockies,* included a map with the "must see" destinations between Jasper and Banff laid out. "This map, for which no geographic accuracy is claimed," Gibbons writes, "has been prepared to instantly locate scenes featured in this publication. The beauty spots included are regarded as photographic musts."[102] In the 1965 issue of *Jasper Tourist News,* photographers were given a "shutterbug guide" – a list of the best places to take photographs in Jasper, including Lac Beauvert, Jasper Park Lodge, and Maligne Canyon. Visitors were also encouraged to photograph bears (though they were warned not to attempt a close-up) and given tips on how to best photograph the many different types of flowers and plants found in the park.[103] Since so many tourists to Jasper expressed interest in capturing picture-perfect souvenir snapshots, photographic tours were often offered to visitors staying at Jasper Park Lodge.[104]

Many local photographers have operated successful businesses in the region, and there has been an ample supply of shops carrying photographic supplies and specializing in photo-finishing services in Jasper National Park. A 1944 illustrated guidebook, for instance, encouraged travellers to Jasper to visit the shop of H.J. Perrier: "Take your Films here for Finishing, and be sure of the finest results! His shop is on the Main Street, opposite the Railway Station, giving train-travellers time to pop over between trains for pictorial souvenirs."[105] Not to be outdone, Jasper Park Lodge also catered to the needs of hobby photographers; film developing was available at the lodge's "novelty shop," where guests could also purchase souvenir postcards and replacement film.[106]

Current visitors to Jasper can take courses and workshops on nature photography offered each summer through the Jasper Institute, the instructional branch of the Friends of Jasper National Park, a non-profit organization dedicated to "promoting understanding, appreciation and respect" in the park.[107] Visitors to the region are also given complimentary maps complete with icons indicating the famous scenic points, ideal locations to get those postcard-perfect holiday snapshots. This promotion of specific scenic views through signified markers has been a constant feature of the tourist experience of Jasper National Park.[108] The result of this practice, as ecocritic Catriona Sandilands argues, is that

> nature becomes a series of photo-opportunities; the tourist has truly "experienced" nature when she has the pictures of it to take home, and these pictures should resemble the ones she saw before she came ... In this commoditizing move, the specificity of the landscape is organized to the facilitation of particular kinds of views – distance, vistas, breathtaking grandeur, wildlife, etc.[109]

Tourist photography, then, is never simply a neutral pastime. Rather, it acts in a self-reflexive manner to legitimize further the ideologies of tourism and systems of environmental knowledge informed by National Park Nature.

CONSUMING LEISURE

Photography, whether used as a promotional tool to advertise Jasper National Park or an activity to enjoy while visiting the park, facilitates consumption of this landscape. This consumption occurs in both a visual and a physical sense, with the two forms being closely interrelated. In this way, both the pursuit of recreational photography and the photographic records of other leisure activities can be considered as part of what Thorstein Veblen referred to as the immaterial "trophies of exploit," evidence that "one's time had not been spent in industrial employment."[110] Tourist photography serves as a means both to verify participation in and to create desire for leisure activities. These concepts are particularly applicable in a discussion of photographic representations of National Park Nature because this type of imagery not only functions as a means of selling the wilderness experience but also allows tourists to identify themselves with this form of consumption and leisured lifestyle, even if temporarily. Photographic postcards with the typical "wish you were here" messages (or, by implication, "I'm here, and you're not!") form a significant aspect of tourist photography in Jasper National Park and vividly underscore this notion.

Ross Mitchell has argued that Veblen's writings have important applications for current environmental analysis in that they offer "insights on the role of humanity in both causing and exacerbating global environmental crises."[111] Veblen's theories of "conspicuous leisure" and "conspicuous consumption" underscore a sense of separation between spaces where leisure is consumed and spaces where work is undertaken or, to put it another way, between Nature and Culture.

RECREATIONAL CLUBS AND ENVIRONMENTAL ADVOCACY

The consumption of goods, services, resources, and landscapes in the pursuit of authentic encounters with Nature and non-human animals has had a significant environmental impact on Jasper National Park. The consumption of images in the context of National Park Nature and wilderness tourism has shaped dominant cultural assumptions about how the landscape of the park should be treated. Often the environmental impacts of tourist activities are occluded through representational techniques that serve to maintain the sense of pristine and unspoiled wilderness so important to the construction of National Park Nature.

The relationship between recreation and the perpetuation of dominant environmental ideologies can be further complicated when we consider that over the course of the past several decades many sport enthusiasts and recreational clubs have become involved with environmental activism campaigns. Groups such as the Alpine Club of Canada have utilized both imagery and direct action political tactics in campaigns aimed to protect the environment in the Canadian Rocky Mountains.[112] In much the same way that Ansel Adams's photographs were intended to show the intrinsic beauty and value of spaces such as Yosemite Valley in the United States, the use of photography as a means to incite a desire to protect this landscape from the ills of development has been (and continues to be) a key component of this dynamic in the Canadian Rockies.

As scholars of sport tourism Joy Standeven and Paul DeKnop have argued, outdoor recreation enthusiasts are motivated to be concerned about the environment in which they play: "The more the natural environment is spoiled, the less possibility there will be for practicing both new and old forms of outdoor activities. Sport tourism is nowadays putting intense pressure on the natural environment, endangering it, and because of that sport tourism is also in danger."[113] From this perspective, then, recreational groups can have a positive environmental impact in that many will actively lobby authorities to keep their favourite recreational region free from development and industrial activity that would alter the environmental character of that region. Recreational activities formed a considerable part of national park tourism over the past several decades, and the presence or absence of particular sportscapes has tremendous economic significance. Scholars such as John Urry have argued that, because of the appeal of recreation, there is a financial incentive to ensure that the landscapes of tourism maintain at least some level of ecological integrity. In this way, contemporary tourism helps to "heighten an environmental consciousness and, indeed, in some cases to improve aspects of the physical environment."[114] The appeal of engaging in recreational activities in a landscape that appears to be environmentally unspoiled is attractive to many tourists, and there is a financial incentive to maintain at least the illusion of an unspoiled environment.

This type of sentiment is not simply a feature of contemporary environmental politics. Historian Jennifer Price has described the different sentiments that accompanied sport hunting and market hunting in the United States during the late nineteenth and early twentieth centuries. As species such as the now extinct carrier pigeon began to dwindle, a number of sportsmen who pursued these species denied that they had contributed to their demise. They laid the blame squarely on so-called market hunters, who killed for profit, not pleasure.[115] Sportsmen, it was argued, did not wish to see the end of a species on which their sport was so dependent. In his history of the conservation movement in the United States, John F. Reiger demonstrates how hunting and sport fishing were integral to broader conservation movements. A large part of this, Reiger argues, was "the growth of group identity."[116] Those who considered themselves to be "true sportsmen" followed a "well-defined code of conduct and thinking" that included both "proper etiquette" and "an aesthetic appreciation of the whole environmental context of sport that included a commitment to its perpetuation."[117] Similarly, Gerard J. van den Broek has pointed out how "special measures" have historically been taken to protect the fox in Britain, "as foxhunting was one of the leisure time activities of the gentry."[118] In a Canadian context, historian Margaret Lewis has shown that sportsmen and sportswomen have helped the conservationist movement in Alberta in a similar way, and she calls the province's hunters and fishermen the region's "first conservationists."[119] According to this pattern of thought, protecting species for the purposes of sport is still a form of environmental protection. Ducks Unlimited, for example, is an organization dedicated to "wetland and habitat conservation," which also happens to support "waterfowl hunting, when conducted in an ethical and sustainable manner, as a legitimate and acceptable use of a renewable resource."[120]

This dynamic has also informed the preservation of land in western Canada. One of the best-known examples is the environmental advocacy of the Alpine Club of Canada (ACC), which has been spurred on by proposed development projects in the Rocky Mountains. As PearlAnn Reichwein explains, the ACC was founded in 1906 with the "dual objectives of opening up the mountains as a 'national playground' while preserving the wildlife, plants, habitat and 'natural beauties of the mountain place' – a noteworthy parallel to the dual mandate of the National Parks."[121] In 1911, when the Dominion Forest Reserves and Parks Act redrew Jasper's boundaries, reducing the park to one-fifth of its original size to allow for expansion of natural resource-based industries in the region, the ACC and the Grand Trunk Pacific Railway lobbied against this reduction of park space.[122] During the 1920s and 1930s, the ACC once again got involved in the protection of park space by lobbying against proposed hydro development projects in the Rocky Mountains.[123]

This connection between recreational pursuits and environmental concerns has been explored by several scholars in recent years. Geographer John Shultis, for instance, has discussed research into the "second-stage ramifications of the recreation experience," pointing out that many of the best-known Nature advocates in North American history credit their interest in and devotion to environmental issues to "life-changing" recreational experiences in their youth.[124] As Shultis writes, "It is hard to underestimate ... the impact of the wilderness wanderings of such writers as Thoreau, Muir, Leopold ... and Edward Abbey on contemporary protected area legislation, policy, and management and thus on society's construction of meanings of nature, wilderness, and protected areas."[125] In their study of the association between forest recreation and cultivation of environmental values, Mark Nord, A.E. Luloff, and Jeffrey C. Bridger distinguish between "appreciative" and "consumptive" forms of outdoor recreation.[126] Appreciative activities "involve attempts to enjoy the natural environment without altering it."[127] Consumptive activities, in contrast, "involve altering the environment in some way and therefore reflect a more utilitarian view."[128] The work of Nord, Luloff, and Bridger emphasizes significant connections between how landscape is used and the perpetuation of environmental knowledge. My analysis differs from theirs in one fundamental way, however. They consider photography to be an appreciative activity, while I insist that tourist photography can, and does, have a large impact on the physical environment of a place. Basic assumptions in the work of Nord, Luloff, and Bridger suggest that it is possible to enjoy the "natural environment" without altering it, an assumption that sees true Nature as unspoiled and untouched and that obscures much of the human impact on this landscape.

The connections between environmental activism and recreational activities are highly complex; many environmentalists are enthusiastic recreationists who attribute their love of Nature to time spent engaging in outdoor leisure activities. This relationship becomes complicated, however, when the environmental impacts of these activities are considered. Hal Clifford notes that it is easy for environmentalists (he includes himself in this category) to find fault with industry activities on ecological grounds but that it is much harder to "look in the mirror" and raise the same questions.[129] Although there is certainly a connection between environmental conservation and recreation in spaces such as Jasper National Park, a move toward more sustainable ways of engaging with this landscape will require a rethinking of this relationship. Recreation is an industry, and, like other industries operating in the Canadian Rockies (among them forestry and mining), its primary focus is on the natural resources in this region. Arguments that stress how recreational advocacy groups are an essential component of conservation efforts in this landscape must also take into account the fact that this industry often competes with other industries for these resources and, by extension, economic profit.

CONCLUSION

The relationship between recreation and the environment is extremely complex. Advertisements for certain types of recreation have had the effect of shaping dominant understandings of nature and, in some cases, have created situations in which certain species or landscapes are protected at the expense of others. The promotion and pursuit of recreational activities in Jasper National Park have resulted in this landscape being conceived of in very specific terms.

Recreational pursuits in the park have long been mediated through the lens of the camera. There is a cyclical process in which advertisements for leisure activities in the park rely on photographic images to attract visitors. The images in these promotions either showcase the scenic spectacles of the region or focus on individuals (or small groups of people) enjoying activities such as skiing or golfing. The sense of harmony between these two representational patterns within the frame of a tourist brochure perpetuates the mythology that it is possible to have both an untouched wilderness and a good time with family and friends in this landscape. The absence of large crowds in visual representations of these spaces also helps reinforce this sentiment. The cycle of image production and consumption continues as visitors use cameras to make images that at once serve as evidence of participation in the advertised activities and visually confirm the scenic and uncrowded qualities for which this landscape is celebrated. Whether these images are recorded on film or through digital technologies matters less than the ideals of National Park Nature they convey. In fact, as rapidly as image-making technologies have shifted (including the introduction of camera phones and the ability to instantaneously share images with family and friends over the Internet), the resulting images have remained remarkably stable.

Representational and promotional strategies continue to perpetuate the notion that a visit to the Canadian Rocky Mountain parks is an antimodern escape to a wilderness playground. As the preceding discussion has argued, however, the consumption of landscape and leisure in Jasper National Park is deeply related to, rather than separate from, the capitalist consumer culture of North American society. Cultural, social, economic, and environmental factors influencing and influenced by recreational activities and the pursuit of leisure in Jasper National Park have been masked historically through dominant representations of this space. As calls for the restoration of ecological integrity to this region increasingly dominate discussion of the Canadian Rocky Mountain parks, the environmental and economic impacts of these popular sportscapes will need to be reconsidered.

4

"The Bears Are Plentiful and Frequently Good Camera Subjects": Photographing Wildlife in Jasper National Park

On 6 May 1944, the *Globe and Mail* of Toronto published a photograph entitled "Wolves Close in on Moose for Kill" (see Figure 30). The photo was supplied to the newspaper by J.A. Rogers, the general superintendent of transportation for Canadian National Railways, then one of the major corporate players in Jasper National Park.[1] "This remarkable picture of life-and-death drama in the wilds of Northwest Canada" was said to have been "taken by a trapper on the Smoky River ... in the northwest section of Jasper Park."[2] Subsequent debate and an investigation revealed that the photograph had been fabricated, that two separate images had been combined to achieve this dramatic scene.

In many respects, the *Globe and Mail* photograph is similar to the 1911 "Nip and Tuck with a Bass" postcard discussed earlier (see Figure 27). Both are "fake" photographs imbued with an additional layer of meaning by the interplay of words and images. But there are major differences between them. The tall-tale postcard is a whimsical souvenir item. Although it alludes to components of the wilderness ideal, no one expected viewers to believe that the lakes and rivers of Jasper National Park contained fish larger than most humans. The *Globe and Mail* photograph, on the other hand, appeared in the context of a news story and was accompanied by a caption intended to lend authenticity to the scene.

Clearly, not all wildlife photography made in Jasper National Park was as fabricated as the *Globe and Mail* image, but, equally, none of the images of non-human animals from the park have been ideologically neutral.

FIGURE 30   This composite photograph appeared in the *Globe and Mail* on 6 April 1944 and intended to show a pack of wolves chasing down a moose. The photograph was supplied to the newspaper by an executive of Canadian National Railways. After the photograph was published in the paper, questions about its authenticity were raised, and after an investigation it was determined to be a fake. *Photographer(s) Unknown, "Wolves Close in on Moose for Kill," 1944. Canadian Science and Technology Museum, X17883.*

Even though it was and remains fairly rare for tourists to engage directly with bears, wolves, or moose on their travels to the Canadian Rocky Mountain parks, most visitors hoped to encounter at least a glimpse of these non-human animals. The promise of such encounters has been re- peated almost endlessly by promoters of park tourism. A 1934 CNR brochure about Jasper claimed that

> one of the great charms of the park is the abundance and fearlessness of its wild life. To wake in the morning and see a deer below one's window, a black bear ambling off into the forest, or, on the trail, to be able to come close to the shyest creatures of the wild, the mountain sheep and goat; to watch the beaver at his busy engineering or the lordly elk, moose and

cariboo making their stately way through the woods, is a pleasure which makes every walk or ride a possible adventure.[3]

The link between wildlife species and National Park Nature is further strengthened by the common practice of naming tourist facilities after non-human animals and using brochures and postcards featuring species not generally found in urban settings – what has come to be known simply as wildlife. Typically, tourism promoters draw on a sense of awe and fascination with specific, and usually photogenic, types of non-human animals to create a particular sense of Nature in the region. Through these types of representational strategies, the term "wildlife" has come to stand for all undomesticated non-human animals in these spaces, even though only a few select species have shaped this definition in the popular imagination.

Representations of wildlife have played a significant role in the construction of the Jasper National Park experience and centre on the cultural constructs of wild and tame, which are continually mediated through representational means. Considering how photographic images have facilitated the construction of these oppositional categories, I discuss how tourism promoters use imagery of non-human animals, with particular focus on the ways in which certain species have come to be understood as part of National Park Nature. Images of wildlife have been part of overall representational conventions of Jasper National Park, and certain species have come to be synonymous with the wilderness experience of the region. However, populations of non-human animals that we tend to associate with Canada's Rocky Mountain parks have, in fact, been a little less natural than current tourist promotions would have us believe.[4]

WILDLIFE PORTRAITS

The current rhetoric of tourism promotion in the Canadian Rocky Mountains focuses on the wildness of faunal species in the parks. A recent Parks Canada brochure attributes the difference between non-human animals in park spaces and those in urban zoos to the relative tameness of zoo animals in comparison with those found in Banff and Jasper. "Is there a difference," the brochure asks,

between a wild bear and one in a zoo? We can only guess what the bear might think. But from our perspective, isn't the very thing that makes wild animals so attractive to us the fact that they are indeed wild? Unfortunately, when animals become used to being around people, they are in danger of losing that very thing that makes them special, their wildness.[5]

By this reckoning, encounters with non-human animals in Jasper National Park will be more authentic than encounters with non-human animals at a zoo or a theme park.

For all that, visual representations of non-human animals within the park tell a different story. In tourist brochures, familiar pictorial codes are adopted and effectively tame "wildlife" according to dominant cultural expectations. Only certain species are represented, and they are represented only in non-threatening and aesthetically pleasing ways. Close-up photography (achieved, presumably, with telephoto lenses) is favoured. Tightly framed scenes crop out elements inconsistent with National Park Nature while zooming in on the eyes and other facial features of these iconic creatures. Such wildlife portraits decontextualize the subject of the photograph from the lived actualities of the individual animal's day-to-day existence.

Current representational trends dictate that these photos be of a solitary animal who becomes representative of an entire species as well as a signifier of wildlife in general. Tourist photography generally presents these select animals as if they were posing for the camera, suggesting that the process of taking the photograph was consensual.[6] Occasionally, an animal is shown engaged in some activity, but this is, again, strictly regulated by cultural expectations. Souvenir postcards, for instance, can depict an elk grazing on grass, or a squirrel nibbling on a nut, but there are few if any examples of a wolf devouring the carcass of a freshly killed deer. Non-human animals, their habits, and their habitats are pictorially removed from the contexts in which they exist and sanitized by this form of tourist photography.

In the wildlife photography that dominates tourist brochures of Jasper National Park, the human values represented in pictures of non-human animals are consistent with the commercial aims of tourism operators. The photographs promise a vacation that is at once tame and wild. Visitors hope to see and photograph animals they would not encounter in urban spaces, yet they do not want to be scared or threatened by them. These expectations have been naturalized through the repetition of certain representational conventions. Today wildlife is central to the Jasper National Park experience, and this "animal economy" is a key component of national park tourism, environmental activism, and overall park management strategies. To quote geographers Jody Emel and Jennifer Wolch, "animals ... are serious business."[7]

The "Zoological Gaze"

From the early days of the fur trade to recent controversial policies regarding the management of wolf populations, certain species of animals have occupied a prominent position in the history and mythology of the Canadian Rockies.[8] Even the iconic cartoon figure of Jasper the Bear has played an important role in defining this region. Jasper the Bear was introduced by Canadian artist James Simpkins and made his first public appearance in the pages of *Maclean's* magazine in 1948.[9] The figure of Jasper the Bear has since become synonymous with Jasper National Park, and having one's photograph taken next to the fibreglass statue of Jasper the Bear that stands along the main street of the Jasper townsite, Connaught Drive, remains a popular tourist activity.

Images of certain types of non-human animals have become normalized as part of the standard promotional rhetoric in the iconography and identity of Jasper National Park. Those with a stake in the tourism industry – from Parks Canada to privately owned businesses specializing in holiday accommodations, recreational opportunities, and souvenir sales – have capitalized on public desire for imagery of wildlife. Postcards and other souvenir items featuring photographs of non-human animals have helped to construct and sustain what sociologist Adrian Franklin has termed the "zoological gaze" or "the manner in which viewing animals has been organized socially over time."[10]

Much of the tourist literature about Jasper speaks of the "friendly boundaries" of the park, which is seen to provide a "haven" protecting non-human animals from the perceived ills of development and civilization.[11] Through this type of representation, Jasper is presented as the antithesis of the hustle and bustle of modern life, and in this context visual culture has gone a long way toward fostering this imaginary divide. Cultural production has long dictated how non-human animals are conceived of and ultimately treated in Western society. From novels and fairy tales to paintings, films, and advertisements, representations of non-human species continually shape the dynamics of interspecies interactions. As I have demonstrated throughout this book, National Park Nature is dependent on a sense of distance between Nature and Culture. In the Nature of the Canadian Rockies, non-human animals such as bears, deer, and bighorn sheep are standard fare and are conceived of as wild and untamed, while non-human animals encountered in spaces characterized by notions of civilization fit into very different systems of representation. In urban centres, non-human animals are generally categorized as pets (cats, dogs), pests (rodents, seagulls), or bugs (ants, spiders, cockroaches), with each group reflecting human desires, behaviours, attitudes, and habits.

Representational categories governing how specific species are understood in relation to human societies are not static but change in relation to shifts in dominant cultural ideologies. This dynamic is not limited to spaces such as Jasper National Park, however. One of the main ways in which North Americans interact with and affect non-human animal populations is through the consumption of meat. In contemporary society, the processes involved in bringing meat to the table are largely hidden; consumer engagement with non-human species is limited to the end product, which tends to be packaged in such a way as to disguise its origins.[12] This stands in marked contrast to the visuality of livestock in urban areas in previous historical periods.[13]

Technologies of representation have played an important part in shaping how certain species have come to be understood in relation to human society. Imagery of non-human animals, of course, predates the photographic era by centuries, and there is a growing body of scholarship exploring the history of picturing animals.[14] Photographic technology, however, has had a significant and unprecedented impact on the construction of the zoological gaze from the mid-nineteenth century onward. Photography made visible many aspects of animal life (both human and non-human) that were previously difficult, if not impossible, for the naked eye to see. One often-cited example is Eadweard Muybridge's nineteenth-century photographic project *Animal Locomotion*. This project turned common activities such as a human walking or a bird flying into a series of photographs made seconds apart. The photographs broke each activity down into a multitude of component motions. Although his work in this area focused on countless animals and activities, Muybridge is best remembered for his photographs demonstrating that when a horse gallops there is a point at which all four of its feet are off the ground, which had been debated because it was so difficult to observe with the naked eye.[15] New technologies continue to influence the ways in which animals are viewed and understood in Western society. A recent example is the introduction of "animal cams," web cameras that give viewers around the world the opportunity to observe pandas, elephants, apes, and polar bears from the comfort of their own homes – a twenty-first-century twist on the armchair adventurer theme.[16]

SEEING THE BEARS

In Jasper National Park, the zoological gaze has been structured predominantly through the medium of photography and has focused on select species of mammals such as black bears and bighorn sheep, non-human animals that best correspond with established ideas of National Park Nature. Certain species have come to be synonymous with the wilderness experience of Jasper National Park, though this, too, has been the product of much human intervention. The populations of non-human animals we currently associate with Canada's Rocky Mountains have fluctuated over time due to human activities, among them hunting and, more recently, parks management policies.

Certain non-human animals have been especially dominant in the rhetoric of National Park Nature and have featured prominently in the tourist photography of Jasper National Park. "Four of a Kind, Jasper Park" (see Figure 31) plays on Western society's traditional fascination with bears. The photograph used on this postcard was taken by G. Morris Taylor and shows five black bears – a mother and four cubs – crossing the railway tracks in the park. Many postcards sent from the Canadian Rocky Mountains have repeated this theme: there are bears on golf courses, bears on hotel properties, small children feeding bears, bears approaching cars on the highway, and, my favourite, a bear sitting in the driver's seat of a car (see Figure 32). According to these examples, which present the wildlife of Jasper National Park as non-threatening and existing entirely for human enjoyment and entertainment, it seems that the CNR's claim that "comical bears are always on hand to greet visitors and pose for pictures" is indeed the case in Jasper National Park.[17]

The juxtaposition of non-human animals with evidence of human activity and technological innovation has been an especially popular component of tourist photography in the Canadian Rocky Mountains. The sense of anthropomorphism evident in these images trivializes these animals at the same time as it underscores the sense of difference thought to exist between human and non-human species. The bear in the car, for instance, appears humorous because automobiles exist outside the realm in which

FIGURE 31   In this undated postcard, the natural world is shown as harmoniously co-existing with human-built technologies. *G. Morris Taylor, "Four of a Kind, Jasper Park," n.d. Collection of the author.*

FIGURE 32   Postcards showing bears engaged in activities that are normally the purview of humans have been especially popular in the Canadian Rockies. *Byron Harmon, "Black Bear," n.d. Collection of the author.*

we have been socially conditioned to expect to encounter such animals. The ideals of National Park Nature, entirely dependent on a sense of separation between Nature and Culture, are not jeopardized by these types of images. The two realms remain distinct even when appearing in the same photograph. It is obvious which of these pictorial subjects is to be read as wild and which is to be understood as evidence of humankind's taming of nature, even though the divisions between the two realms are not as clear-cut as they first appear to be. Yet the juxtaposition of Nature and Culture (or wild and tame) in the same pictorial frame strengthens dominant cultural understandings of both in that each serves as a counterpoint to the other. One factor that makes landscapes such as Jasper National Park unique in the minds of tourists is that this is a space where the two realms seem to coexist harmoniously.

Human interaction with bears in park spaces has not been limited to images on souvenir postcards. In the first few decades after Jasper was established as a national park, tourists were encouraged to engage with the bears of the region. In the 1920s, advertisements in the *Edmonton Journal* encouraged people to ride the train to Jasper to see and feed the bears in the park.[18] CNR actively promoted this type of wilderness encounter and facilitated means for park visitors to interact with these animals. One promotional pamphlet produced by CNR during the 1930s gave information about a special taxi service for tourists staying at Jasper Park Lodge; for fifty cents, guests could take a taxi from the front door of the lodge to "see the bears."[19]

There are countless photographic postcards and tourist snapshots showing people happily engaging with bears in the Canadian Rockies – an activity that is somewhat shocking to our twenty-first-century sensibilities. Joe Weiss's photograph "Hello You" (see Figure 33) shows a small child posed next to a bear cub in Jasper National Park. The juxtaposition of a human child with an animal "child" would no doubt have made this a popular postcard image. The positions of the two figures within the photographic frame is also significant. The child, dressed in white, stands on the walkway that runs alongside the cottage behind the two figures. Both the path and the cottage can be read as evidence of human domestication of this space. Conversely, the black bear stands on the grass, which, though carefully maintained and manicured, signifies Nature. Despite the physical closeness of the two figures, the mythical divide that separates Nature from Culture is played out in this photograph. Even though physical proximity to and direct engagement with the bear by the child

"HELLO YOU"

FIGURE 33   Photographs of encounters between humans and bears are a hallmark of a previous era in Jasper National Park, since these kinds of interactions are no longer encouraged in Canadian national parks. *Joe Weiss, "Hello You" (Loretta North with a bear at Jasper Park Lodge), 1930s. Jasper-Yellowhead Museum and Archives, PA 73-3, Jasper-Yellowhead Historical Society Historian's Photograph Collection.*

in this image seem rather alarming to viewers in the twenty-first century, the ideals that fuelled the making of this image – that humans and non-human animals can peacefully coexist in this space – continue to inform tourist photography in the Canadian Rocky Mountain parks.

Photographs found in postcards, brochures, and guidebooks influenced how visitors to Jasper conceived of and interacted with non-human animals they encountered on their mountain holidays. As Thomas Dunlap has noted, in the context of Canadian national parks, non-human animals have often been seen as simply part of the landscape:

Canada established National Parks in the late nineteenth century as places for scenery and relaxation ... When park officials did think of animals, they thought in terms of scenery. Their ideal was a large ruminant, majestic, graceful, with horns or antlers, posing in a family group in the middle distance against the backdrop of mountain peaks.[20]

In the Rocky Mountain parks in particular, a sense of wildlife existing entirely for the enjoyment of tourists anxious to experience an authentic wilderness encounter and to bring home an album full of snapshots providing evidence of this experience seems to have dominated early tourism management decisions in the region.

As early as the 1930s, however, there were concerns about human interactions with non-human species in the Rocky Mountain national parks.[21] In particular, there were concerns over tourists feeding bears. A number of "injuries to incautious visitors" who offered tasty morsels to these animals led to a 1951 revision of the National Park Game Regulations.[22] This legislative addition "prohibited the touching, feeding or enticing of bears with candy or food," and, as national park historian W.F. Lothian notes, "general observance of the new regulation was more evident after several park visitors paid a fine in court following their conviction for feeding the bears."[23] Even those who chose not to offer food to these animals could find themselves in danger of a violent encounter with a bear that had been attracted to an area frequented by humans because of food and garbage smells. In 1958, a young girl who was visiting Jasper National Park with her family was killed by a black bear, an incident that prompted renewed efforts to reduce factors thought to be attracting bears to campsites and other spaces where tourists gathered.[24] Bears, too, often suffered as a result of this relationship. On 31 May 1930, the *Banff News* reported a heart-wrenching tale of a bear cub killed after being struck by a car. The young cub had apparently been enjoying a snack provided by the occupants of one car when it was run over by an oncoming vehicle. The paper reported that

> the mother bear enraged pursued the automobile for a distance and then returned to her cub. She nuzzled the lifeless body, voicing sad cries. A fascinated crowd saw the bereaved mother sadly pick up the bruised little body and carry it away into the bush far from curious eyes.[25]

Human encounters with bears can end tragically, and these examples underscore the importance of regulatory efforts aimed at reducing such incidents. Yet images of illegal behaviour continued to circulate. A postcard sent from the Canadian Rockies in June 1969 (see Figure 34) showed a

Piggy Back Bear, Banff National Park, Alta., Canada.

Photo: Jean Powell

FIGURE 34 This hand-coloured photographic postcard shows a mother and her cub leaning against a car in the Canadian Rockies. *Jean Powell, "Piggy Back Bear," n.d. Collection of the author.*

mother bear and her cub standing up against a car stopped along the side of the road.[26] The pre-printed caption on the back of the card reads, "This is a very cute and unusual picture but *Please do not feed the Bears* as it is very dangerous." The juxtaposition of image and text in this instance demonstrates the uneasy relations between National Park Nature and national park policies.[27]

Policies toward predator species have changed in recent years. Postcards and other forms of tourist photography featuring bears, elk, and sheep remain popular but are now presented in a slightly different light. Images of children sharing their lunches with animals along the roadside have faded to the status of historical artifact, though the notion of humans existing in harmony with cute, cuddly, photogenic fauna remains a dominant theme in visual representations of Jasper National Park. Further, the same select species continue to stand as representatives for the entire wildlife population, in essence reducing the highly complex ecosystem to a series of photo-ops with a select few charismatic megafauna.

Hunting with a Camera

The tourism industry has drawn repeatedly on photogenic animals such as elk, mountain goats, marmots, and bears to promote the Canadian Rocky Mountains, and tourists have been encouraged to "hunt with the camera" while in Jasper National Park.[28] Throughout the twentieth century, illustrated guidebooks produced by Parks Canada and Canadian National Railways published tips on wildlife photography alongside stock photographs of bears, elk, deer, and other faunal tourist attractions, and a 1942 publication proclaimed that in Jasper "animals become so tame that they may be posed easily for pictures, especially deer, elk, mountain sheep, goats and bear."[29] When this sentiment is compared with the above-quoted 2003 Parks Canada brochure in which the level of wildness of non-human animals living in the national parks is compared with that of those living in zoos, it becomes apparent that notions of wild and tame in the context of Canadian national parks have not remained consistent throughout the history of these spaces.

Photographer W.J. Oliver was one of the most vocal advocates of hunting with a camera, and this sentiment informed much of the work he produced for the parks branch. This was also the underlying theme in two films made by Oliver, *Hunting without a Gun* (1933) and *Stalking Big Game* (1934), and of a lecture he delivered on CBC Radio in 1937.[30] Both the films and the radio address underscored the notion of wildlife appreciation through visual culture, and in this context the lens of the camera became a critical tool for experiencing and appreciating Nature in the Canadian Rockies. This sentiment remains a crucial part of contemporary tourism promotions for the region. For instance, in the 2009-10 issue of *Experience the Mountain Parks,* a free magazine that serves as a "visitors' guide to Alberta and British Columbia," an article on the wildlife in the mountain parks reminds tourists to keep their cameras "ready for action."[31]

As Matthew Brower has argued, this type of photography can be contextualized as a form of hunting, as it preserves "the moment of the animal's capture" and yields products to be "circulated and displayed as trophies."[32] Promotions encouraging hunting with a camera[33] foster human behaviour that obeys federal laws, since hunting in its traditional form is illegal in Jasper National Park.[34] Pictorial, rather than taxidermic, trophies provide evidence of an authentic wilderness experience, and in this way park borders are reinforced through technology; within Jasper, one is required to hunt with a camera, while outside park borders the weapon of choice can be a firearm. By directing visitors to adopt a different set of behavioural codes and conventions – the collection of "camera trophies" instead of traditional forms of hunting – park officials and tourism promoters signify and solidify a sense of difference in this landscape.

In addition to facilitating authentic tourist experiences, during the late 1960s hunting with a camera began to be used as a means of wildlife preservation and environmental education. In the fall of 1971, the film *Death of a Legend,* a joint effort of the Canadian Wildlife Service and the National Film Board of Canada, premiered.[35] The film was produced by award-winning filmmaker Bill Mason and was comprised of footage of wolves from various North American destinations, including Jasper – a site that producers thought would be especially beneficial to the project.[36] The film also included biological information aimed at providing scientific understanding of the *"real"* wolf,"[37] though, as historian Tina Loo discusses, Mason's primary focus was on the non-human animals themselves. The scientific research depicted in this film was relegated to a supporting role.[38] This intentional focus away from human technologies and the pursuit of knowledge was part of what Loo calls "a growing disquiet about the modern world" during the mid-twentieth century.[39]

As *Death of a Legend* demonstrates, wildlife conservation and environmental activist groups have often adopted representational strategies dependent on visual technologies to educate the public and to gain support for their various campaigns. There is a long history of the camera being used in campaigns to protect non-human animals, often with great success.

A recent controversy over the establishment of an open-pit coal mine adjacent to Jasper National Park has highlighted tensions between local conditions and the ideals of National Park Nature, with the protection of wildlife habitats as one of the major points of contestation. In the late 1990s, Cardinal River Coals brought forth a proposal to build a mine near the borders of the park.[40] The proposal was ultimately permitted to go ahead, but it sparked public outcry and lengthy legal challenges.[41] The dynamics of this conflict, including both the 900 local jobs affected by it and its proximity to a national park, set the stage for a bitter and complex battle.[42] Further, designation of the Canadian Rocky Mountain parks as UNESCO World Heritage Sites attracted international attention to the matter.[43] In 1997, the World Heritage Committee of the United Nations urged the Canadian government to reconsider approval given to the Cheviot project.[44] A number of conservation groups concerned about the mine attempted to stop its development by targeting "the regulatory and enforcement agencies overseeing the mine, the federal and provincial endangered species provisions and the mine's parent companies."[45] In the end, however, the mine went ahead under the direction of Teck Coal in 2005.[46]

In this highly charged debate, mine workers in the nearby town of Hinton were pitted against environmental groups. Local workers who supported the Cheviot project wore T-shirts with the slogan "Our future. Our jobs. Our environment," while nationally recognized environmental groups such as the Canadian Parks and Wilderness Society (CPAWS), the Canadian Nature Federation, and the Sierra Club of Canada launched offensives against the development on the grounds that it would be environmentally destructive, particularly in terms of habitat loss.[47] The juxtaposition of local, federal, and international interests in this region has made this a particularly complex debate.

Wildlife (or, perhaps more specifically, the representation of wildlife) has been at the heart of the Cheviot controversy. As Karen Jones has noted, wolves have become "ambassador species" in the ongoing debate, with both sides embracing dominant ideologies and popular mythologies about *Canis lupus* to mobilize support for their positions:

> Industrialists and their environmentalist opponents clashed over whether the Cheviot project would be compatible with, or catastrophic to, local wildlife. Their activities reflected widely different notions about naturalness and value, and yet both groups cast Canis lupus as a symbol of ecological vibrancy and wild nature. Pro-Cheviot interests co-opted the resilient grey wolf for green public relations, while environmentalists fought to defend a lupine landscape from industrial encroachment. Both reflected a post-war identification of wolves with vibrant ecosystems.[48]

Representations of the wolf on both sides of this debate have less to do with the specifics of the animal and more to do with the symbolic ideologies surrounding the species as a result of several decades of cultural representation. That two such divergent positions are able to couch their arguments in a language of scientific authority with regard to wildlife populations in this region signifies just how subjective the production of environmental knowledge can be.

Bears are also near the centre of this controversy. A central concern of environmental groups opposed to the mining project is that it would cut through grizzly bear habitats and migration paths.[49] Data released by the Jasper Environmental Association in 2006 indicate that the population of grizzlies in the region surrounding the mine has diminished.[50] As a result, the wildlife portrait aesthetic often employed by the tourism industry has also been used in photographs of bears to elicit sympathy and support for the anti-Cheviot position.

That environmental activist groups and tourism promoters draw on similar iconic codes of representation speaks volumes about the dominance of certain ways of representing wildlife in Western society. Activist photography often juxtaposes elements of Nature and Culture in the same frame. However, the context in which these images appear influences how they are understood. So does the interpretation of intertextual relationships that exist between word and image in these examples. A particularly poignant example of a visual protest against the mine development near Jasper was produced by the Western Canada Wilderness Committee. The words *Stop the Cheviot Mine!* were placed over a black-and-white photograph depicting a family of bears climbing on a large piece of mining equipment. The text clearly situates this image in the realm of environmental activism, and this photograph disrupts the sense of harmony that characterizes wildlife photography in the region. It is different from Taylor's "Four of a Kind" postcard (see Figure 31). Both images show a family of black bears engaging with human-built machinery. The train in the Taylor photograph is symbolic of tourism and a familiar and expected means of mediating human experiences of Nature in this space. The heavy machinery of the Western Canada Wilderness Committee's photograph, on the other hand, appears jarringly out of place in this landscape, and this is particularly effective in symbolizing the destruction of National Park Nature.

"A Fed Animal Is a Dead Animal"

Scenes of environmental or interspecies discord are rarely featured in tourist photography. Early postcards of Jasper have much in common with the ones for sale in park souvenir shops today. Although it is rare to find contemporary postcards showing direct engagement between humans and non-human animals in the ways that Weiss's "Hello You" (see Figure 33) or Harmon's "Black Bear" (see Figure 32) cards do, the sense of interspecies harmony that informed these images remains firmly entrenched in Rocky Mountain tourist photography. When this formula is disrupted, the results are visually jarring.

In recent years, postcards used in a wide variety of activist and educational campaigns have deliberately disrupted these pictorial codes. In 1993, CPAWS launched a postcard campaign aimed at halting development in Banff National Park. Subscribers to *Borealis,* the official publication of CPAWS, were given postcards featuring photographs of recent construction projects in Banff bearing captions such as "Banff: Is This a National Park?" and "Not All Postcards from Banff Are Pretty" and information about the rate of commercial development in the park.[51] Such imagery relies on the well-known format of the picture postcard but challenges the inferences typically associated with the popular souvenir postcard. The blend of the familiar and the unexpected makes this an effective tool for environmental activism.

The link between environmental education and tourism promotion has been further solidified by a recent postcard campaign aimed at encouraging more sustainable relationships between tourists and wildlife in the region.

"A Fed Animal is a Dead Animal"

"Wilde Tiere füttern—ein tödliches Vergnügen"

"Nourrir un animal, c'est le condamner à mourir"

「自分で餌を見つけることができない野生動物は死ぬほかない。」

Bear Photo/Photo de l'ours: Terry Berezan

FIGURE 35   Feeding wildlife in Canadian national parks is now illegal, but it seems that not all visitors to the parks are getting the message. This postcard is an attempt to educate visitors on why this practice is outlawed. *Steve Agar, "A Fed Animal Is a Dead Animal," 1999.*

In the early 1990s, Steve Agar, owner of Pipestone Photos in Lake Louise, created a postcard (see Figure 35) bearing the caption "A Fed Animal Is a Dead Animal" in four languages to discourage tourists from engaging in the common yet highly dangerous practice of feeding wildlife.[52] Most of the images used on this card are tourist snapshots culled from rolls of film dropped off for developing at participating photography businesses in the Canadian Rocky Mountain parks. The caption shifts the currency of these photographs from tourist souvenirs to material objects of environmental education. Although these cards are distributed and consumed in a manner different from traditional postcards – Agar's postcard is distributed free of charge by photo-finishing businesses – the fact that such a familiar format is being used in this manner speaks volumes about the power of visual culture to shape attitudes and behaviours.

Drivers for Wildlife

The Drivers for Wildlife awareness campaign to reduce vehicle-animal collisions in the Rocky Mountain parks has also employed photographic imagery in powerful and groundbreaking ways. On average, 170 large

Figure 36   The Drivers for Wildlife campaign is an effort to reduce collisions between vehicles and animals in places such as Banff and Jasper National Parks. Part of this campaign involves incorporating photographs of wildlife on road signs. *Cheryl Williams, photographer, "Drivers for Wildlife Road Sign," 2010.*

mammals were killed on the roads of Jasper National Park each year between 1992 and 2006.[53] Part of the Drivers for Wildlife campaign involves new highway signage. Some of the standard signs indicating speed limits in the park have been redesigned and now feature photographic images of wildlife (see Figure 36). The Friends of Jasper National Park, a nonprofit organization dedicated to raising funds for and awareness of park issues, sells bumper stickers with the same photographic images and the caption "Drive as if Their Lives Depended on It."[54]

This campaign focuses on the species of animals most closely associated with the park through tourist photography – wolves, bighorn sheep, and grizzly bears – the charismatic megafauna that have become symbols of National Park Nature through various representational techniques. Representations of these animals in the Drivers for Wildlife campaign are consistent with the ways in which tourists have come to know these nonhuman animals through genres such as the picture postcard.

The campaign eschews images of roadkill, which would detract from the idyllic experience of National Park Nature for most park visitors. Yet more graphic imagery may be a more effective way to achieve social change. In Canada, federal legislation requires cigarette packages to be labelled with graphic health warnings, including photographs showing the effects of smoking on human organs. These much-criticized labels appear to be working; a recent study by the Canadian Cancer Society found that package warnings had encouraged over 40 percent of smokers to attempt to quit the habit.[55] As a representative of a high-profile antismoking lobby group commented, "Words can't describe the harm tobacco does. That's why we need pictures."[56] The Drivers for Wildlife campaign images do seem to reduce animal-vehicle accidents, but unlike the tobacco ads this photographic campaign stops short of alienating those who consume the imagery and its referent product. The graphic warnings on the cigarette labels clearly are intended to decrease the pleasure of smoking. The Drivers for Wildlife campaign, on the other hand, is careful not to detract from the ideals of National Park Nature in its use of imagery.

CONCLUSION

This chapter has explored some of the ways in which the non-human animals of Jasper National Park have been represented by the tourist industry and environmental activist groups and revealed just how deeply entrenched dominant ideologies of non-human species have become. The significance, as art historian Steve Baker explains, is that "representations do have consequences for living animals."[57] The ways in which animals have been pictured in spaces such as Jasper National Park influence how they have been conceived of and, ultimately, treated, there and elsewhere. In the case of wolves, for decades they were seen as a threat to National Park Nature and were eradicated from park spaces through federally sanctioned programs. The fake photograph in the *Globe and Mail* with which this chapter opened demonstrates the degree to which imagery shapes dominant cultural conceptions of animals. By offering evidence of the supposed ferociousness of *Canis lupus,* this image both fed into and fuelled dominant cultural connotations of the species. As Andrea Gullo, Unna Lassiter, and Jennifer Wolch have argued, "Social constructions of animals alter over time and space, and in turn ultimately shape and reshape public policy, which affects animal life chances."[58] Films such as *Death of a Legend* and the use of wolf imagery as part of the anti-Cheviot campaigns can be seen as examples of this perceptual shift.

The examples discussed in this chapter demonstrate that images of wildlife used in the context of Jasper National Park – and indeed in almost any other so-called wilderness space – are a vital component in the cultural construction of National Park Nature and dominant ideologies about non-human species. Wildlife photography is repeatedly used in divergent contexts such as tourism and environmental activism. That both forms of activity rely so heavily on wildlife photography demonstrates the significant place that non-human species hold in cultural ideals of Nature.

This chapter expands upon ideas I explored in a previous article. See J. Keri Cronin, "'The Bears Are Plentiful and Frequently Good Camera Subjects': Picture Postcards and the Framing of Interspecific Encounters in Canada's Rocky Mountain Parks." *Mosaic* 39, 4 (2006): 77-92.

5

Fake Nature

The circulation and consumption of photographs corresponding with the ideals of National Park Nature have created and sustained cultural expectations. However, as Susan G. Davis has argued in her study of Sea World – another type of tourist destination designed around human experiences and expectations of non-human animals – when considering cultural representations of nature and non-human species "the gaps between what we are shown and what we can't see" need to be considered, particularly in light of ongoing dialogue surrounding environmental concerns in the twenty-first century.[1] Keeping Davis's observation in mind, this chapter explores the seemingly contradictory notion of "fake nature" and relates it to the cultural construction of destinations such as Jasper National Park. First I introduce the idea of fake nature by discussing the "Ocean Dome" in Miyazaki, Japan, and the Disney Wilderness Lodge in Orlando, Florida, before expanding the concept by exploring how ideas of Nature are created and sustained in the culturally charged spaces of museums. This discussion focuses on the new installation at the Royal Alberta Museum (RAM) entitled Wild Alberta.[2] Billed as a "new centre for environmental education that encourages visitors to see the world through different eyes," this installation uses display technologies and techniques such as wildlife dioramas and interactive computer terminals to convey environmental knowledge through the authoritative voice of the museum.[3] Finally, I situate National Park Nature in this discussion by considering it against fake nature sites and the display techniques used in museums to show how all three replicate ideologies of Nature, organize vision, and impart environmental knowledge.

A Makeover for Mother Nature

In recent years, fake nature sites have become increasingly popular tourist destinations. Although these sites take different physical forms, their general defining characteristic is that they are human-built facilities designed to mimic specific aspects of the non-human world. These sites have been described as "eye-popping innovations that have given a holiday make-over to old Mother Nature."[4] Japan's famed Ocean Dome offered a human-built beach lauded as an "utterly updated version of the Garden of Eden."[5] Opened in 1993 and closed in 2007, and equipped with the "world's largest retractable roof," Ocean Dome offered visitors over 12,000 square metres of sandy "seashore," and 13,500 tonnes of unsalted and chlorinated "ocean" water that was kept at a constant twenty-eight degrees Celsius.[6] This site, part of the $1.8 billion Seagaia entertainment complex in Miyazaki, was popular with sunbathers and surfers alike.[7] One of the most ironic and intriguing things about Ocean Dome was its proximity to a more traditional (not entirely human-built) beach. As cultural critic David Boyle noted, "There was something about building a virtual version of a beach just over a fence, through a small wood and across a motorway from a real one which made my head spin."[8] The "real" beach that Boyle speaks of, of course, has also been shaped by human hands and by dominant cultural ideologies regarding nature, albeit, some would argue, not to the same extent as the sanitized version offered by the architects of Ocean Dome.

The Disney Wilderness Lodge in Orlando is another "entertainment complex" that is part of the fake nature phenomenon. Part of the world-famous Disney World theme park, Wilderness Lodge is described as a "relaxing mountain retreat" in spite of its location near the centre of one of the busiest urban areas in central Florida. Streams, geysers, "cowboys-and-Indians décor and frontier-style cooking" attempt to replicate the highlights of the most popular American national parks in one convenient location.[9] In his discussion on the Disney Wilderness Lodge, environmental philosopher and thoughtful student of environmental restoration Eric Higgs compares this facility to Jasper Park Lodge and the "themed" experiences that drive much Nature tourism in the twenty-first century. Higgs is concerned with the "real consequences" of these ways of experiencing Nature.[10] Much like the Ocean Dome complex, the facilities and attractions offered at the Disney Wilderness Lodge are presented as an improvement on conventional ways of experiencing Nature, and, as promotions for the lodge proclaim, this resort "celebrates the majesty of the unspoiled wilderness."[11] As Higgs argues, however, these "contradictory messages about wild nature ... result in a compounded problem. Not only is the myth of wilderness promulgated ... but nature is also rendered as something subject to our ultimate control."[12]

The more I learned about these multi-million-dollar developments, the more familiar they seemed to me; these are sites where the picture postcard fantasy is brought to life and the "wilderness ideal" has come full circle. In her discussion of the use of imagery in the tourism industry, Lucy Lippard argues that, "eventually, most tourists can be tempted to accept the post-card image over their own lived experience."[13] So-called fake nature sites take this idea one step further and attempt to tailor the "lived experience" to match the "postcard image." In a sense, people flock to these mega-plexes because real Nature (if we may momentarily call it that) does not live up to the dominant cultural expectations, created in large part by the consumption of tourist photography, of what it should be. This is a com-plex process because, as Higgs points out, "the Wilderness Lodge is changing what people understand wilderness or nature to be and this in turn shapes their views of the real thing."[14]

In his famous collection of essays *Travels in Hyperreality*, Umberto Eco discusses the play in contemporary consumer culture between the search for the authentic and its manifestation in the "absolute fake."[15] He sees creation of the "hyperreal" becoming a dominant cultural trend in West-ern societies and describes how a destination such as that designed by the Walt Disney Corporation "not only produces illusion, but ... stimulates the desire for it."[16] In other words, there is a highly complex reflexive re-lationship between fake nature sites and their supposedly natural referents, with each being continually judged according to criteria perceived to be embodied by the other. Although fake nature sites may be dismissed as trivial or frivolous, their very existence reveals dominant cultural ideologies of Nature.

FAKE NATURE IN MUSEUMS

In contrast to the perceived frivolity of fake nature tourist destinations, museums have long histories as purveyors of cultural capital and have conventionally been regarded as institutions of both education and social reform.[17] Even though display techniques and protomuseums such as the seventeenth and eighteenth centuries' "cabinets of curiosity" date back several centuries, the museum as it exists today – like photography and national parks – is a product of nineteenth-century modernity. In *The Birth of the Museum,* Tony Bennett argues that, in addition to facilitating the Victorian fascination with scientific classification and order, museums became a vehicle of "cultural governance" in the nineteenth century and were expected to "help form and shape the moral, mental and behavioural characteristics of the population."[18] Further, museums have played a predominant role in defining ideologies of national identity in the Western world.[19]

Natural history displays became particularly popular in the nineteenth century and played an instrumental role in the discursive shifts occurring within various fields of scientific knowledge. One of the most common and defining didactic tools employed in these types of museum exhibits was the diorama. The word *diorama* has been used to refer to several variations of visual spectacle since the early nineteenth century, but the most common use of the word (and the one that continues to be employed today) is in reference to a specific type of museological exhibit.[20] Art historian Karen Wonders explains that

> dioramas are natural history scenarios which typically contain mounted zoological specimens arranged in a foreground that replicates their native surroundings in the wild. Ideally, the three-dimensional foreground merges imperceptibly into a painted background landscape, creating an illusion – if only for a moment – of atmospheric space and distance.[21]

Dioramas, in the form described by Wonders, remain popular in several North American and European natural history museums.

Their significance here is related to how these illusionary displays create a particular way of seeing and understanding nature through a re-creation of what is purported to be an "authentic" landscape scene. The tension between the obvious artificiality of these exhibits and the three-dimensional "realism" presented to viewers through this installation technique makes this type of display of particular interest. Further, connections can be made between the rise of these types of displays and the perception of disappearing "wilderness" in North America that accompanied late-nineteenth-century modernity. Wonders has argued that the use of dioramas is "a vivid way of bringing nature into the museum," a significant observation regarding a geographical space perceived to be disappearing at an alarming rate.[22]

Like all museum displays, dioramas featuring aspects of nature and the non-human world can hold various meanings. The location of these kinds of natural history exhibits in densely populated urban spaces has tended to serve as a *memento mori* for that which was thought to have disappeared from that locale. The association of these exhibits with the frontier space of western Canada and the United States, however, often signified very different ways of understanding nature. George Colpitts has demonstrated that in the context of western Canada these types of displays helped to perpetuate the sense that this was a land of wild abundance:

> Boosters were taken with the idea of a western Eden and, while their efforts to keep streams stocked and breeding areas productive met with limited success, it was really in exhibitions and museum dioramas that they communicated the concept most effectively. There, they arranged wildlife to show Canada as a region where humans were relieved of want and, hence, relieved of the poverty identified with urban Chicago and London.[23]

Since the rise of the popular environmental movement during the 1970s, debate about the role of the museum in dealing with ecological issues has increased. Natural history museums, in particular, have begun to incorporate environmental themes.[24] "Environmental exhibitions," defined as those that explicitly address "the degradation of the environment," have begun to appear in North American museums in recent years,[25] and Canadian institutions have been lauded for being "at the forefront of change" in planning and installing exhibitions with ecological themes.[26]

WILD ALBERTA

Through display techniques such as the diorama, the space of the museum facilitates what political theorist Timothy Luke has termed "indirect access" to Nature.[27] In recent decades, several exhibits have been redesigned to incorporate rising societal concerns over the state of the physical environment, and the "museology of the environment" has become an important curatorial consideration.[28] However, this link between museums and the physical environment is not unique to the late twentieth and early twenty-first centuries. Early in the twentieth century, the newly formed Canadian prairie provinces enthusiastically embraced the natural history museum as a tool to promote settlement and to showcase the abundance and availability of natural resources.[29] Recent changes to these cultural spaces continue to reflect shifts in the dominant ways of understanding the western Canadian landscape.

The Royal Alberta Museum recently joined internationally renowned institutions such as the Berne Museum and the Field Museum in Chicago in "updating" its diorama exhibits.[30] This "metamorphosis" has resulted in *Wild Alberta*, an installation that claims to take a much more ecologically focused approach to Alberta's natural history than has been found at the RAM. The dioramas at the centre of *Wild Alberta* are the same ones that comprised the *Habitat Gallery* for the past several decades, but they have been recontextualized in accordance with the themes and aims of the new installation. As with all museum displays, the emphasis is on what is made visually accessible through the various exhibition techniques incorporated. ("The natural world takes on new meanings when seen from these different perspectives," the promotional material reads.[31]) As in other cultural representations of Nature, however, what is absent from this installation is as significant as what is included.

Wild Alberta is divided into five distinct "zones" representing ecosystems found in the province: the Boreal Zone, the Prairie Zone, the Water Zone, the Parkland Zone, and the Mountain Zone. The zones are connected to one another by a circular walkway, and each display incorporates a carefully planned repertoire of the sights, sounds, and smells that one might experience during a visit to the region they depict.[32] One of the main goals of the exhibit is to demonstrate how "human culture is shaping the modern wilderness and how our actions, both positive and negative[,] have an impact," and this is expressed through a combination of textual and visual materials.[33] Exhibit labels describe the habitats and habits of "feature creatures" found in the installation space, while larger text panels explore themes of ecological conservation and human impacts on Alberta's physical environment.

Jasper National Park is represented in the Mountain Zone of *Wild Alberta* by a diorama that features two taxidermic bighorn sheep positioned in front of a painting of the Athabasca Glacier (see Figure 37), a well-known geological attraction found along the Icefields Parkway. The painted backdrop is based on a photographic image taken several decades ago, and the text panels accompanying this diorama draw the viewer's attention to the differences between the painted representation and a more recent photograph of the same region. The glacier has receded a noticeable distance, an effect attributed to global climate change. In spite of promotional

FIGURE 37   The Wild Alberta installation at the Royal Alberta Museum includes a diorama representing bighorn sheep in Jasper National Park. *Cheryl Williams, photographer, bighorn sheep diorama, "Wild Alberta," 2010.*

FIGURE 38   The Wild Alberta installation at the Royal Alberta Museum featured an exhibit focusing on urban wildlife in 2008. This exhibit is no longer part of the installation. *Keri Cronin, photographer, "Urban Ecology, Wild Alberta," 2008.*

materials describing the bighorn sheep as symbolizing "wild and unspoiled places," the focus of this exhibit is on the "hidden impacts" that human activity has had on the landscape of the Canadian Rockies.[34]

In his discussion of museums that have recently "updated" their natural history exhibits to incorporate new environmental sensibilities, Peter Davis, professor of museology at Newcastle University, wonders which criteria are used to determine the new look of these displays:

> If the intention is to re-create reality (as originally intended) should dioramas be brought up to date? Should the background to a tropical rainforest exhibit feature the scars and blaze of deforestation? Should the foreground of a Rocky Mountain diorama contain human footprints, discarded packaging or rusting Coke cans? This would certainly be more honest, but would destroy a display of some historical significance.[35]

What is included in these installations often changes in response to shifts in environmental ideologies; however, as Davis notes, even within this context there seem to be limits to what curators are willing to portray. Parallels can be drawn between these displays and the tourist photography of the region. Both function within specific cultural and economic agendas, and neither includes the marks and detritus of human presence in the area.

Difficult decisions inform the choice of items to include in displays. *Urban Ecology*, a recent addition to the RAM exhibition gallery, features stuffed crows, magpies, and other "scavenger" animals arranged to suggest that they are feasting on the contents of a tipped-over garbage can (see Figure 38). Litter is strewn through the installation, and "No Parking" and "No Skateboarding" signs reinforce the illusion that this scene represents part of the urban concrete jungle. This addition to the Wild Alberta gallery contrasts markedly with the ways in which Nature has typically been presented in the museum. Such "pests" – particularly when they are portrayed engaging in behaviour that raises the ire of many city-dwelling homeowners – are not usually thought of as "wild animals" in the same way that a moose, coyote, or grizzly bear would be. The *Urban Ecology* installation unsettles dominant assumptions about what is and is not deemed acceptable within natural history museums and draws attention to the subjective nature of the processes of creating and curating an exhibition.

Several factors have limited the extent to which museums have been able to tackle environmental issues. One is the desire to minimize controversy.

Culturally charged, government-run museums often try to avoid debates over their exhibits.[36] The RAM, a provincially funded institution in a province with high economic dependency on natural resource industries such as forestry, mining, and oil and gas production, appears to be following this pattern with regard to environmental issues.

The Wild Alberta installation does not completely ignore the persistent conflicts between Nature and industry that have characterized labour and environmental relations in the province for decades. An interactive computer terminal allows visitors to try their hand at being a forestry boss. Participants decide how best to balance ecological and economic decisions using interactive computer software that tabulates profit margins, job losses, and environmental impacts of individual decisions made by visitors to the gallery. Even with these sorts of "educational" components, however, the overarching message of the RAM exhibits is that economic and environmental interests harmoniously coexist due to wise management decisions made by trained experts.

Wild Alberta was a joint effort between the RAM (under the direction and management of Alberta Community Development, a branch of the provincial government) and the Federation of Alberta Naturalists. Corporate sponsorship came from companies such as Alberta-Pacific Forest Industries (ALPAC), Toronto Dominion Bank, and Weyerhaeuser, whose support is recognized, prominently, at the entrance to the installation. Further funding came in July 2007, when a "special partnership" between the Forest Resource Improvement Association of Alberta and the Friends of the Royal Alberta Museum Society yielded a $1.25 million donation for the Wild Alberta exhibits and educational outreach programs to "help Albertans better understand our forests."[37]

Yet the involvement of these corporate entities in an exhibition that has been described as "one of the most significant exhibitions about Alberta's natural world" inevitably raises questions about the production of environmental knowledge through cultural representations.[38] The "logic of maximization" that drives capitalist society necessarily raises contradictions between profit motive and environmental protection.[39]

Weyerhaeuser, an international "forest products company," has operations in eighteen countries and generates nearly $20 billion in sales each year.[40] In 1999, the company purchased MacMillan Bloedel, a move that made it "Canada's largest forest products company."[41] In spite of claims that Weyerhaeuser's activities improve the "quality and health of our forests" through programs such as hand-planting seedlings and selectively applying fertilizers, environmental activists continually express concern about the activities of this global corporation. In British Columbia, for instance, Weyerhaeuser's pulp mill operations have been criticized for releasing pollutants such as chlorine dioxide and sulphur oxides into the air.[42] The Washington-based logging company has been described as "the number one destroyer of old-growth forests in North America" and has been targeted by well-known environmental activist groups such as the Sierra Club of Canada and the Rainforest Action Network.[43] Weyerhaeuser spends a significant amount of money and effort in attempts to convince consumers and investors that it is an environmentally friendly corporation. However, these claims are refuted by organizations such as Greenpeace International, the Multinational Monitor, and the Council on Economic Priorities, which claim that Weyerhaeuser masks the effects of its operations by the skilful and persistent use of "greenwashing" techniques.[44]

The Wild Alberta exhibit has been widely publicized in both the Edmonton media and publications produced by Travel Alberta highlighting Alberta's tourist attractions. The high-profile nature of this installation coupled with its perceived environmental message provides a stage for companies such as Weyerhaeuser to profess their commitment to environmentally sustainable operations. As a Weyerhaeuser company spokesperson stated of the Wild Alberta installation, "We chose to direct our support to the woodland caribou display to reflect our stewardship and commitment to the conservation of this endangered species."[45] The presentation of this display and the inclusion of the Weyerhaeuser name in an exhibition intended to educate Albertans about human impacts on the physical environment of the province give the message that this is a corporation that places high value on the ecological health of the region. Not surprisingly, there is no mention of Weyerhaeuser's logging operations in Canada's boreal forests, a habitat for the still-living relatives of the woodland caribou present in the exhibit through the science of taxidermy and the visual technology of the diorama.[46]

Weyerhaeuser is not the only corporate sponsor of Wild Alberta that has raised the ire of environmental activists in western Canada. Both the Toronto Dominion Bank and Alberta-Pacific Forest Industries have been the targets of protest campaigns in recent years. Environmental advocacy groups have argued that Toronto Dominion "funds the destruction" of old-growth forests because it has been a shareholder in both International Forest Products and West Fraser Timber, two corporations that, according to Greenpeace, have been "responsible for the greatest level of destruction in BC's ancient rainforests."[47] Similarly, questions have been raised about the corporate practices of Alberta-Pacific Forest Industries.

The Alberta-based, Japanese-owned company operates a pulp mill near Athabasca. Described as "the world's largest bleached kraft pulp mill," the facility was approved by the Alberta government in 1990 in spite of concerns expressed by members of the public, environmental organizations, and Alberta's scientific community.[48] Concerns over the widespread release of pollutants generated by the mill's operations continue to be raised, in particular as a means to counter efforts by ALPAC to use the media as a vehicle to convince Albertans that its operations are environmentally sound and pose no health risk to either human or non-human inhabitants of the region.

These concerns focus attention on the various ways in which the environmental knowledge presented in galleries and museums is shaped by dominant political, cultural, and economic interests. As Davallon, Grand-mont, and Schiele argue,

> What the public is invited to view is the result of a decision-making process greatly swayed by contingent factors which are exterior to the museum's criteria itself. This certainly contributes to the fact that themes which are put on display by a museum are an expression of the social imaginary in terms of the environment.[49]

Although attention is paid to human impacts on the physical environment in the Wild Alberta exhibit, the displays stop short of implicating RAM sponsors and of challenging any visitors who work for or consume the products and services provided by them. Thus, the exhibition offers a very subjective view of environmental issues in Alberta – even as this position is neutralized by the perceived authority and objectivity of the museum as a cultural institution of knowledge, research, and higher learning.

Other factors also shape the ways in which environmental knowledge is produced in the space of the museum. Scholars such as Kay Anderson and Donna Haraway have demonstrated that the "visual technologies" used in such natural history displays replicate and reinforce pre-existing power relations among various groups of human actors as well as between humans and non-human animals.[50] As Anderson argues, exhibitions of natural history are geared to a specific type of viewer, "a historically specific type of (white) masculine [viewer] that is unseen ... the privileged eye (I), the bearer of reason, the author, the knower."[51] Moreover, the physicality of the exhibition space replicates hierarchies and dominant power relations between humans and non-human animals. Not only are select types of animals represented, but also the presentation of these animals behind glass and positioned to be "gazed upon" reinforces the position of power that human beings have traditionally held in this relationship. Finally, in these types of exhibitions, dominant ideologies of Nature and non-human animals are presented as objective and indisputable facts. Within the context of the museum, the idea of Nature as a cultural construct is relegated to "background" status, if included at all.[52]

FAKE NATURE IN NATIONAL PARKS?

In much the same way as National Park Nature in Jasper is created and sustained by dominant cultural ideals surrounding notions of wilderness, recreation, and wildlife, fake nature sites and museum displays frame nature in culturally specific ways. All three types of spaces are governed by a sense of tension between what is perceived to be "authentic" and what is deemed to be "inauthentic." In this equation, spaces such as Jasper are positioned at one end of this authenticity spectrum, while entities such as human-engineered oceans are situated at the other. The inauthenticity of spaces such as Ocean Dome or the Disney Wilderness Lodge is constantly measured against what is perceived to be genuine Nature found in spaces such as Jasper National Park. This comparison, however, presents an ideological conundrum. If, as this book has attempted to demonstrate, dominant ideologies of what constitutes an unmediated and natural experience in Jasper (and, indeed, in all national parks) are themselves highly constructed and selected, then how can these divergent assumptions be sustained?

In popular thinking, national parks occupy a space between the educational function associated with museums and the entertainment function of destinations such as Ocean Dome. However, *all* representations of nature, be they postcards of the Canadian Rockies or glass-enclosed dioramas located in busy urban centres, are necessarily dependent on dominant social, cultural, and economic ideologies. By definition, then, certain aspects, representations, and features of nature become celebrated at the expense of others. In other words, representations attempting to portray Nature as an unmediated, wild, and pristine space will always be different from what they purport to be. Simply put, national parks cannot offer a more authentic Nature experience than what a museum or theme park can.

In his discussion on zoos and animal theme parks in the United States, Umberto Eco describes how sites such as Marine World and the San Diego Zoo frame human encounters with the non-human world. "The oscillation

between a promise of uncontaminated nature and a guarantee of negotiated tranquility is constant," Eco writes of his experience in these popular
tourist destinations.[53] This sentiment, I suggest, is characteristic of National Park Nature as well. In spaces such as Jasper National Park, the
promise of "uncontaminated nature" has been the cornerstone of cultural representations and consumer advertisements since the park was first
established in 1907. Further, the concept of "negotiated tranquility"
underpins dominant ways of engaging with this space. Whether this negotiation takes the form of scenic drives, a round of golf on the Jasper Park
Lodge course, or mediated encounters with symbolic wildlife such as bears,
there exists a promise of interspecies harmony that will be achieved by all
who visit the park. Things that disrupt this harmony – road construction,
large numbers of fellow golfers, and the possibility of a less-than-serene
meeting with a wild animal – tend not to be the subjects of most tourist
photography. In much the same way that "undesirable" qualities such as
jellyfish, rain, and "harmful" UV rays were excluded from the fake nature
found at Ocean Dome, so too are dominant pictorial representations of
the Canadian Rockies sanitized to correspond to tourist desires and expectations.[54] Commercial renderings such as the "Jasper Wonderful by
Nature" campaign set up the landscape of Jasper National Park as if it were
a glass-encased museum display – static and existing entirely to be gazed
upon. Like the fake nature found in museum displays, however, this is a
select way of seeing this landscape and the result of complex cultural,
historical, social, and economic influences.

CONCLUSION

This comparison of National Park Nature and fake nature makes clear
that representations shape environmental knowledge, attitudes, assumptions, and behaviours. In her discussion of the American marine theme
park Sea World, Susan G. Davis argues that, instead of debating the merits
of fake nature versus real nature, political and cultural issues related to the
construction of Nature in all its forms should be emphasized:

> It is the uses to which nature simulations are put that we should worry
> about, the stories about environmental crisis that are left untold and the
> limits on our ability to imagine solutions. What is invisible at Sea World,
> and places like it, are the selective ways nature is shaped into something
> that can be looked at.[55]

In "fake nature" sites such as Sea World, the Disney Wilderness Lodge, and Ocean Dome, this shaping of Nature is relatively evident. Museums and national parks, however, also participate in similar processes. As we have seen, the production of environmental values, knowledge, and awareness in these spaces is determined by many external factors. These factors are often not immediately apparent but need to be part of ongoing dialogues about human–non-human relationships and environmental sustainability in the twenty-first century.

Conclusion

This book has explored some of the pictorial themes that have influenced how the landscape of Jasper National Park has been imaged and imagined over the course of its history. In the years since this landscape was first set aside as a federal forest reserve, images of "wilderness," "recreation," and "wildlife" have dominated the visual culture of Jasper National Park. Wilderness images tend to be photographs of scenic vistas from which people are either absent or a minor compositional detail. Recreation-themed images emphasize the aesthetic pleasures of the mountain landscape but also visually promise fun-filled adventures and athletic pursuits. In this pictorial formula, human leisure activity is presented as having little or no environmental impact and as an essential way of having an authentic encounter with Nature. Potential visitors are invited to situate themselves in the frame, and the small groups of people depicted in dominant representations of Rocky Mountain recreation underscore that this is not a crowded landscape, so it will be a pleasant experience to share with an intimate group of family or friends. Photographs of non-human animals that are used in visual promotions of this space also tend to follow particular representational patterns. In tourist brochures and picture postcards, images of certain species dominate, with bears being the most common.

In spite of social, technological, and political changes that have occurred in the century or so of the park's existence, predominant patterns of visual representation that have defined Jasper National Park for so many have remained surprisingly constant. This play between change and visual continuity is one of the most interesting aspects of National Park Nature and speaks to enduring values regarding nature and non-human animals. In contrast to representations that characterize the park as pristine wilderness, this landscape and, in fact, all North American national parks, need to be reconceptualized as culturally constructed commodities. The repetition of a particular way of seeing and understanding these spaces – what I have referred to as National Park Nature – serves to occlude the commodification of nature within park borders and instead presents these spaces as environmentally pristine and free of human intervention. This gap between what is pictured and the actual conditions of the physical environment has resulted in significant cultural and ecological consequences. The construction of Nature and Culture as two distinct entities has continued to reinforce significant discrepancies between landscape representations and realities, even as environmental concerns have received increased media and popular attention in recent years. It is because of the severity of these concerns that dominant understandings of Nature and non-human animals need to be called into question.

As I have argued throughout this book, camera images (photography and film) have been influential in the construction of National Park Nature as the mechanical nature of the camera continues to mask and neutralize the subjective values that have transformed the landscape of Jasper National Park into both cultural icon and tourist commodity. Here I follow geographer Steven Hoelscher, who characterizes photography as "uniquely positioned to naturalize cultural constructions."[1] From the use of photographic reproductions in illustrated guidebooks and souvenir postcards to promotions encouraging tourists to take up Nature photography as a hobby while visiting this world-famous destination, a specific way of seeing the landscape of the Canadian Rockies has been created through photographic technology. This way of seeing is taken to be objective, even though analysis of the processes of production and consumption of these images reveals that they are as constructed as the representations and displays found in "fake nature" theme parks and museum displays.

National Park Nature in Jasper has been shaped in large part through photographic representations. This body of imagery is diverse; however, specific and consistent ideologies of nature and non-human animals have been constructed and sustained through the widespread circulation of these pictorial renditions of National Park Nature. In short, the notion that this space is separate and environmentally different from the rest of Canada is perpetuated through dominant representational strategies. Human encounters with non-human species and participation in recreational activities in this landscape of leisure are presented as means to mediate an authentic wilderness experience, and, as such, the environmental consequences of these activities are pictorially and ideologically negated.

As a tourist destination within the internationally renowned Canadian national park system, Jasper National Park is most often represented in relation to the tourism industry. In consequence, most of the images investigated in this book are drawn from brochures, postcards, advertisements, and other forms of cultural representation that visualize the vacation experience in the Canadian Rockies. As Susan G. Davis has argued, when this type of material is used in the context of a so-called wilderness destination, it serves to "circulate arguments about what nature is and how humans ought to think and feel about it, through the culture of consumption."[2] In other words, values espoused by consumer culture are deeply embedded in tourist photography and the production of National Park Nature. To experience Nature in Jasper National Park is to consume a carefully manufactured cultural product.

The environmental implications of tourist photography in spaces such as Jasper need to be considered on two fronts. First, as "images of ecology," pictures used by entities such as Travel Alberta, Parks Canada, and Canadian National Railways have served to naturalize certain ways of seeing and relating to this landscape.[3] This is significant not only because it creates a situation in which dominant values and behaviours are allowed to continue unchallenged but also because it does not easily permit alternative ways of conceiving of human relationships with this landscape. Second, an analysis of the "ecology of images" resulting from the depiction of National Park Nature in the Canadian Rockies reveals that the consumption and circulation of these images can result in unintended environmental consequences. Part of this observation relates to the fact that the technologies of image production necessary to manufacture this wilderness industry are themselves often fraught with environmental concerns. For example, the photographic industry is not environmentally benign. Although changes have been implemented to help bring this industry in line with twenty-first-century environmental standards, the visual technology responsible for much of the rhetoric of "nature loving" and "wilderness appreciation" is also responsible for high volumes of pollution and toxic waste.[4]

This book does not argue against national parks per se. They are culturally significant spaces with complex human and natural histories and need to be recognized as such. Like many Canadians, I enjoy spending time in destinations such as Jasper National Park; to read the preceding arguments as a condemnation of national parks is to miss the point entirely. What I am arguing for, however, is the need to raise questions about how these spaces have been represented. I do not wish to suggest that to be an environmentally responsible citizen one must refuse to participate in the visual economy of photography. In addition to being an overly simplistic, knee-jerk reaction to the arguments presented here, this would be an impossible goal to achieve in our image-driven society. Moreover, photographic images can act as powerful agents of social, cultural, and environmental change.

So what would the visual culture of Jasper National Park look like if we were to move away from the current model, which replicates the values of National Park Nature through the lenses of countless cameras? First, we would have to be prepared to let go of the notion that this is an "untouched" or a "pristine" space. As the case studies in this book have shown, both environmental lobby groups and tourism operators have much invested in presenting the landscape in these terms. However, this mythology of an "untrammelled" wilderness is, ultimately, unproductive in terms of environmental dialogue. Achieving ecological integrity in this landscape requires complex negotiations between human and non-human species and a critically self-reflexive awareness of how these dynamics have played out historically. We have much to learn from past human encounters in this space, but we must first adjust our dominant representational patterns so that these encounters become visible. One important way in which this is already taking place in Jasper National Park is the awareness-raising efforts of groups, such as the Council of Elders of the Descendants of Jasper Park, who are actively working to include Métis culture and history in dominant representations of the region.[5]

This conceptual shift away from a pristine landscape need not exclude visually striking images of the flora, fauna, geological features, and landscapes of the park. Indeed, these features are what attract so many of us to the Canadian Rockies, and professional and amateur photographers alike delight in capturing their own versions of these images on their cameras and video recorders. Likewise, I am not arguing that souvenir shops suddenly replace all the postcards featuring the shimmering shores of Maligne Lake with photographs of roadkill, pollution, or construction sites. Rather, as consumers of this landscape, we need to be open to alternative ways of visualizing the park and to recognize that our presence in it is inextricably linked with the ecological conditions of the region.

Similarly, those who produce and package Jasper National Park as a commodified vacation experience need to be willing to abandon marketing models that continue to distance Nature from Culture.

Perhaps we can look to other realms of visual and cultural production for inspiration on these fronts. Two examples of late-twentieth-century Canadian art immediately come to mind here. Both Jin-me Yoon's photographic project *Souvenirs of the Self* (1991) and Shawna Dempsey and Lorri Millan's performance piece *Lesbian National Parks and Services* (1997-present, Figure 39) engage with the landscape of the Canadian Rockies in ways that differ from those perpetuated by National Park Nature. In both projects, the bodies of the artists challenge long-held associations between nature, nation, and identity in Canada.[6] "For whom do wilderness mythologies exist?" these projects ask. We can also consider the approach of contemporary photographers such as Edward Burtynsky and Martin Parr. Burtynsky's large-format landscape photographs of industrial sites are at once aesthetically stunning and psychologically unsettling, a post-industrial version of the sublime. In Burtynsky's work, Nature and Culture powerfully collide. What would happen if a similar approach was used in photographing the landscape of Jasper National Park? Can we even conceive of what this might look like? To answer yes is to open the door to new ways of picturing this landscape; to answer no indicates the visual stronghold that ideologies of National Park Nature have on our cultural imagination. Likewise, Parr, a British photographer, turns the tables on the usual relationship between tourist and landscape in projects such as *Small World* (1996) in that the subjects of his photographs are the camera-wielding tourists in famous vacation sites such as the Grand Canyon and the Pantheon.[7] If we were to turn our cameras on ourselves in a similar fashion while visiting Banff and Jasper National Parks, what would we see?

In addition to reframing the tourist experience, the medium of photography can be used to educate people about ecological change. One such project is the Rocky Mountain Repeat Photography Project, which studies changes in the landscape of the Canadian Rockies through photography. In this project, Eric Higgs and Jeanine Rhemtulla compared a body of photographs taken of the Rocky Mountain landscape in the early twentieth century with photographs they took in the late 1990s. The early-twentieth-century negatives were made by Morrison Parsons Bridgland, a dominion land surveyor.[8] Higgs and Rhemtulla painstakingly researched Bridgland's survey route and rephotographed the same landscape views from the same locations eight decades later in order to compare changes

FIGURE 39   A number of contemporary artists are engaging with themes of nature in their work, asking questions about who benefits when mythologies of nature and landscape continue to be repeated. *Shawna Dempsey and Lorri Millan, photograph from* Lesbian National Parks and Services *performance (1997-present).*

in the landscape.⁹ A similar photographic approach was used in Cliff White
and E.J. (Ted) Hart's recent publication *The Lens of Time: A Repeat Photography of Landscape Change in the Canadian Rockies*. White, a biologist,
and Hart, a Rocky Mountains historian, drew on a wide range of historical photographs to complete their project. Like Higgs and Rhemtulla's
repeat photography project, this comparative approach was intended to
study changes in the Rocky Mountain landscape. For instance, a 1907
hand-tinted lantern slide of Mount Athabasca and the Athabasca Glacier
taken by Mary Schäffer was compared with a 2004 photograph of the
same location. Among the many changes visible in the comparison of these
two images is that the later image includes human-built structures such
as the Icefields Parkway.¹⁰ There is also obvious glacial recession visible in
the 2004 image. Another comparison that White and Hart undertook was
with Horetzky's photograph taken at Jasper House in the early 1870s (see
Figure 4).¹¹ In the 2004 image of the same site, there is no visible evidence
that this is where the post had once stood (though it is now designated as
a national historic site). This pairing serves as a good reminder that photographs tell only part of the story and that they are influenced by many
external factors. The historical images that both of these repeat photography
projects draw on, for instance, were entirely shaped by late-nineteenth-
century and early-twentieth-century ideas about science, aesthetics, and
politics. The circumstances that brought Morrison Parsons Bridgland,
Mary Schäffer, and Charles Horetzky to this landscape with their cameras
were fraught with sociopolitical notions about diverse issues such as resource extraction, geological surveying, natural history, nation building,
and wilderness conservation. A late-twentieth-century and early-twenty-
first-century repetition of these images brings with it, of course, further
contemporary concerns regarding "the environment" and the role of
government agencies such as Parks Canada.

Shifting ideologies and technologies of representation also shape the
ways in which non-human animals are pictured in the context of Jasper
National Park. A recent initiative by park managers saw the reintroduction
of wolves into one of the most heavily visited tourist sites, the golf course
at Jasper Park Lodge. By reconfiguring boundary fences, Parks Canada
staff are now actively encouraging the presence of the once-despised wolf
on the meticulously manicured greens as a means of keeping the elk
population in check. The presence of "habituated elk" has been of increasing concern to park staff because injuries resulting from human-elk encounters are on the rise.¹² In 1994, for instance, 103 reports of this nature

were recorded.[13] Wolf attacks on humans, on the other hand, continue to
be virtually non-existent in the Rocky Mountain parks.

As part of this reintroduction initiative, the presence of wolves and other
large carnivores is monitored through the use of motion-sensitive cameras.[14]
Use of such cameras has allowed Parks Canada biologists to track movement patterns of non-human animals in the vicinity of the golf course at
Jasper Park Lodge.[15] A second and equally important aspect of this project
is comprised of education, communication, and outreach efforts aimed
at teaching park visitors both about the animals central to this study and
how interaction between human and non-human animals in this landscape
can have significant ecological impacts. For example, illustrated signs asking park visitors to participate in a program of "voluntary trail restriction"
were deemed to be an effective way of reducing human traffic in the areas
central to this reintroduction effort.[16] The *Where Is the Wildlife?* poster (see
Figure 40) is another aspect of these outreach efforts. The poster, comprised
of images taken by the "infrared-triggered, remote wildlife cameras" during the relocation study, urges visitors to the park to give these non-human
animals "the room they need."[17] As was the case with Steve Agar's "A Fed
Animal Is a Dead Animal" postcard, here images originally intended for
one purpose are recontextualized for another.

The intersection of imagery and ecology in the culturally charged space
of Jasper National Park results in a highly complex situation that has far-
reaching implications for the many species that inhabit this region. I
cannot pretend to offer a quick-fix solution to many of the issues raised
in these chapters. The complexities of this dynamic necessitate that a re-
conceptualization of National Park Nature will have to involve dialogue
among a wide range of social actors. Any solution arrived at by an individual approaching this topic from one methodological viewpoint will
necessarily be incomplete. Instead, I have attempted to raise questions
about the dominant representations of this space in order to unsettle
persistent assumptions about Nature in the context of the Canadian Rocky
Mountains. By demonstrating connections between imagery and ideology
in the picturing of this landscape, I hope that this book will offer new
ecoanalytical frameworks for ongoing discussion of the issues raised here.

FIGURE 40   Parks Canada biologists are using camera-based technology to study the
movement patterns of wolves and other large animals near the Jasper Park Lodge golf
course. These images are also used in education and outreach. *Parks Canada, "Where Is
the Wildlife?" poster, 2004.* ▶

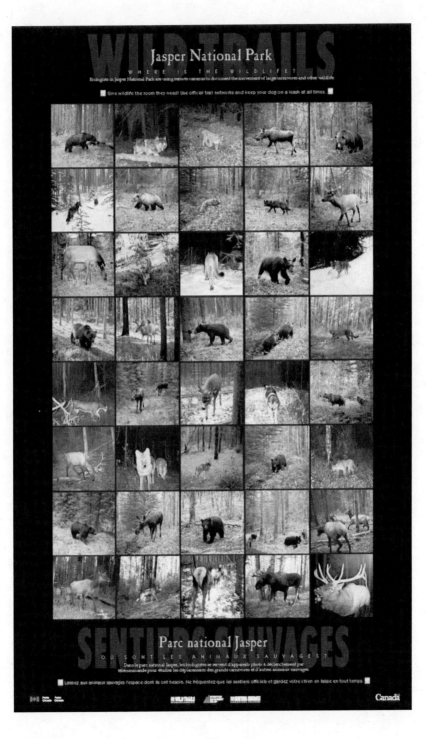

My conclusion, therefore, is a simple one: the picturing of animals (human and non-human) and landscapes is a process that necessarily shapes and is shaped by human ideologies. These cultural representations have environmental implications that need to be included in discussions about how to maintain a sense of ecological integrity in these regions. Debates focused entirely on what Richard White has termed "our hopeless fixation on purity" will continue to replicate a sense of division between Nature and Culture and, as such, will not yield adequate ways of reframing human relationships with nature and non-human animals.[18]

Imagery and ecology are interrelated on a number of fronts: the ideas underpinning the particular discussion in these pages can be applied to virtually all other realms of visual material. As this book has shown, cultural representations of Nature both shape dominant understandings of place and obfuscate the imbalance of power between human and non-human actors. The unsettling of these assumptions will be the project of an environmentally informed approach to studies of art history and visual culture. An ecocritical art historical methodology, for instance, will need to consider the various ways in which a certain image or body of imagery shapes environmental knowledge and values; how an image or body of imagery can work to either validate or disrupt status quo conceptions of Nature and non-human animals; how museums and art galleries function within environmental discourse; and how environmental impacts are associated with image-making techniques.

Notes

FOREWORD

1 The words of Prime Minister John A. Macdonald are taken from Leslie Bella, *Parks for Profit* (Montreal: Harvest House, 1987), 14. On the CPR publicity campaign, see E.J. Hart, *The Selling of Canada: The CPR and the Beginnings of Canadian Tourism* (Banff: Altitude Publishing, 1983).

2 Hart, *The Selling of Canada*, 26.

3 Hart, *The Selling of Canada*, 26, 55-65.

4 Macdonald is quoted by R. Craig Brown, "The Doctrine of Usefulness: Natural Resources and National Park Policy in Canada, 1887-1914," in *Conference on the National Parks Today and Tomorrow: Proceedings,* ed. J.G. Nelson and R.C. Scace (Calgary: University of Calgary, 1968), 94-110. For the *Baedeker Guide,* see Christopher Armstrong, Matthew Evenden, and H.V. Nelles, *The River Returns: An Environmental History of the Bow* (Montreal: McGill-Queen's University Press, 2009), 277, and see chapter 10, "Building Banff," 271-96, for a more general discussion of these developments.

5 The numbers are from Bella, *Parks for Profit*, 20-21, and Hart, *The Selling of Canada*, 88.

6 Mary T.S. Schäffer, *Old Indian Trails of the Canadian Rockies* (Vancouver: Rocky Mountain Books, 2007), 2. Also available as E.J. Hart, ed., *A Hunter of Peace: Mary T.S. Schäffer's Old Indian Trails of the Canadian Rockies: Incidents of Camp and Trail Life, Covering Two Years Exploration through the Rocky Mountains of Canada* (Banff: Whyte Museum of the Canadian Rockies, 1980).

7 Stewardson Brown, *Alpine Flora of the Canadian Rocky Mountains. Illustrated with Water-Colour Drawings and Photographs by Mrs Charles Schäffer* (New York and London: GP Putnam and Sons/The Knickerbocker Press, 1907). The volume is dedicated to "lovers of Alpine Florae" and "the memory of Dr Charles Schäffer, one of the pioneer botanists of the Canadian Rockies, and who early recognized this region as a new and interesting field for study."

8 Schäffer, *Old Indian Trails*, 1, 2.

9   See the comments of R.H. Campbell, the director of forestry for the Canadian Department of the Interior, reported in Peter J. Murphy, "'Following the Base of the Foothills': Tracing the Boundaries of Jasper Park and its Adjacent Rocky Mountains Forest Reserve," in *Culturing Wilderness in Jasper National Park: Studies in Two Centuries of Human History in the Upper Athabasca River Watershed,* ed. I.S. MacLaren (Edmonton: University of Alberta Press, 2007), 87-88.

10 Schäffer, *Old Indian Trails,* 6.

11 Schäffer, *Old Indian Trails,* 124.

12 Schäffer, *Old Indian Trails,* 121-23.

13 The substance of this paragraph is drawn from Murphy, "'Following the Base of the Foothills'," which provides much more detail.

14 PearlAnn Reichwein and Lisa McDermott, "Opening the Secret Garden: Mary Schäffer, Jasper Park Conservation, and the Survey of Maligne Lake, 1911," in *Culturing Wilderness,* ed. MacLaren, 155-98, quotations from 166 and 167. The survey was reported in "Mrs. Schäffer's Discovery and Survey of Lake Maligne, Canadian Rockies," *Geographical Journal* 39, 4 (April 1912): 397-81, which included a map of the survey and pictures of the lake.

15 The phrase is from The Rocky Mountains Park Act of 1887. See Parks Canada, "Parks Canada Guiding principles and Operational Policies: Preface; Early History," http://www.pc.gc.ca/, and can also be found in many accounts of the development of Canada's National Parks.

16 [J.B. Harkin], "Report of the Commissioner of Dominion Parks," in *Annual Report of the Department of the Interior for the Fiscal Year ending March 31, 1914,* Canada, Department of the Interior (Ottawa: 1915), 4.

17 See, more broadly, Katie Pickles, *Transnational Outrage: The Death and Commemoration of Edith Cavell* (Basingstoke and New York: Palgrave MacMillan, 2007).

18 This paragraph draws in substantial part from C.J. Taylor, "The Changing Habitat of Jasper Tourism," in *Culturing Wilderness,* ed. MacLaren, 199-231; quotations from 204 and 205-6.

19 *Cue Magazine,* 5 July 1941, cited by Taylor, "The Changing Habitat," 207.

20 Superintendent of Jasper National Park, 1937, cited by Taylor, "The Changing Habitat," 214. More generally, compare with Paul S. Sutter, *Driven Wild: How the Fight against Automobiles Launched the Modern Wilderness Movement* (Seattle: University of Washington Press, 2002) and David Louter, *Windshield Wilderness: Cars, Roads, and Nature in Washington's National Parks* (Seattle: University of Washington Press, 2006).

21 Taylor, "The Changing Habitat," 216.

22 Numbers from Taylor, "The Changing Habitat," 226-27.

23 Reichwein and McDermott, "Opening the Secret Garden," 184-88, quotation on 185.

24 Schäffer, *Old Indian Trails,* vi.

25 Reichwein and McDermott, "Opening the Secret Garden," 186.

26 Much of the detail of this paragraph is drawn from Karen R. Jones, *Wolf Mountains: A History of Wolves along the Great Divide* (Calgary: University of Calgary Press, 2002), 107-13.

27 Jones, *Wolf Mountains,* 111.

28 [Alexander Burgess] Deputy Minister of the Interior, cited by Jones, *Wolf Mountains,* 110.

29 C.J. Taylor, "Legislating Nature: The National Park Act of 1930," in *To See Ourselves/To Save Ourselves: Ecology and Culture in Canada,* ed. R. Lorimer, M. M'Gonigle, J-P. Revéret, and S. Ross (Montreal: Association for Canadian Studies, 1991), 128.

30 W.F. Lothian, *A Brief History of Canada's National Parks* (Ottawa: Environment Canada, Parks Canada, 1987); Janet Foster, *Working for Wildlife: The Beginnings of Preservation in Canada* (Toronto: University of Toronto Press, 1978 and 1998). The bureaucrat as hero phrase comes from Alan MacEachern, "Voices Crying in the Wilderness: Recent Works in Canadian Environmental History," *Acadiensis* 31, 2 (2002): 217-18.

31 The longer Harkin quote is from his undated "The Origin and Meaning of the National Parks of Canada," and is found in Jones, *Wolf Mountains*, 147. For more on Harkin see E.J. (Ted) Hart, *J.B. Harkin: Father of Canada's National Parks* (Edmonton: University of Alberta Press, 2010).

32 As discussed in Alan MacEachern, *Natural Selections: National Parks in Atlantic Canada, 1935-1970* (Montreal: McGill-Queen's University Press, 2001), 30-32.

33 MacEachern, *Natural Selections*, 30.

34 Jasper Environmental Association, *Report to Parks Canada and the Public on the Current State of Jasper National Park, with Reference to Observations and Recommendations from 2002,* 29 January 2007, http://www.jasperenvironmental.org/, and CPAWS, Northern Alberta Chapter, "The Future of Jasper National Park," http://cpawsnab.org/.

35 Stephen J. Pyne, *How the Grand Canyon Became Grand: A Short History* (New York: Viking Penguin, 1998), xiii, which my phrasing echoes. The *Chasm of the Colorado* is a painting by Thomas Moran, made on the north rim of the canyon in 1873 and purchased by the US Congress (see Pyne, *How the Grand Canyon*, 89, 91, 92).

36 Mark Daniel Barringer, *Selling Yellowstone: Capitalism and the Construction of Nature* (Lawrence, KS: University Press of Kansas, 2002), 1-7.

37 These mythologies are discussed in many places. See, among others, R. Cole Harris and John Warkentin, "Conclusion" in *Canada before Confederation: A Study in Historical Geography* (New York: Oxford University Press, 1974); Margaret Atwood, *Survival: A Thematic Guide to Canadian Literature* (Toronto: Anansi, 1972); John Smith, *The Generall Historie of Virginia, New-England, and the Summer Isles: With the Names of the Adventurers, Planters, and Gov- ernours from Their First Beginning Ano: 1584 to This Present 1624. With the Procedings of Those Severall Colonies and the Accidents That Befell Them in All Their Journyes and Discoveries. Also the Maps and Descriptions of All Those Countryes, Their Commodities, People, Government, Customes, and Religion Yet Knowne. Divided Into Six Bookes. By Captaine John Smith, Sometymes Governour in Those Countryes and Admirall of New England* (London: Printed by I.D. and I.H. for Michael Sparkes, 1624), quotation on page 2; F. Scott Fitzgerald, *The Great Gatsby* (New York: Charles Scribner's Sons, 1925), 182. See also Louise H. Westling, *The Green Breast of the New World: Landscape, Gender and American Fiction* (Athens, GA: University of Georgia Press, 1996) and Michael S. Cross, ed., *The Frontier Thesis and the Canadas: The Debate on the Impact of the Canadian Environment* (Toronto: Copp Clark Publishing, 1970).

38 See Roderick Nash, *Wilderness and the American Mind* (New Haven: Yale University Press, 1967) and William Cronon, "The Trouble with Wilderness; or, Getting Back to the Wrong Nature," *Environmental History* 1 (1996): 7-28, for important context here.

39 Susan G. Davis, *Spectacular Nature: Corporate Culture and the Sea World Experience* (Berke- ley: University of California Press, 1997), 11. Cited on 143.

CHAPTER I: GROUNDING NATIONAL PARK NATURE

1 Parks Canada, *Jasper National Park of Canada Management Plan* (Ottawa: Parks Canada, 2010), 1.

2 Karen R. Jones, *Wolf Mountains: A History of Wolves along the Great Divide* (Calgary: University of Calgary Press, 2002), 163.

3 Jeff Waugh, *Cheadle and Milton's Northwest Passage* (1996), http://www.jaspernationalpark. com/.

4 Greg Gillespie, "'I Was Well Pleased with Our Sport among the Buffalo': Big-Game Hunters, Travel Writing, and Cultural Imperialism in the British North American West, 1847-72," *Canadian Historical Review* 83, 4 (2002): 582; William Fitzwilliam Milton and W.B. Cheadle, *The North-West Passage by Land*, 6th ed. (London: Cassell, Petter, Galpin, [1870]).

5 I.S. MacLaren, "Cultured Wilderness in Jasper National Park," *Journal of Canadian Studies* 34, 3 (1999): 13; Lynda Jessup, "The Group of Seven and the Tourist Landscape in Western Canada, or the More Things Change ... ," *Journal of Canadian Studies* 37 (2002): 155.

6 Paul Kane, *Wanderings of an Artist among the Indians of North America, from Canada to Vancouver's Island and Oregon, through the Hudson's Bay Company's Territory and Back Again* (London: Longman, Brown, Green, Longmans, and Roberts, 1859). See also I.S. MacLaren, "Henry James Warre's and Paul Kane's Sketches in the Athabasca Watershed, 1846," in *Culturing Wilderness in Jasper National Park: Studies in Two Centuries of Human History in the Upper Athabasca River Watershed*, ed. I.S. MacLaren (Edmonton: University of Alberta Press, 2007), 41-70.

7 Canadian National Railways, *Jasper National Park* (Montreal: Canadian National Railways, 1927), Jasper-Yellowhead Museum and Archives (hereafter JYMA), Accn#994.45.1.1, CNR Tourism Brochures folder. An article in the October 1930 issue of the *Canadian Geographical Journal* on Jasper National Park also reproduced several A.Y. Jackson paintings of various aspects of the Jasper landscape, including *The Athabaska Valley, Amethyst Lake, Maligne Lake, Mount Edith Cavell*, and *Pyramid Mountain*. A footnote to the article indicates that these images were reproduced with permission from Canadian National Railways. See R.W. Cautley, "Jasper National Park," *Canadian Geographical Journal* 1, 6 (1930): 466-80. See also Jessup, "The Group of Seven and the Tourist Landscape."

8 Arthur Conan Doyle, "Jasper National Park on the Athabaska Trail," 18 June 1914, JYMA. Photographs of Conan Doyle's visit can be found in Library and Archives Canada (hereafter LAC), Department of Mines and Resources Collection.

9 Digital images of these scrapbooks are part of the online exhibition entitled "Picturing a Canadian Life: L.M. Montgomery's Personal Scrapbooks and Book Covers," http://lmm. confederationcentre.com. I would like to thank Elizabeth Epperly for bringing these scrapbooks to my attention.

10 Thomas Wharton, *Icefields* (Edmonton: NeWest Publishers, 1995).

11 Linda Goyette, "Jasper by Starlight," *Canadian Geographic Travel* (May 2007): 68-78.

12 Recent scholarly work on Jasper National Park has opened up new avenues of critical inquiry. See, for instance, Eric Higgs, *Nature by Design: People, Natural Processes, and Ecological Restoration* (Cambridge, MA: MIT Press, 2003), and I.S. MacLaren, ed., *Culturing Wilderness in Jasper National Park: Studies in Two Centuries of Human History in the Upper Athabasca River Watershed* (Edmonton: University of Alberta Press, 2007).

13 Patricia Jasen, *Wild Things: Nature, Culture, and Tourism in Ontario, 1790-1914* (Toronto: University of Toronto Press, 1995), 13.

14 Throughout this book, I adopt the linguistic model utilized by Neil Evernden in *The Social Creation of Nature:* that is, nature (non-capitalized) is used in reference to "the great amorphous mass of otherness that encloaks the planet," whereas Nature (capitalized) refers

to the cultural "system or model" of understanding, organizing, controlling, and shaping ideologies of the world around us. Neil Evernden, *The Social Creation of Nature* (Baltimore: Johns Hopkins University Press, 1992), xi.

15 I use the phrase "non-human animal" throughout this book to signify both the power and the limitation of language to describe the complexity of relationships among humans and other species. The phrase is intended to serve as a linguistic reminder that, while there are significant differences among the many species categorized as "animals," human beings are part of and not separate from this category. Admittedly, "non-human animal" still conveys a sense of "otherness" and has its limitations. Further, the meaning of the phrase has changed over time. For instance, in contemporary cultural studies, it tends to be used in the manner in which I use it here – as a marker of connectedness among species, standing in contrast to those analyses that take a "man versus beast" approach. However, in previous historical periods, particularly in the decades following publication of Charles Darwin's *On the Origin of Species* in 1859, the descriptor "non-human" could also be used as a means to emphasize differences among species. See, for instance, John Fiske, "The Progress from Brute to Man," *North American Review* 117, 241 (1873): 316. For more on the limitations of language in discussions of varying types of animals, see Erica Fudge, *Animal* (London: Reaktion Books, 2002), 160-64.

16 Bruce Braun, *The Intemperate Rainforest: Nature, Culture, and Power on Canada's West Coast* (Minneapolis: University of Minnesota Press, 2002), 261.

17 Daniel Botkin, *Discordant Harmonies: A New Ecology for the Twenty-First Century* (Oxford: Oxford University Press, 1990), 6. This analogy has recently taken on a new layer of meaning; amid ongoing debates about "the death of nature," the Eastman Kodak company has announced that it will no longer be manufacturing Kodachrome film. See "Kodak Is Taking Kodachrome Film Away," 22 June 2009, http://www.cbc.ca/.

18 See, for instance, the essays in William Cronon, ed., *Uncommon Ground: Rethinking the Human Place in Nature* (New York: W.W. Norton and Company, 1995).

19 Braun, *The Intemperate Rainforest,* 129.

20 John Barrell, *The Dark Side of the Landscape: The Rural Poor in English Painting, 1730-1840* (Cambridge, UK: Cambridge University Press, 1980).

21 Malcolm Andrews, *Landscape and Western Art* (Oxford: Oxford University Press, 1999), 175.

22 T.J. Jackson Lears, *No Place of Grace: Antimodernism and the Transformation of American Culture, 1880-1920* (New York: Pantheon Books, 1981), xiii.

23 William Cronon, "The Trouble with Wilderness; or, Getting Back to the Wrong Nature," in *Uncommon Ground: Rethinking the Human Place in Nature,* ed. William Cronon (New York: W.W. Norton and Company, 1995), 69-90.

24 "Rocky Mountains," *Our Alberta* (Summer 2008): 19.

25 Braun, *The Intemperate Rainforest,* 146.

26 Lucy Lippard, *On the Beaten Track: Tourism, Art, and Place* (New York: New Press, 1999), 136.

27 Michael C. Hall and John Shultis, "Railways, Tourism, and Worthless Lands: The Establishment of National Parks in Australia, Canada, New Zealand, and the United States," *Australian-Canadian Studies* 8 (1991): 64. See also Leslie Bella, *Parks for Profit* (Montreal: Harvest House, 1987), 1.

28 David Suzuki and Dave Robert Taylor, *The Big Picture: Reflections on Science, Humanity, and a Quickly Changing Planet* (Vancouver: Greystone Books, 2009), 73.

29 Kevin Van Tighem, "Parks at Risk (Book Review of Rick Searle's *Phantom Parks*)," *Alternatives Journal* 27, 3 (2001): 38.

30 Marc Bekoff, *The Animal Manifesto: Six Reasons for Expanding Our Compassion Footprint* (Novato, CA: New World Library, 2010), 40.

31 Stéphane Castonguay, "Naturalizing Federalism: Insect Outbreaks and the Centralization of Entomological Research in Canada, 1884-1914," *Canadian Historical Review* 85, 1 (2004): 1.

32 Brenda Shepherd and Jesse Whittington, "Response of Wolves to Corridor Restoration and Human Use Management," *Ecology and Society* 11, 2 (2006): http://www.ecologyandsociety.org/.

33 Ed Struzik, "Call of the Wild Once Again Echoes through Jasper; Since Culls Virtually Killed Off the Predators, Park Elk Have Spiralled out of Control – So that Today, Wolves Are Welcome Once More," *Edmonton Journal,* 25 May 2008, E6.

34 Ibid.

35 John Korobanik, "Restroom for Campers No Longer Maligned; Powered by Six Solar Panels, New Jasper Facility Is Virtually a Self-Contained Sewage Treatment Plant," *Edmonton Journal,* 30 August 2007, F2.

36 Ibid.

37 Parks Canada, *Jasper National Park Management Plan,* sections 3.2 and 9.5, updated 15 April 2009, http://www.pc.gc.ca/. See also W.F. Lothian, *A History of Canada's National Parks – Volume III* (Ottawa: Parks Canada, 1979), 59.

38 Parks Canada, *Jasper National Park Management Plan,* section 3.1, updated 15 April, 2009, http://www.pc.gc.ca/.

39 Rick Searle, *Phantom Parks: The Struggle to Save Canada's National Parks* (Toronto: Key Porter Books, 2000), 27-29.

40 Ibid., 185.

41 Cameron French, "Environmentalists Applaud Canadian Parks Plan," Reuters News Service, 4 September 2002, http://enn.com/.

42 Donald Dawson, "Plans for Ten New Canada Parks Met with Skepticism," *National Geographic News,* 10 October 2002, http://news.nationalgeographic.com/.

43 Ibid.

44 Ed Struzik, "Can Our Parks Be Saved?" *Edmonton Journal,* 26 December 2004, F5.

45 Braun, *The Intemperate Rainforest,* 112.

46 See, for instance, Kevin McNamee, "Prime Minister Protects Two Candidate National Parks," *Nature Alert* 7, 1 (1997): 4.

47 Canadian Parks and Wilderness Society, *What's Happening in Our Mountain Parks?* (Calgary: Canadian Parks and Wilderness Society, 2002), 3; Richard West Sellars, "Science or Scenery? A Conflict of Values in the National Parks," *Wilderness* 52 (1989): 29-38.

48 Suzuki and Taylor, *The Big Picture,* 72.

49 Parks Canada, *Jasper National Park Management Plan,* section 3.9, updated 15 April, 2009, http://www.pc.gc.ca/.

50 Ibid., section 3.10.

51 John Urry, *Consuming Places* (London: Routledge, 1995), 189.

52 Timothy W. Luke, "Nature Protection or Nature Projection: A Cultural Critique of the Sierra Club," *Capitalism, Nature, Socialism* 8, 1 (1997): 44.

53 Cronon, "The Trouble with Wilderness"; Simon Schama, *Landscape and Memory* (Toronto: Random House, 1995).

54 William Cronon, "Foreword," in *Uncommon Ground: Rethinking the Human Place in Nature,* ed. William Cronon (New York: W.W. Norton and Company, 1995), 21.

55 See, for instance, John Beardsley, *Earthworks and Beyond* (New York: Abbeville Press, 1989); Vittorio Fagone, *Art in Nature* (Milan: Mazzotta, 1996); John K. Grande, *Balance: Art and Nature* (Montreal: Black Rose Books, 1994); and Jeffrey Kastner, ed., *Land and Environmental Art* (London: Phaidon Press, 1998).

56 A number of recent publications have begun to address the relationships between imagery and ecology. See, for instance, Tim Bonyhady, *The Colonial Earth* (Melbourne: Melbourne University Press, 2002); Alan C. Braddock and Christoph Irmscher, *A Keener Perception: Ecocritical Studies in American Art History* (Tuscaloosa: University of Alabama Press, 2009); Finis Dunaway, *Natural Visions: The Power of Images in American Environmental Reform* (Chicago: University of Chicago Press, 2005); and Greg Thomas, *Art and Ecology in Nineteenth Century France: The Landscapes of Théodore Rousseau* (Princeton: Princeton University Press, 2000).

57 W.J.T. Mitchell, "Interdisciplinarity and Visual Culture," *Art Bulletin* 77, 4 (1995): 543.

58 Joan M. Schwartz and James R. Ryan, "Introduction: Photography and the Geographical Imagination," in *Picturing Place: Photography and the Geographical Imagination,* ed. Joan M. Schwartz and James R. Ryan (London: I.B. Tauris, 2003), 5.

59 Tim Bonyhady, "Artists with Axes," *Environment and History* 1, 2 (1995): 221-39.

60 Bonyhady, *The Colonial Earth,* 199-202.

61 Dunaway, *Natural Visions,* xv.

62 There is, however, a growing body of scholarship exploring the relationship between photographic practices and environmental issues. See, for instance, Claude Baillargen, ed., *Imaging a Shattering Earth: Contemporary Photography and the Environmental Debate* (Rochester, MI: Meadow Brook Art Gallery [in association with CONTACT Toronto Photography Festival], 2006); Carol Diehl, "The Toxic Sublime," *Art in America* 94, 2 (2006): 118-23; and Meaghan Lowe, "Dreamworld and Reality: An Exploration of Environmental Aesthetics in Contemporary Photography," *Topia* 21 (2009): 105-20. See also J. Keri Cronin, "A Tale of Two Parks: Photography, Pollution, and 'the Pecuniary Canons of Taste,'" in *Thorstein Veblen's Contributions to Environmental Sociology: Essays in the Political Ecology of Wasteful Industrialism,* ed. Ross Mitchell (Lewiston, NY: Edwin Mellen Press, 2007), 257-86.

63 Stephanie Croft, "Pin-Up Protest: Salt Spring Women Bared All in a Fundraising Calendar," *Alternatives Journal* 27, 2 (2001): 28.

64 Denis Cosgrove, *Apollo's Eye: A Cartographic Genealogy of the Earth in the Western Imagination* (Baltimore: Johns Hopkins University Press, 2001), 261.

65 Yaakov Jerome Garb, "The Use and Misuse of the Whole Earth Image," *Whole Earth Review* 45 (1985): 18-25.

66 The environmental movement has not been a cohesive, homogeneous social movement. The concept of a "green spectrum" is a useful analytical tool in this regard as it allows different political positions that exist between environmental groups to be articulated. For more on the range of dynamics that informs environmental politics, see John S. Dryzek and David Schlosberg, "Introduction," in *Debating the Earth: The Environmental Politics Reader,* ed. John S. Dryzek and David Schlosberg (Oxford: Oxford University Press, 1998), 1-3. The range of the green spectrum in a Canadian context is explored by well-known writer and environmental activist Farley Mowat in *Rescue the Earth! Conversations with the Green Crusaders* (Toronto: McClelland and Stewart, 1990).

67 Joel Connelly, "A Growing Awareness: Environmental Groups and the Media," *Aperture* 120 (1990): 41.

68 Two of the best-known examples have been the use of graphic images exposing the violence of the seal hunt on the east coast of Canada and images of Russian whaling ships at work in the Atlantic Ocean. For more on Greenpeace's use of imagery, see Jim Bohlen, *Making Waves: The Origins and Future of Greenpeace* (Montreal: Black Rose Books, 2001), and Stephen Dale, *McLuhan's Children: The Greenpeace Message and the Media* (Toronto: Between the Lines, 1996).

69 Deborah Bright, "Of Mother Nature and Marlboro Men: An Inquiry into Cultural Meanings of Landscape Photography," in *The Contest of Meaning: Critical Histories of Photography,* ed. Richard Bolton (Cambridge, MA: MIT Press, 1991), 129.

70 Deborah Bright, "The Machine in the Garden Revisited: American Environmentalism and Photographic Aesthetics," *Art Journal* 51 (1992): 64.

71 Ibid.

72 Denis Cosgrove, "Images and Imagination in 20th Century Environmentalism: From the Sierras to the Poles," *Environment and Planning A* 40, 8 (2008): 1864.

73 For more on this dynamic in the context of the American environmental movement, see Finis Dunaway, "Gas Masks, Pogo, and the Ecological Indian: Earth Day and the Visual Politics of American Environmentalism," *American Quarterly* 60, 1 (2008): 67-99.

74 Government of Canada, "National Historic Parks Wildlife and Domestic Animals Regulation (SOR/81-613)," *Canada Gazette Part II* 115, 15 (23 July 1981): 2317.

75 Paul Kopas, *Taking the Air: Ideas and Change in Canada's National Parks* (Vancouver: UBC Press, 2007), 178.

76 Alberta Provincial Tourist and Publicity Bureau, *See Alberta First* (Edmonton: Provincial Tourist and Publicity Bureau, 1938), JYMA, 994.45.1.1, Doris Kensit Fonds.

77 *Pleasurable Places in the Wide Open Spaces* (Vancouver: Traveller's Digest, 1944); *Jasper in June: A Vacationtime Superb in the Canadian Rockies* (Edmonton: Hamly Press, n.d.), JYMA, 84.161.72 Jasper Yellowhead Museum and Archives Book and JYMA 2005.44.13a Jasper National Park Travel Brochure and Memorabilia Collection.

78 Steven Hoelscher, "The Photographic Construction of Tourist Space in Victorian America," *Geographical Review* 88, 4 (1998): 558.

79 Ibid., 549.

80 Tina Loo, "Making a Modern Wilderness: Conserving Wildlife in Twentieth-Century Canada," *Canadian Historical Review* 82 (2001): 94.

81 Bill Gibbons, *Photographing the Canadian Rockies* (Banff: British Photographic Laboratories of Canada, 1948), 5.

82 Jaakko Suvantola, *Tourist's Experience of Place* (Burlington, VT: Ashgate, 2002), 182.

83 John Urry, "Sensing Leisure Spaces," in *Leisure/Tourism Geographies: Practices and Geographical Knowledge,* ed. David Crouch (London: Routledge, 1999), 39.

84 Christopher B. Steiner, "Authenticity, Repetition, and the Aesthetics of Seriality: The Work of Tourist Art in the Age of Mechanical Reproduction," in *Unpacking Culture: Art and Commodity in Colonial and Postcolonial Worlds,* ed. Ruth B. Phillips and Christopher B. Steiner (Berkeley: University of California Press, 1999), 99.

85 Sylvie Beaudreau, "The Changing Faces of Canada: Images of Canada in *National Geographic,*" *American Review of Canadian Studies* 32, 4 (2002): 529.

86 Steiner, "Authenticity, Repetition, and the Aesthetics of Seriality," 92.

87 Michael Payne, "The Fur Trade on the Upper Athabasca River, 1810-1910," in *Culturing Wilderness in Jasper National Park: Studies in Two Centuries of Human History in the Upper*

Athabasca River Watershed, ed. I.S. MacLaren (Edmonton: University of Alberta Press, 2007), 4.

88　I.S. MacLaren, "Introduction," in *Culturing Wilderness in Jasper National Park: Studies in Two Centuries of Human History in the Upper Athabasca River Watershed,* ed. I.S. MacLaren (Edmonton: University of Alberta Press, 2007), xxv; Peter J. Murphy, "Homesteading in the Athabasca Valley to 1910: An Interview with Edward Wilson Moberly, Prairie Creek, Alberta, 29 August 1980," in *Culturing Wilderness in Jasper National Park: Studies in Two Centuries of Human History in the Upper Athabasca River Watershed,* ed. I.S. MacLaren (Edmonton: University of Alberta Press, 2007), 128.

89　Parks Canada, *Jasper National Park of Canada: State of the Park Report* (Ottawa: Parks Canada, 2008), iv.

90　Parks Canada, *Japer National Park: State of the Park Report,* iv-v.

91　Parks Canada, *Jasper National Park of Canada Management Plan* (Ottawa: Parks Canada, 2010), vi.

92　*Setting a New Direction for Canada's National Parks,"* vol. 2 of *"Unimpaired for Future Generations"? Protecting Ecological Integrity within Canada's National Parks* (Ottawa: Parks Canada Agency, 2000), v.

93　Randy Boswell, "Two of Canada's Natural Wonders, Nahanni, Rocky Mountain Parks, under Threat, Says UNESCO," *CanWest News,* 29 August 2006, 1.

94　Joan M. Schwartz, *"The Geography Lesson*: Photographs and the Construction of Imaginative Geographies," *Journal of Historical Geography* 22 (1996): 16-45. The concept of "imaginative geography" is associated with the work of Edward Said. See, for instance, Edward Said, "Imaginative Geography and Its Representations: Orientalizing the Oriental," in *Orientalism,* by Edward Said (New York: Pantheon Books, 1978), 49-73.

95　George Altmeyer, "Three Ideas of Nature in Canada," in *Consuming Canada: Readings in Environmental History,* ed. Chad Gaffield and Pam Gaffield (Toronto: Copp Clark, 1995), 98. Altmeyer points out that between 1901 and 1911 "Canada's urban population increased by 62 percent and the rural population by only 17 percent." The government of Canada established Jasper Forest Park in 1907.

96　Richard Tresidder, "Tourism and Sacred Landscapes," in *Leisure/Tourism Geographies: Practices and Geographical Knowledge,* ed. David Crouch (London: Routledge, 1999), 144-45. Tresidder deliberately avoids giving a concrete definition for "sacred landscapes," as he argues that this is arrived at through a process of individual reflexivity. However, he does point out that "we can see many tourism sites as a refuge from modernity, in which we can find the organic, the primitive, the original and the expressive. These elements enable landscape to become defined as 'sacred'" (138).

97　Michael Karlberg, "News and Conflict: How Adversarial News Frames Limit Public Understanding of Environmental Issues," *Alternatives Journal* 23, 1 (1997): 22-27.

98　Evernden, *The Social Creation of Nature,* x.

Chapter 2: "Jasper Wonderful by Nature"

1　Leslie Bella, *Parks for Profit* (Montreal: Harvest House, 1987), 9.

2　Richard White, "The New Western History and the National Parks," *George Wright Forum* 13, 3 (1996): 31.

3　Kathy Kennedy, "Jasper Overcrowding Brings Hiking Quotas," *Edmonton Journal,* 19 June 1976, 37.

4　John Urry, *Consuming Places* (London: Routledge, 1995), 180.

5 Canadian National Railways, *Jasper National Park* (Montreal: Canadian National Railways, 1927), 4.

6 Ibid.

7 Cyndi Smith, *People, Places, and Events: A History of Jasper National Park* (Jasper: Jasper-Yellowhead Historical Society, 1983), 2. In 1821, the North West Company became part of the famed Hudson's Bay Company.

8 "Jasper's Early Visitors Knew 'Togetherness,'" *Jasper Tourist News* (summer 1960): 1.

9 Colleen Skidmore discusses contemporary readings of Schäffer's photography, writing, and life in her edited volume *This Wild Spirit: Women in the Rocky Mountains of Canada* (Edmonton: University of Alberta Press, 2006), especially 279-90.

10 J.G. Nelson, "Parks and Protected Areas and Sustainable Development," in *Changing Parks: The History, Future, and Cultural Context of Parks and Heritage Landscapes,* ed. John S. Marsh and Bruce W. Hodgins (Toronto: Natural History/Natural Heritage, 1998), 291.

11 I.S. MacLaren, "Cultured Wilderness in Jasper National Park," *Journal of Canadian Studies* 34 (1999): 7.

12 Smith, *People, Places, and Events,* 1. See also Eric Higgs, *Nature by Design: People, Natural Processes, and Ecological Restoration* (Cambridge, MA: MIT Press, 2003), 23.

13 F.W. Howay, "A Short Historical Sketch of Jasper Park Region," *Sierra Club Bulletin* 14 (1929): 28-33; J.G. MacGregor, *Overland by the Yellowhead* (Saskatoon: Western Producer Book Service, 1974).

14 W.F. Lothian, *A Brief History of Canada's National Parks* (Ottawa: Environment Canada, Parks Canada, 1987), 52.

15 Ibid.

16 C.J. Taylor, "The Changing Habitat of Jasper Tourism." In *Culturing Wilderness in Jasper National Park: Studies in Two Centuries of Human History in the Upper Athabasca River Watershed,* ed. I.S. MacLaren (Edmonton: University of Alberta Press, 2007), 199.

17 Hanneke Brooymans, "Jasper Hopes to Open Gates to More Visitors," *Edmonton Journal,* 25 November 2009, B2.

18 A study done in the 1980s found that over 50 percent of photographs used in this manner were empty of human presence, and in the instances where people were included they were more often than not found at the periphery of a scene dominated by breathtaking mountain vistas and other such "scenic" views. For more on this study, see Douglas C. Nord, "Canada Perceived: The Impact of Canadian Tourism Advertising in the U.S.A.," *Journal of American Culture* 9 (1986): 23-30.

19 Parks Canada, *Jasper National Park of Canada: State of the Park Report* (Ottawa: Parks Canada, 2008), iii.

20 Ibid., 9.

21 Ibid.

22 Ibid., vi.

23 Ibid., 4.

24 Smith, *People, Places, and Events,* 1.

25 Ibid.

26 Higgs, *Nature by Design,* 23-24.

27 Peter J. Murphy, "Homesteading in the Athabasca Valley to 1910: An Interview with Edward Wilson Moberly, Prairie Creek, Alberta, 29 August 1980," in *Culturing Wilderness in Jasper National Park: Studies in Two Centuries of Human History in the Upper Athabasca River Watershed,* ed. I.S. MacLaren (Edmonton: University of Alberta Press, 2007), 127.

28 Ibid., 128.
29 In their exploration of the erasure of Aboriginal peoples from lands claimed by settler societies in North America, scholars such as Jonathan Bordo, Maureen Sherlock, John Sandlos, and Mark David Spence have demonstrated how cultural hegemony is asserted through dominant landscape representations in the context of North American nature. These authors argue that the symbolic removal of human presence in imagery is often linked to the actual removal of those who previously inhabited the lands in question. See Jonathan Bordo, "Jack Pine – Wilderness Sublime or the Erasure of the Aboriginal Presence from the Landscape," *Journal of Canadian Studies* 27 (1992): 98-128; John Sandlos, *Hunters at the Margin: Native People and Wildlife Conservation in the Northwest Territories* (Vancouver: UBC Press, 2007); Maureen P. Sherlock, "The Accidental Tourist," in *Eye of Nature,* ed. Daina Augaitis and Helga Pakasaa (Banff: Walter Phillips Gallery, 1991), 123-37; and Mark David Spence, "Dispossessing the Wilderness: Yosemite Indians and the National Park Ideal, 1864-1930," *Pacific Historical Review* 65, 1 (1996): 27-59.
30 For more on these types of souvenir items, see Valda Blundell, "Aboriginal Empowerment and the Souvenir Trade in Canada," *Annals of Tourism Research* 20 (1993): 64-87.
31 Joan M. Schwartz, "The Geography Lesson: Photographs and the Construction of Imaginative Geographies," *Journal of Historical Geography* 22, 1 (1996): 16-45.
32 Recent curatorial projects have attempted to recontextualize these kinds of images. For instance, between the autumn of 1999 and the winter of 2002, the exhibition "Emergence from the Shadow" (curated by Jeff Thomas) was on display at the Canadian Museum of Civilization. This exhibition featured survey photographs taken by the Geological Survey of Canada as well as photographic works by contemporary artists of Aboriginal heritage. Two major objectives were undertaken in this exhibition: the linking of past and present, and the use of images of Native peoples by Euro-Canadians as a site of empowerment and exploration for contemporary First Nations audiences. The exhibit still exists in an online form at http://www.civilization.ca/.
33 Travel Alberta would not, however, consent to having this photograph reproduced in this book.
34 Canadian National Railways, "Jasper: Gem of the Canadian Rockies," *Canadian National Magazine* 24, 5 (1938): 1.
35 Ibid.
36 Urry, *Consuming Places,* 137; J.A. Walter, "Social Limits to Tourism," *Leisure Studies* 1 (1982): 295-304.
37 Urry, *Consuming Places,* 137.
38 Ibid., 138.
39 For more on the relationship between the automobile and wilderness tourism, see David Louter, *Windshield Wilderness: Cars, Roads, and Nature in Washington's National Parks* (Seattle: University of Washington Press, 2006), and Paul S. Sutter, *Driven Wild: How the Fight against Automobiles Launched the Modern Wilderness Movement* (Seattle: University of Washington Press, 2002).
40 Sherri Zickefoose, "National Park Fees Frozen," *Calgary Herald,* 10 May 2009, B3.
41 Sharon Zukin et al., "From Coney Island to Las Vegas in the Urban Imaginary: Discursive Practices of Growth and Decline," *Urban Affairs Review* 33, 5 (1998): 627-54.
42 Neil Evernden, *The Social Creation of Nature* (Baltimore: Johns Hopkins University Press, 1992), 23.
43 Much work has been done on the use of imagery in this way by Canadian Pacific Railway. See, for instance, E.J. Hart, *Trains, Peaks, and Tourists: The Golden Age of Canadian*

Travel (Banff: EJH Literary Enterprises, 2000); Lynda Jessup, "The Group of Seven and the Tourist Landscape in Western Canada, or the More Things Change ... ," *Journal of Canadian Studies* 37 (2002): 144-79; and Dennis Reid, *"Our Own Country Canada": Being an Account of the National Aspirations of the Principal Landscape Artists in Montreal and Toronto, 1860-1890* (Ottawa: National Gallery of Canada, 1979).

44 Ian Urquhart, ed., *Assault on the Rockies: Environmental Controversies in Alberta* (Edmonton: Rowan Books, 1998).

45 Jasper Environmental Association, *Report to Parks Canada and the Public on the Current State of Jasper National Park, With Reference to Observations and Recommendations from 2002*, 29 January 2007, http://www.jasperenvironmental.org/.

46 *Jasper: Visitor's Choice, Winter 2002/2003* (Vancouver: Visitor's Choice Publications, 2002), 10.

47 Canadian National Railways, "Choose a Canadian National Vacation This Year – Vacation at Jasper National Park," *World's Work Magazine* (April 1927): n. pag.

48 Nord, "Canada Perceived," 24.

49 Ibid., 26.

50 Ibid.

51 *Our Jasper* (promotional brochure) (Jasper: Mountain Park Lodges, c. 2003).

52 Parks Canada, *Parks Canada: First Priority. Progress Report on the Implementation of the Recommendations of the Panel on the Ecological Integrity of Canada's National Parks* (Ottawa: Parks Canada, 2001), iii.

53 *Setting a New Direction for Canada's National Parks*, vol. 2 of *"Unimpaired for Future Generations"? Protecting Ecological Integrity within Canada's National Parks* (Ottawa: Parks Canada Agency, 2000), 1-9.

54 Jasper Environmental Association, *Report*.

55 The government of Canada established Jasper Forest Park in 1907. In July 1911, the Dominion Forest Reserves and Parks Act designated Jasper as a "dominion park," and in 1930 the National Parks Act gave Jasper its current status as a Canadian national park. For more on the establishment of national parks in Canada, see Sid Marty, *A Grand and Fabulous Notion: The First Century of Canada's Parks* (Toronto: NC Press, 1984).

56 I.C. Adams, "Good Post Cards Still Profitable," *Camera Craft* 10, 11 (1913): 502.

57 Canadian National Railways, *Across Canada: The Canadian Scene in Map and Pictures* (Montreal: Canadian National Railways, 1961), JYMA, Accn#994.45.1.1, CNR Tourism Brochures folder.

58 E. Palmer, "Seeing the Sights: Popular Places to Experience Classic Mountain Scenery and Adventure," *Where Rocky Mountains* (summer 1996): 12; quoted in Shelagh J. Squire, "Rewriting Languages of Geography and Tourism: Cultural Discourses of Destinations, Gender, and Tourism History in the Canadian Rockies," in *Destinations: Cultural Landscapes of Tourism*, ed. Greg Ringer (London: Routledge, 1998), 80.

59 *Totem Pole* (postcard) (Jasper: J.A. Weiss, c. 1944). This postcard is dated 25 December 1944 and postmarked in Jasper. It is addressed to a Mr. and Mrs. A.W. Shorey in Newburg Junction, Carleton, and bears a three-cent postage stamp. Part of the author's personal collection. For more on the life and photography of Joe Weiss, see Helen Collinson, *One Man's Mountains: Joe Weiss in Jasper* (Edmonton: University of Alberta Collections, 1979).

60 The pole, which dates to the late nineteenth century, had deteriorated to the point where conservators were unable to repair it. It was removed in April 2009 as a safety precaution and was repatriated to Haida Gwaii in the summer of 2010. Parks Canada, "Jasper Raven Totem Pole Returns to Haida Gwaii," 21 June 2010, http://news.gc.ca/.

61 Aldona Jonaitis, "Northwest Coast Totem Poles," in *Unpacking Culture: Art and Commodity in Colonial and Postcolonial Worlds,* ed. Ruth B. Phillips and Christopher B. Steiner (Berkeley: University of California Press, 1999), 105.

62 Graeme Wynn, "'Shall We Linger along Ambitionless?': Environmental Perspectives on British Columbia," *B.C. Studies* 142-43 (2004): 26.

63 Lucy Lippard, *On the Beaten Track: Tourism, Art, and Place* (New York: New Press, 1999), 138.

64 Peter Osborne, *Travelling Light: Photography, Travel, and Visual Culture* (Manchester: Manchester University Press, 2000), 92.

65 Marguerite Shaffer, *See America First: Tourism and National Identity* (Washington, DC: Smithsonian Institution Press, 2001), 265.

66 "You Should Be Here," *Travel Alberta* (Summer 2003): 67.

67 Travel Alberta, "Marketing Opportunities – In Province," n.d. (ca. 2003), http://industry.travelalberta.com/.

68 Alberta Economic Development, *Tourism – Alberta, Canada,* February 2004, http://industry.travelalberta.com.

69 Travel Alberta, *Maximum Opportunity Regions: Travel Alberta Partnership Planner, 2003-2005* (Edmonton: Travel Alberta, 2003), 3, 7. For the purposes of tourism marketing, Alberta is broken into six distinct "tourism destination regions" (TDRs): Alberta South, Calgary and Area, Canadian Rockies, Alberta Central, Alberta North, and Edmonton and Area. For more on these regions, see Travel Alberta's industry-specific website, http://www.industry.travelalberta.com.

70 Canada, Department of Mines and Resources, *Jasper National Park in the Canadian Rockies* (Ottawa: National Parks Bureau, [1940s]).

71 For discussion of the CPR's use of visual culture in its promotional material, see Margery Tanner Hadley, "Photography, Tourism, and the CPR," in *Essays on the Historical Geography of the Canadian West: Regional Perspectives on the Settlement Process,* ed. L.A. Rosenvall and S.M. Evans (Calgary: University of Calgary, 1987), 48-69; Hart, *Trains, Peaks, and Tourists;* and Brock Silversides, *Waiting for the Light: Early Mountain Photography in British Columbia and Alberta, 1865-1939* (Saskatoon: Fifth House Publishers, 1995).

72 Canadian National Railways, *Jasper National Park, Canadian Rockies* (Montreal: Canadian National Railways, 1953), 16.

73 "To Advertise Banff," *Banff Crag and Canyon,* 13 October 1917, 8.

74 "Harmon's Photographs Published in England," *Banff Crag and Canyon,* 5 June 1925, 1.

75 Silversides, *Waiting for the Light,* 4.

76 "Harmon's Images of Civilization and Wilderness," *Banff Crag and Canyon,* 24 August 1988, 3. In the summer 2002 *Our Alberta* magazine, for instance, readers are told about Harmon's life and work in an article accompanied by an example of his mountain photography. See Jill Sawyer, "The Ultimate Alberta," *Our Alberta* 20, 1 (2002): 11.

77 I.S. MacLaren, Eric S. Higgs, and Gabrielle Zezulka-Mailloux, *Mapper of Mountains: M.P. Bridgland in the Canadian Rockies* (Edmonton: University of Alberta Press, 2005), 169-81.

78 Canada, *Jasper National Park* (1940s), 3.

79 Ibid., 10.

80 Robert J.C. Stead, *Canada's Mountain Playgrounds* (Ottawa: Department of Mines and Resources, 1935), 5.

81 Parks Canada, *Welcome to National Parks* (Ottawa: Parks Canada, 1986), 2; Parks Canada, *The Mountain Guide to Banff, Jasper, Kootenay, Yoho, Glacier, and Mount Revelstoke National Parks of Canada* (Ottawa: Parks Canada, 2003), 3.

82 Warren Allmand, "W.J. Oliver Photographer, 1887-1954," in *Footloose in the National Parks: W.J. Oliver* (Ottawa: Parks Canada, 1978), 1.

83 One of Oliver's most celebrated films made in Jasper National Park was the 1938 production entitled *Jasper of the Lakes*. This film has been described as a "picturization of a poem" by the same name written by Jasper school teacher T.P. O'Connor. Both the poem and the film describe the scenic beauty of Jasper throughout the four seasons. A copy of O'Connor's poem can be found in the Joan Cavers fonds of the Glenbow Archives in Calgary, and a copy of the film is housed in the National Film Archives. For more on this production, see Sheilagh S. Jameson, *W.J. Oliver: Life through a Master's Lens* (Calgary: Glenbow Museum, 1984), 67, 100.

84 LAC, National Parks Collection 1960-124, album 18. The albums in this collection also contain photographs that Oliver took in Jasper in 1923 and 1927.

85 Canada, *Jasper National Park* (1940s), 4.

86 Stead, *Canada's Mountain Playgrounds*, 11.

87 Letter from Mabel B. Williams, Department of the Interior, to W.J. Oliver, 11 November 1923, LAC, MG30-D402, vol. 1.

88 Letter from J.C. Campbell, Director of Publicity for Canadian National Parks, to W.J. Oliver, 29 November 1923, LAC, MG30-D402, vol. 1.

89 Harper Cory, "W.J. Oliver, Cameraman to Nature," *Photography* 6, 62 (1937): 6-7. Oliver was also the cameraman for the famed Grey Owl films. For more on the story of Grey Owl and his position as Canadian icon, see Daniel Francis, *National Dreams: Myth, Memory, and Canadian History* (Vancouver: Arsenal Pulp Press, 1997), 142, 146-49.

90 Cory, "W.J. Oliver," 6.

91 Richard West Sellars, "Science or Scenery? A Conflict of Values in the National Parks," *Wilderness* 52 (1989): 35.

92 MacLaren, "Cultured Wilderness," 36.

93 Ibid., 38. For more on the revisitation of the fire suppression policies, see Canadian Parks and Wilderness Society, *What's Happening in Our Mountain Parks?* (Calgary: Canadian Parks and Wilderness Society, 2002), 11.

94 Parks Canada, *Jasper National Park of Canada Management Plan* (Ottawa: Parks Canada, 2010), v.

95 Carol Crawshaw and John Urry, "Tourism and the Photographic Eye," in *Touring Cultures: Transformations of Travel and Theory*, ed. Chris Rojek and John Urry (London: Routledge, 1997), 182-83.

96 Urry, *Consuming Places*, 183.

97 Lisa M. Benton and John Rennie Short, *Environmental Discourse and Practice* (Oxford: Blackwell Publishers, 1999), 197. See also Timothy W. Luke, "Nature Protection or Nature Projection: A Cultural Critique of the Sierra Club," *Capitalism, Nature, Socialism* 8, 1 (1997): 37-63.

98 William Cronon, "The Trouble with Wilderness; or, Getting Back to the Wrong Nature," in *Uncommon Ground: Rethinking the Human Place in Nature,* ed. William Cronon (New York: W.W. Norton and Company, 1995), 69-90.

99 William Cronon, "Foreword," in *Uncommon Ground: Rethinking the Human Place in Nature,* ed. William Cronon (New York: W.W. Norton and Company, 1995), 22.

100 For a discussion on some of the concerns related to the environmental assessment process, see Jasper Environmental Association, "Environmental Assessments: Mitigation Magic," n.d., http://www.jasperenvironmental.org/.

101 John T. Faris, *Seeing Canada* (Philadelphia: J.B. Lippincott Company, 1924).

102 "Jasper Seeks Policy for Filmmakers in Park," *Bow Valley This Week*, 3-10 August 1993, 1. For discussion on the various Hollywood movies filmed in this landscape, see "Jasper Scenery Hollywood's Choice," *Jasper Tourist News* (summer 1960): 6, and MacLaren, "Cultured Wilderness," 32-36.

103 William Cronon, "Foreword: Why Worry about Roads," in *Driven Wild: How the Fight against Automobiles Launched the Modern Wilderness Movement*, ed. Paul S. Sutter (Seattle: University of Washington Press, 2002), xii. For more on automobile tourism in North American national parks, see Alexander Wilson, "The View from the Road: Nature Tourism in the Postwar Years," *Border/Lines* 12 (1988): 10-14, and Alexander Wilson, *The Culture of Nature: North American Landscape from Disney to the Exxon Valdez* (Toronto: Between the Lines, 1991).

104 Louter, *Windshield Wilderness*.

105 David W. Schindler, "The Eastern Slopes of the Canadian Rockies: Must We Follow the American Blueprint?" in *Rocky Mountain Futures: An Ecological Perspective*, ed. Jill S. Baron (Washington, DC: Island Press, 2002), 287.

106 David Nye, "Technologies of Landscape," in *Technologies of Landscape: From Reaping to Recycling*, ed. David Nye (Amherst: University of Massachusetts Press, 1999), 1.

CHAPTER 3: AN INVITATION TO LEISURE

1 Canadian National Railways, "Magnificent Jasper Park in the Heart of the Canadian Rockies," *Maclean's Magazine*, 1 May 1934, 57.

2 John Bale, "Parks and Gardens: Metaphors for the Modern Places of Sport," in *Leisure/ Tourism Geographies: Practices and Geographical Knowledge*, ed. David Crouch (London: Routledge, 1999), 50.

3 "Report of the Commissioner of Dominion Parks," in Department of the Interior, *Annual Report* (1914), 4, quoted in C.J. Taylor, *Negotiating the Past: The Making of Canada's National Historic Parks and Sites* (Montreal: McGill-Queen's University Press, 1990), 27.

4 Geoff Wall, "Outdoor Recreation and the Canadian Identity," in *Recreational Land Use: Perspectives on Its Evolution in Canada*, ed. G. Wall and J. Marsh (Ottawa: Carleton University Press, 1982), 419-34.

5 "Canadian Rockies," in *Your Official Alberta Vacation Guide* (2002), 25.

6 Thorstein Veblen, *The Theory of the Leisure Class* (1899; reprint, New York: Dover Thrift Editions, 1994).

7 I expand on this notion in another publication. See J. Keri Cronin, "A Tale of Two Parks: Photography, Pollution, and 'the Pecuniary Canons of Taste,'" in *Thorstein Veblen's Contributions to Environmental Sociology: Essays in the Political Ecology of Wasteful Industrialism*, ed. Ross Mitchell (Lewiston, NY: Edwin Mellen Press, 2007), 257-86.

8 For discussion on the forced labour used to build many of the roads and related facilities in Canada's mountain parks, see Bill Waiser, *Park Prisoners: The Untold Story of Western Canada's National Parks, 1915-1946* (Saskatoon: Fifth House Publishers, 1995).

9 Richard White, "'Are You an Environmentalist or Do You Work for a Living?'" in *Uncommon Ground: Rethinking the Human Place in Nature*, ed. William Cronon (New York: W.W. Norton and Company, 1995), 171.

10 Hal Clifford, *Downhill Slide: Why the Corporate Ski Industry Is Bad for Skiing, Ski Towns, and the Environment* (San Francisco: Sierra Club Books, 2002), x, 53.

11 Bale, "Parks and Gardens," 50-51.
12 Kate Jaimet, "Ignoring Nature's Call," *Ottawa Citizen,* 9 December 2006, B1.
13 Ibid.
14 Ibid.
15 Canadian National Railways, *Canadian Rockies: Jasper, Mount Robson, and the Fiords of the North Pacific* (Montreal: Canadian National Railways, 1934), 9.
16 Canadian National Railways, *Jasper National Park* (Montreal: Canadian National Railways, 1927), 32.
17 Gabrielle Zezulka-Mailloux, "Laying the Tracks for Tourism: Paradoxical Promotions and the Development of Jasper National Park," in *Culturing Wilderness in Jasper National Park: Studies in Two Centuries of Human History in the Upper Athabasca River Watershed,* ed. I.S. MacLaren (Edmonton: University of Alberta Press, 2007), 242.
18 The CNR brochures list features such as orchestra concerts, a ballroom, motion pictures, church services, a "fully equipped medical department," a heated outdoor swimming pool, world-class dining facilities, and souvenir shops as part of the Jasper Park Lodge experience. See, for instance, Canadian National Railways, *What to Do at Jasper and Mount Robson* (Montreal: Canadian National Railways, 1930), 24-25; Canadian National Railways, *Canadian Rockies and the Pacific Coast* (Montreal: Canadian National Railways, 1938), 1; and Canadian National Railways, *Jasper National Park in the Canadian Rockies* (Montreal: Canadian National Railways, 1939), 20-22.
19 In 1988, the lodge was purchased by Canadian Pacific Hotels and Resorts. See Cyndi Smith, *Jasper Park Lodge: In the Heart of the Canadian Rockies,* rev. ed. (Waterton Park, AB: Coyote Books, 1989), 11, 78.
20 Liz Wylie, "Canoeing and Canadian Art," *Queen's Quarterly* 103, 3 (1996): 615-27. See also Daniel Francis, *National Dreams: Myth, Memory, and Canadian History* (Vancouver: Arsenal Pulp Press, 1997), 128-51, and John Murray Gibbon, *The Romance of the Canadian Canoe* (Toronto: Ryerson Press, 1951).
21 Catherine Volpé and Paul E. Burton, *Tourism: New Realities – A Canadian Perspective* (Toronto: Prentice Hall, 2000), 22; Alan MacEachern, *Natural Selections: National Parks in Atlantic Canada* (Montreal: McGill-Queen's University Press, 2001), 66.
23 James A. Barclay, *Golf in Canada: A History* (Toronto: McClelland and Stewart, 1992), 368.
24 "Golf at the Fairmont Jasper Park Lodge," n.d., http://www.fairmont.com/; *The Fairmont Jasper Park Lodge Golf Club: The Wild Side of the Rockies* (Jasper, AB: The Fairmont Jasper Park Lodge and the Jasper Park Lodge Golf Club, 2009), 10.
25 Jasper Chamber of Commerce, "Bing Crosby's Victory in Totem Golf Rivalled Best Hollywood Scripts," in *Jasper Tourist News – Your Companion in Jasper* (Jasper: Jasper Chamber of Commerce, 1965), 14.
26 The Fairmont Jasper Park Lodge, "Golf: Jasper Park Lodge Club," n.d., http://www.fairmont.com/.
27 Alec Brownlow, "A Wolf in the Garden: Ideology and Change in the Adirondack Landscape," in *Animal Spaces, Beastly Places: New Geographies of Human-Animal Relations,* ed. Chris Philo and Chris Wilbert (London: Routledge, 2000), 152.
28 Ibid.
29 In recent years, Parks Canada has been attempting to reverse some of the problems related to habitat fragmentation in this region and to reintroduce predator species in the vicinity of the Jasper Park Lodge golf course. For more information, see Brenda Dobson et al., *The Effectiveness of Wildlife Corridor Restoration: Fairmont Jasper Park Lodge Golf Course, Jasper National Park* (Ottawa: Parks Canada, 2004).

30 Brian Kendall, "Go Ahead, Tree Huggers, Hit the Links," *Globe and Mail*, 30 April 2010, T11.
31 *The Fairmont Jasper Park Lodge Golf Club: The Wild Side of the Rockies*, 10.
32 Cathy Ellis, "Golf Stars Event Dismays Conservationists; 2010 Skins Game OK'd For Banff," *Calgary Herald*, 3 July 2009, A16.
33 Letter from F.C. Badgley, Director of Canadian Government Motion Picture Bureau, to W.J. Oliver, 30 October 1931, LAC, MG30-D402, vol. 1.
34 Ibid.
35 Sheilagh S. Jameson, *W.J. Oliver: Life through a Master's Lens* (Calgary: Glenbow Museum, 1984), 99-101.
36 Ibid.
37 Letter from Russell H. Bennett to W.J. Oliver, 16 May 1932, LAC, MG30-D402, vol. 1.
38 W. Ward Marsh, "Travel Pictures Prompt the Old Vacation Urge," *Cleveland Plain Dealer* [1932], LAC, MG30-D402, vol. 1.
39 Ibid.
40 Cynthia Elyse Rubin and Morgan Williams, *Larger than Life: The American Tall-Tale Postcard, 1905-1915* (New York: Abbeville Press, 1990), 46.
41 Ibid., 109. As I have been informed by numerous fishing enthusiasts in the course of discussing this postcard, one does not fish for bass in the lakes and rivers of Jasper National Park.
42 Ernest Voorhis, "Fishing in Canada," *Canadian Travel* 13, 2 (1928): 33. For more on the cultural ideologies surrounding sport fishing and how these ideologies were perpetuated through pictorial means, see Lynda Jessup, "Landscapes of Sport, Landscapes of Exclusion: The 'Sportsman's Paradise' in Late-Nineteenth-Century Canadian Painting," *Journal of Canadian Studies* 40, 1 (2006): 71-123.
43 Tina Loo, "Making a Modern Wilderness: Conserving Wildlife in Twentieth-Century Canada," *Canadian Historical Review* 82 (2001): 93.
44 Lynda Jessup, "The Group of Seven and the Tourist Landscape in Western Canada, or the More Things Change ... ," *Journal of Canadian Studies* 37 (2002): 164. See also Jonathan Frow, "Tourism and the Semiotics of Nostalgia," *October* 57 (1991): 123-51.
45 Canadian National Railways, *Jasper National Park in the Canadian Rockies* (Montreal: Canadian National Railways, 1940), 14, JYMA, Accn#994.45.1.1, CNR Tourism Brochures folder.
46 Jasper Chamber of Commerce, "Fishermen Best When It Comes to Relaxing," in *Jasper Tourist News – Your Companion in Jasper* (Jasper: Jasper Chamber of Commerce, 1965), 4.
47 Richard White, *The Organic Machine: The Remaking of the Columbia River* (New York: Hill and Wang, 1995), 34. John Urry has discussed how the "solitudinous contemplation" of Nature, a key aspect of the "romantic tourist gaze," is a significant component of tourism predicated on antimodern values. See John Urry, *Consuming Places* (London: Routledge, 1995), 186. For more on the exclusionary nature of the visual culture of fishing in Canada, see Jessup, "Landscapes of Sport, Landscapes of Exclusion."
48 White, *The Organic Machine*, 34.
49 Canadian National Railways, *What to Do in Jasper National Park* (Montreal: Canadian National Railways, 1935), 3. A government-sponsored hatchery was established in Jasper in 1941; however, descriptions of "artificially propagated" fish in the park's lakes and rivers predate this development by several years. See V.E.F. Solman, J.P. Currier, and W.C. Cable, "Why Have Fish Hatcheries in Canada's National Parks?" in *Transactions of the 17th North American Wildlife Conference* (Washington, DC: Wildlife Management Institute, 1952), 226.

50 Ed Struzik, "Is It Possible to Restore Altered Fish Populations to Their Natural State? A New Study in Jasper National Park May Provide an Answer," *Outdoor Canada* 29, 1 (2001): 11.

51 Alberta Provincial Tourist and Publicity Bureau, *Alberta* (Edmonton: Provincial Tourist and Publicity Bureau, 1939), 4, LAC, MG30-D402, vol. 1, file Printed Material 1939.

52 Jasper Chamber of Commerce, "Fishermen Best When It Comes to Relaxing," 3.

53 John F. Reiger's influential study *American Sportsmen and the Origins of Conservation,* 3rd ed. (Corvallis: Oregon State University Press, 2001), traces the relationship between sports such as hunting and fishing and the broader wilderness and wildlife conservation movement in the United States.

54 "Finds Jasper Waters Teeming with Fine Fish," *Calgary Herald,* n.d., LAC, MG30-D402, vol. 1, file Scrapbook of Clippings, 1918-47. See, for instance, Canadian National Railways, *What to Do at Jasper National Park,* 3, and Canadian National Railways, *Jasper National Park, Canadian Rockies* (Montreal: Canadian National Railways, 1942), 18.

55 Canada, Department of the Interior, *The National Parks of Canada: A Brief Description of Their Scenic and Recreational Attractions* (Ottawa: Department of the Interior, 1936), 17.

56 Voorhis, "Fishing in Canada," 29.

57 Tina Loo makes a similar observation about the exclusion of fish in dominant representations of wildlife. See Tina Loo, *States of Nature: Conserving Canada's Wildlife in the Twentieth Century* (Vancouver: UBC Press, 2006), 4.

58 Eric Higgs, *Nature by Design: People, Natural Processes, and Ecological Restoration* (Cambridge, MA: MIT Press, 2003), 31. See also Philip Dearden, "Endangered Species and Terrestrial Protected Areas," in *Politics of the Wild: Canada and Endangered Species,* ed. Karen Beazley and Robert Boardman (Oxford: Oxford University Press, 2001), 75-93.

59 Kathy Kennedy, "It Pays to Stay off the Beaten Track," *Edmonton Journal,* 19 June 1976, 37.

60 Parks Canada, *The Mountain Guide to Banff, Jasper, Kootenay, Yoho, Glacier, and Mount Revelstoke National Parks of Canada* (Ottawa: Parks Canada, 2003), 4.

61 Struzik, "Is It Possible to Restore Altered Fish Populations," 11.

62 Alberta Provincial Tourist and Publicity Bureau, *Alberta,* 5.

63 Letter from W.H. Robinson, Supervisor of Photographic Service and Exhibits of Canadian National Railways, to W.J. Oliver, 1 March 1939, LAC, MG30-D402, vol. 1.

64 Prior to installation of the T-bar lift in 1964, skiers rode snowmobiles up to the top of the mountain runs. As one guidebook notes, "Despite the lack of modern improvements and lifts, almost 2,000 skiers rode the snowmobiles during the winter of 1963-64." Jasper Chamber of Commerce, "Jasper Park Moves into Skiing's Big Leagues," in *Jasper Tourist News – Your Companion in Jasper* (Jasper: Jasper Chamber of Commerce, 1965), 17.

65 Ibid.

66 "Marmot Basin: A Mountain for Everyone" (advertisement), *Where: Canadian Rockies* (winter 2008-9): 32.

67 *Jasper's Marmot Basin 25th Anniversary* (Jasper: Marmot Basin Ski Lifts, 1989).

68 Marmot Basin Ski Hill, "Ski Marmot Basin: Skiing and Snowboarding in Jasper National Park," n.d., http://www.skimarmot.com.

69 Clifford, *Downhill Slide,* 181.

70 Hal Clifford, "Downhill Slide," *Sierra Magazine* (January-February 2003), http://www.sierraclub.org/.

71 Annie Gilbert Coleman, "From Snow Bunnies to Shred Betties: Gender, Consumption, and the Skiing Landscape," in *Seeing Nature through Gender,* ed. Virginia Scharff (Lawrence: University Press of Kansas, 2003), 212.

72 *Ski Jasper's Marmot Basin* (Jasper: Marmot Basin Ski Lifts, 1995).

73 Christiane Gachelin-Ribault, "Skiing, Culture, and the Environment: Mountains Are Not Made for Crowds, Some Say, but Can Mountain Communities Live without Tourism?" *Ecodecision* 20 (1996): 49.

74 George Koch and John Weissenberger, "Jumbo Controversy: A Visionary Architect Wants to Bring a World-Class Ski Resort to a Logged-Over B.C. Valley. Eco-Freaks Respond with 'Grizzlies Not Gondolas' Bumper Stickers," *National Post,* 19 December 2003, FP11.

75 Ben Gadd, "Why Ski Areas Don't Belong in National Parks," 2006, http://www.jasperenvironmental.org/.

76 Dennis Hryciuk, "Get Rid of Ski Hills in Parks, Jasper Environmentalist Says," *Edmonton Journal,* 15 December 1998, A5.

77 Dayle Parker, "Ski Resorts Take the High Road on Environmental Protection," *Edmonton Journal,* 2 March 2006, E2.

78 The tension between the government of Alberta and the federal government over control and operation of parks in that province has a long history. See Paul Kopas, *Taking the Air: Ideas and Change in Canada's National Parks* (Vancouver: UBC Press, 2007), 33.

79 "Let's Develop the Parks: Alberta Gov't," *Banff Crag and Canyon,* 25 November 1987, 1-2.

80 Ardith Finnegan, "CPAWS to Fight for National Parks," *Banff Crag and Canyon,* 10 June 1992, 5.

81 Jasper Environmental Association, "Marmot Basin: A Slippery Slope for Wildlife," updated 20 May, 2009, http://www.jasperenvironmental.org/.

82 Ibid.

83 Ibid.

84 Ibid.

85 Sid Marty, *A Grand and Fabulous Notion: The First Century of Canada's Parks* (Toronto: NC Press, 1984), 99. For more on the history of parks legislation in Canada, see Ian Attridge, "Canadian Parks Legislation: Past, Present, and Prospects," in *Changing Parks: The History, Future, and Cultural Contexts of Parks and Heritage Landscapes,* ed. John S. Marsh and Bruce W. Hodgins (Toronto: Natural Heritage/Natural History, 1998), 221-37.

86 Robert J.C. Stead, *Canada's Mountain Playgrounds* (Ottawa: Department of Mines and Resources, n.d.), 1.

87 Canada, Department of Resources and Development, *Banff and Jasper National Parks* (Ottawa: Department of Resources and Development, 1951), 1.

88 "Court Defends Harlequins and Parks," *Sierra Legal Defence Fund Newsletter* 24 (1999): 1.

89 Stephen Legault, "Making Waves: Commercial Rafters on Alberta's Maligne River Are Crowding out the Harlequin Ducks," *Outdoor Canada* 25, 3 (1997): 13.

90 "Rafters Oppose River Closure," *Banff Crag and Canyon,* 14 July 1993, 3.

91 "Jasper National Park Update," *News for the Wild (Canadian Parks and Wilderness Society Newsletter)* (summer 2002): 8; Jill Seaton, "Bogged down in the Tonquin Valley," *Prairie Sierran* 1, 4 (1997-98): 5-6.

92 "Jasper Park Must Step up Pace of Development," *Banff Crag and Canyon,* 21 September 1988, 12.

93 Kathy Kennedy, "Jasper Overcrowding Brings Hiking Quotas," *Edmonton Journal,* 19 June 1976, 37.
94 Ibid.
95 Urry, *Consuming Places,* 136.
96 Sierra Legal Defence Fund, "Media Release – Federal Government Announcement Good News for National Parks and Marine Conservation Areas," 2001, http://sierralegal.org.
97 "Jasper National Park Update," 8.
98 Canadian National Railways, *Jasper National Park, Canadian Rockies* (Montreal: Canadian National Railways, 1953), 14, JYMA, Accn#994.45.1.1, CNR Tourism Brochures folder.
99 *Jasper's Marmot Basin 25th Anniversary.*
100 Urry, *Consuming Places,* 132-33.
101 Canadian National Railways, *Jasper National Park, Canadian Rockies* (1942), 23, JYMA, Accn#994.45.1.1, CNR Tourism Brochures folder.
102 Bill Gibbons, *Photographing the Canadian Rockies* (Banff: British Photographic Laboratories of Canada, 1948), 2.
103 *Jasper Tourist News – Your Companion in Jasper* (Jasper: Jasper Chamber of Commerce, 1965), 15.
104 In 1941 and 1942, for instance, the magazine *Popular Photography* sponsored photographic tours and workshops in Jasper. These events were led by Ivan Dmitri, a "famed artist-photographer," and offered visitors "field instructions in various phases of composition and exposure" as well as evening lectures and roundtable discussions on a number of photography-related topics. See Canadian National Railways, *Jasper National Park, Canadian Rockies* (1942), 23-24, JYMA, Accn#994.45.1.1, CNR Tourism Brochures folder.
105 *Pleasurable Places in the Wide Open Spaces* (Vancouver: Traveller's Digest, 1944), 61.
106 Canadian National Railways, *Jasper National Park in the Canadian Rockies* (Montreal: Canadian National Railways, 1938), 36, JYMA, Accn#994.45.1.1, CNR Tourism Brochures folder.
107 Friends of Jasper National Park, "Jasper Institute: Natural History Field Courses in the Canadian Rockies," n.d., http://www.friendsofjasper.com/.
108 Mike Crang discusses the use of "spatial semiotics" in the context of tourism. See Mike Crang, "Knowing, Tourism, and Practices of Vision," in *Leisure/Tourism Geographies: Practices and Geographical Knowledge,* ed. David Crouch (London: Routledge, 1999), 240.
109 Catriona Sandilands, "Ecological Integrity and National Narrative: Cleaning up Canada's National Parks," *Canadian Woman Studies* 20 (2000): 140.
110 Veblen, *The Theory of the Leisure Class,* 29.
111 Ross E. Mitchell, "Thorstein Veblen: Pioneer in Environmental Sociology," *Organization and Environment* 14 (2001): 390.
112 PearlAnn Reichwein, "'Hands off Our National Parks': The Alpine Club of Canada and Hydro-Development Controversies in the Canadian Rockies, 1922-1930," *Journal of the Canadian Historical Association* 6 (1995): 129-55.
113 Joy Standeven and Paul DeKnop, *Sport Tourism* (Champaign, IL: Human Kinetics, 1999), 236.
114 Urry, *Consuming Places,* 183.
115 Jennifer Price, *Flight Maps: Adventures with Nature in Modern America* (New York: Basic Books, 1999), 45.
116 Reiger, *American Sportsmen and the Origins of Conservation,* 3.
117 Ibid.

118 Gerard J. van den Broek, "The Sign of the Fly: A Semiotic Approach to Fly Fishing," *American Journal of Semiotics* 3, 1 (1984): 74. See also Michael Woods, "Fantastic Mr. Fox? Representing Animals in the Hunting Debate," in *Animal Spaces, Beastly Places: New Geographies of Human-Animal Relations,* ed. Chris Philo and Chris Wilbert (London: Routledge, 2000), 182-202.

119 Margaret Lewis, *To Conserve a Heritage* (Calgary: Alberta Fish and Game Association, 1979), xi. Lewis refers to hunters and fishermen (gender emphasis deliberate) who fit with European and Euro-Canadian ideologies of these sports. Traditional forms of hunting, trapping, and fishing by First Nations peoples are not considered by Lewis.

120 Ducks Unlimited Canada, "Our Position on Hunting," n.d., http://www.ducks.ca/.

121 Reichwein, "'Hands off Our National Parks,'" 130.

122 Jasper was restored to 4,400 square miles in 1914. The current size of the park is slightly smaller and was set in 1930 as part of the National Parks Act. See Karen R. Jones, *Wolf Mountains: A History of Wolves along the Great Divide* (Calgary: University of Calgary Press, 2002), 283n47.

123 Reichwein, "'Hands off Our National Parks,'" 129-55.

124 John Shultis, "Recreational Values of Protected Areas," in *The Full Value of Parks: From Economics to the Intangible,* ed. David Harmon and Allen D. Putney (Lanham, MD: Rowman and Littlefield, 2003). See also Farley Mowat, *Rescue the Earth! Conversations with the Green Crusaders* (Toronto: McClelland and Stewart, 1990), in which Mowat interviews a number of leading figures in the Canadian environmental movement, many of whom credit their passion for environmental issues to time spent in wilderness areas and the pursuit of outdoor recreational activities.

125 Shultis, "Recreational Values of Protected Areas," 67.

126 Mark Nord, A.E. Luloff, and Jeffrey C. Bridger, "The Association of Forest Recreation with Environmentalism," *Environment and Behavior* 30, 2 (1998): 235-46.

127 R.E. Dunlap and R.B. Heffernan, "Outdoor Recreation and Environmental Concern: An Empirical Examination," *Rural Sociology* 40 (1975): 19-20.

128 Nord, Luloff, and Bridger, "The Association of Forest Recreation with Environmentalism," 238.

129 Clifford, *Downhill Slide,* 77.

CHAPTER 4:
"THE BEARS ARE PLENTIFUL AND FREQUENTLY GOOD CAMERA SUBJECTS"

1 Karen R. Jones, *Wolf Mountains: A History of Wolves along the Great Divide* (Calgary: University of Calgary Press, 2002), 174-75.

2 "Wolves Close in on Moose for Kill," *Globe and Mail,* 6 May 1944, 4.

3 Canadian National Railways, *Canadian Rockies: Jasper, Mount Robson, and the Fiords of the North Pacific* (Montreal: Canadian National Railways, 1934), 9, JYMA, Accn#994.45.1.1, CNR Tourism Brochures folder.

4 Dick Dekker, "The Not-So-Natural History of Jasper National Park," *Park News* 23, 4 (1987-88): 26-29; David W. Schindler, "The Eastern Slopes of the Canadian Rockies: Must We Follow the American Blueprint?" in *Rocky Mountain Futures: An Ecological Perspective,* ed. Jill S. Baron (Washington, DC: Island Press, 2002), 285-99.

5 Parks Canada, *The Mountain Guide to Banff, Jasper, Kootenay, Yoho, Glacier, and Mount Revelstoke National Parks of Canada* (Ottawa: Parks Canada, 2003), 10.

6 In the Spring of 2010, Dr. Brett Mills, senior lecturer at the University of East Anglia, made headlines with his pronouncement that filming and photographing non-human animals without their consent is a breach of their privacy. For more on this see Richard Alleyne, "Wildlife Documentaries Invade Animal Privacy Rights, Claims Leading Academic." *The Telegraph* (29 April 2010), http://www.telegraph.co.uk.

7 Jody Emel and Jennifer Wolch, "Witnessing the Animal Moment," in *Animal Geographies: Place, Politics, and Identity in the Nature-Culture Borderlands,* ed. Jennifer Wolch and Jody Emel (London: Verso, 1998), 2, 17.

8 For a discussion of the changing yet always controversial policies regarding *Canis lupus* within the borders of Jasper National Park, see Jones, *Wolf Mountains.* For discussions of the history as well as the current socio-economic impacts of the fur industry, see Julia V. Emberley, *The Cultural Politics of Fur* (Ithaca: Cornell University Press, 1997), and Chantal Nadeau, *Fur Nation: From the Beaver to Brigitte Bardot* (London: Routledge, 2001).

9 Seth (Gregory Gallant), "Jasper the Bear Sheds a Tear," *National Post,* 11 February 2004, AL08.

10 Adrian Franklin, *Animals and Modern Culture: A Sociology of Human-Animal Relations in Modernity* (London: Sage Publications, 1999), 7.

11 Canadian National Railways, *Jasper National Park in the Canadian Rockies* (Montreal: Canadian National Railways, 1939), 19, JYMA, Accn#994.45.1.1, CNR Tourism Brochures folder.

12 This topic has gained much currency lately as books such as Michael Pollan's *The Omnivore's Dilemma* and Jonathan Safran Foer's *Eating Animals* have brought debates about social, cultural, and ethical dimensions of consuming animal bodies to a mainstream audience. See Jonathan Safran Foer, *Eating Animals* (New York: Little, Brown and Company, 2009), and Michael Pollan, *The Omnivore's Dilemma: A Natural History of Four Meals* (New York: Penguin Press, 2006).

13 Diana Donald, "'Beastly Sights': The Treatment of Animals as a Moral Theme in Representations of London, c. 1820-1850," *Art History* 22, 4 (1999): 515.

14 See, for instance, Steve Baker, *Picturing the Beast: Animals, Identity, and Representation* (1993; reprint, Urbana: University of Illinois Press, 2001); Janetta Rebold Benton, *The Medieval Menagerie: Animals in the Art of the Middle Ages* (New York: Abbeville Press, 1992); Erica Fudge, ed., *Renaissance Beasts: Of Animals, Humans, and Other Wonderful Creatures* (Champaign: University of Illinois Press, 2003); William H. Peck, "Animal Symbolism in Ancient Egyptian Art," *Sculpture Review* 52, 2 (2003): 8-15; Nigel Rothfels, ed., *Representing Animals* (Bloomington: Indiana University Press, 2002).

15 Marta Braun and Elizabeth Whitcombe, "Marey, Muybridge, and Londe: The Photography of Pathological Locomotion," *History of Photography* 23, 3 (1999): 218-24.

16 For instance, the "panda cam," "polar bear cam," "ape cam," and "elephant cam" can be accessed through www.sandiegozoo.com. As has been the case in the development of many new visual technologies throughout history, the introduction of animal web cams has allowed people to observe things that they would not otherwise have had the opportunity to see. The panda cam at the San Diego Zoo was set up to follow the growth and development of Mei Sheng, a male giant panda cub born at the zoo in the summer of 2003. Long before Mei Sheng was placed on display at the zoo, interested viewers could watch him as he slept, nursed, and took his first steps in the special birthing den set up as part of the zoo's Giant Panda Conservation and Research Program.

17　Canadian National Railways, *Jasper National Park, Canadian Rockies* (Montreal: Canadian National Railways, 1953), 25.

18　Jones, *Wolf Mountains,* 168.

19　Canadian National Railways, *Jasper National Park in the Canadian Rockies* (Montreal: Canadian National Railways, 1938), 29, JYMA, Accn#994.45.1.1, CNR Tourism Brochures folder.

20　Thomas R. Dunlap, "Ecology, Nature, and Canadian National Park Policy: Wolves, Elk, and Bison as a Case Study," *Canadian Issues* 13 (1991): 140.

21　Parks Canada, "Evolution of Bear Management in the Mountain National Parks," 2003, http://www.pc.gc.ca/.

22　W.F. Lothian, *A History of Canada's National Parks – Volume II* (Ottawa: Parks Canada, 1977), 35.

23　Ibid.

24　Stephen Herrero, *Bear Attacks: Their Causes and Avoidance* (Guilford, CT: Lyons Press, 1988), 94; Parks Canada, "Evolution of Bear Management."

25　Edward Cavell and John Whyte, *Rocky Mountain Madness: A Historical Miscellany* (Canmore, AB: Altitude Publishing, 2001), 98.

26　This photograph was taken by Jean Powell, and I have found a number of different versions of this postcard, each with slight variations in the pre-printed captions as well as in compositional choices such as how the image is cropped or what colour the car is tinted.

27　In 1981, changes to the National Historic Parks Wildlife and Domestic Animals Regulations made it illegal to feed all wildlife in Canada's national parks.

28　Canadian National Railways, *Jasper National Park in the Canadian Rockies* (1938), 13.

29　Alberta Publicity and Travel Bureau, *The Alberta Vacation Cruise* (Edmonton: Publicity and Travel Bureau, 1942), 11.

30　For more on these productions, see Sheilagh S. Jameson, *W.J. Oliver: Life through a Master's Lens* (Calgary: Glenbow Museum, 1984), 62, 94, 99-101, and William J. Oliver, "Hunting with a Camera," transcript of broadcast on CBC Radio, 1937, LAC, MG30-D402, vol. 1.

31　"Wildlife of the Mountain Parks," in *Experience the Mountain Parks: A Visitor's Guide to Alberta and British Columbia* (2009-10), 47.

32　Matthew Brower, "Trophy Shots: Early North American Photographs of Nonhuman Animals and the Display of Masculine Prowess," *Society and Animals* 13, 1 (2005): 14.

33　Tim Bonyhady has explored the origins of the notion of "hunting with a camera" and discusses instances of technological innovation aimed at perpetuating this shift in specific interactions. Bonyhady, for instance, describes "photographic guns" developed in France during the late nineteenth century to aid in making pictures of birds in flight. Tim Bonyhady, *The Colonial Earth* (Melbourne: Melbourne University Press, 2002), 212. See also James R. Ryan, "'Hunting with the Camera': Photography, Wildlife, and Colonialism in Africa," in *Animal Spaces, Beastly Places: New Geographies of Human-Animal Relations,* ed. Chris Philo and Chris Wilbert (London: Routledge, 2000), 203-21.

34　Illegal hunting, or poaching, remains a significant problem in the Rocky Mountain parks. See Philip Dearden, "Endangered Species and Terrestrial Protected Areas," in *Politics of the Wild: Canada and Endangered Species,* ed. Karen Beazley and Robert Boardman (Oxford: Oxford University Press, 2002), 86, and "Open Season on Poachers," *Canadian Geographic* 112, 1 (1992): 10-11.

35 Jones, *Wolf Mountains*, 184, 187. The film was first shown at Ottawa's National Arts Centre and then on CBC Television. See Gordon Stoneham, "Film Probes 'Bad Guy' Reputation of Wolves," *Saturday Citizen*, 25 September 1971, 29.

36 *Death of a Legend* received critical acclaim, and Mason received several international awards for the project, including the 1972 Red Ribbon Award at the 14th American Film Festival held in New York.

37 Jones, *Wolf Mountains*, 186-87.

38 Tina Loo, *States of Nature: Conserving Canada's Wildlife in the Twentieth Century* (Vancouver: UBC Press, 2006), 177.

39 Ibid., 10.

40 Ed Struzik, "Sierra Club Opposes Cheviot Mine Project; U.S. Conservation Lobby Urges PM to Say No," *Edmonton Journal*, 10 September 1997, B5.

41 Randy Boswell, "Two of Canada's Natural Wonders, Nahanni, Rocky Mountain Parks, under Threat, Says UNESCO," *CanWest News*, 29 August 2006, 1; Judy Gelfand, "Nature Canada Takes Mining Company and Feds to Court over Cheviot Mine," *Nature Canada* 33, 4 (2004-5): 35; Larry Johnsrude, "Cheviot Road Illegal – Activists," *Edmonton Journal*, 25 January 2005, A6; Larry Johnsrude, "Cheviot Road Less Damaging than Rail Line: Mine Official," *Edmonton Journal*, 26 January 2005, B6; Dustin Walker, "Groups Worried about Mining Road's Impact on Grizzlies," *Jasper Booster*, 24 March 2004, http://www.jasperbooster.com/. The Cheviot Creek pit is now managed by Teck Coal as part of its Cardinal River Operations. For more information on this mine, see http://www.teck.com.

42 Stephen Legault, "Coal Miner's Fodder," *Canadian Geographic* 117, 2 (1997): 20.

43 Shannon Curry, "UNESCO Questions Cheviot Mine Approval," *Alternatives Journal* 24, 4 (1998): 2.

44 Kevin McNamee, "The World's Treasures," *Nature Canada* 29, 1 (2000): 18-23. McNamee demonstrates how groups opposed to this form of conservation and international involvement have often couched pro-development and capitalist sentiments in the language of sovereignty. As McNamee notes, in 1994 the now defunct Reform Party of Canada challenged the inclusion of Tatshenshini-Alsek Park in the previously established Kluane-Wrangell-St. Elias World Heritage Site on the grounds that UN involvement would undermine Canada's ability to make decisions about the appropriate use of land within its own borders.

45 Jasper Environmental Association et al., "Conservation Groups Shift Focus in Tacking Mine Next-Door to Jasper National Park," 30 September 2005, www.sierraclub.ca/.

46 Jasper Environmental Association, "Cheviot Mine: Grizzlies vs. Coal," 2006, www.jasper-environmental.org.

47 Kevin McNamee, "Canadian Nature Federation Intervenes in Cheviot Mine Hearings," *Nature Canada* 26, 1 (1997): 23.

48 Jones, *Wolf Mountains*, 193-95.

49 Ed Struzik, "New Plan to Open Cheviot Coal Mine: Controversial Mine Borders Jasper National Park," *Edmonton Journal*, 15 June 2002, A1. See also Ian Urquhart, ed., *Assault on the Rockies: Environmental Controversies in Alberta* (Edmonton: Rowan Books, 1998).

50 Jasper Environmental Association, "Cheviot Mine."

51 Harvey Locke, "Is Banff an Endangered Space?" *Borealis (Magazine of the Canadian Parks and Wilderness Society)* 4, 1 (1993): 3.

52 Michael Mugford, "Wildlife Protection: Parks Canada Joins Forces with Photofinishers," *Photo Life* 24, 5 (1999): 22.

53 Parks Canada, *Jasper National Park of Canada: State of the Park Report* (Ottawa: Parks Canada, 2008), 12. See also Jim Bertwistle, "A Description and Analysis of Wildlife Mortality on Transportation Corridors in Jasper National Park, Canada" (MSc thesis, University of Alberta, 2002), and Friends of Jasper National Park, "Drivers for Wildlife," *Nature Calls* (newsletter of the Friends of Jasper National Park) (fall-winter 2003): 2. Significantly, trains also play a large part in the animal carnage within park boundaries. Both CN freight trains and Via Rail passenger trains pose significant risks to wildlife. CN has made efforts in recent years to clean up things such as grain spilled from its cargo cars so that animals will not be attracted to the rail lines as a source of food. For more information, see John Cotter, "Canada's Mountain Parks Try Different Ways to Reduce Wildlife Carnage," *Canadian Press NewsWire*, 6 February 2005, 1.

54 Friends of Jasper National Park, "Drivers for Wildlife," 2.

55 Debra Martens, "Graphic Tobacco Warnings Having Desired Effect," *Canadian Medical Association Journal* 166, 11 (2002): 1453.

56 Action on Smoking and Health, "Graphic Health Warnings Needed to Deter Smokers," 10 January 2002, http://www.ashaust.org.au/.

57 Steve Baker, "Animals, Representation, and Reality," *Society and Animals* 9 (2001): 197.

58 Andrea Gullo, Unna Lassiter, and Jennifer Wolch, "The Cougar's Tale," in *Animal Geographies: Place, Politics, and Identity in the Nature-Culture Borderlands,* ed. Jennifer Wolch and Jody Emel (London: Verso, 1998), 141.

Chapter 5: Fake Nature

1   Susan G. Davis, *Spectacular Nature: Corporate Culture and the Sea World Experience* (Berkeley: University of California Press, 1997), 11.

2   The Royal Alberta Museum was formerly known as the Provincial Museum of Alberta. The name of the institution changed in honour of a visit to the museum by Queen Elizabeth II in May 2005.

3   Provincial Museum of Alberta, "Wild Alberta at the Museum," 2003, http://www.RAM. edmonton.ab.ca/.

4   Ron Gluckman, "The Great Indoors," in *In Search of Wild Adventure: A Wild Travel Anthology,* ed. Brad Olsen (San Francisco: CCC Publishing, 1999), 117.

5   Ibid.

6   "Surfing Indoors," *The Economist,* 18 December 1993, 86.

7   Phoenix Seagaia Resort, "Announcement of Termination of Ocean Dome Operations on October 1, 2007," 7 August 2007, http://www.seagaia.co.jp/.

8   David Boyle, *Authenticity: Brands, Fakes, Spin, and the Lust for Real Life* (London: HarperCollins, 2003), xiv.

9   Eric Higgs, *Nature by Design: People, Natural Processes, and Ecological Restoration* (Cambridge, MA: MIT Press, 2003), 48.

10 Ibid., 54.

11 Walt Disney World Resort, "Disney's Wilderness Lodge," n.d., http://disneyworld.disney. go.com/.

12 Higgs, *Nature by Design,* 54.

13 Lucy Lippard, *On the Beaten Track: Tourism, Art, and Place* (New York: New Press, 1999), 138.

14 Higgs, *Nature by Design,* 51.

15 Umberto Eco, *Travels in Hyperreality* (New York: Harcourt Brace Jovanovich, 1986), 8.
16 Ibid., 44.
17 For an in-depth analysis of the history of these concepts, see Tony Bennett, *The Birth of the Museum: History, Theory, Politics* (London: Routledge, 1995).
18 Ibid., 2, 21.
19 Sharon Macdonald, "Introduction," in *Theorizing Museums,* ed. Sharon Macdonald and Gordon Fyfe (Oxford: Blackwell Publishers, 1996), 7. See also the essays in Ivan Karp and Steven D. Lavine, eds., *Exhibiting Cultures: The Poetics and Politics of Museum Display* (Washington, DC: Smithsonian Institution Press, 1991).
20 The word *diorama* was coined in 1822 by L'ouis J.M. Daguerre and is derived from the Greek words *dia* ("through") and *horama* ("what is seen"). For more on the etymology and shifting meanings of this word, see Karen Wonders, *Habitat Dioramas: Illusions of Wilderness in Museums of Natural History* (Uppsala: Uppsala University, 1993), 12.
21 Ibid., 9.
22 Ibid., 17.
23 George Colpitts, "Wildlife Promotions, Western Canada Boosterism, and the Conservation Movement, 1890-1914," *American Review of Canadian Studies* 28, 1-2 (1998): 109-10.
24 Peter Davis, *Museums and the Natural Environment* (London: Leicester University Press, 1996), 1.
25 Jean Davallon, Gérald Grandmont, and Bernard Schiele, *The Rise of Environmentalism in Museums* (Quebec: Museé de la Civilisation, 1992), 17.
26 Davis, *Museums and the Natural Environment,* 78.
27 Timothy W. Luke, "Nature Protection or Nature Projection: A Cultural Critique of the Sierra Club," *Capitalism, Nature, Socialism* 8, 1 (1997): 51-52.
28 Davallon, Grandmont, and Schiele, *The Rise of Environmentalism in Museums,* 18.
29 Colpitts, "Wildlife Promotions," 105.
30 Davis, *Museums and the Natural Environment,* 75.
31 Provincial Museum of Alberta, "Wild Alberta."
32 For instance, a recorded soundtrack with "Nature" sounds such as the call of a swan, moose, or coyote is piped into the exhibit space, with appropriate sounds corresponding to the visual displays in each region. Further, the exhibit aims to emulate Nature by replicating certain smells associated with Alberta's wilderness. In the water zone, for instance, one can detect the smell of mud, and in the prairie zone the smell of sage grass wafts through the display area. Provincial Museum of Alberta, *Wild Alberta Media Kit* (Edmonton: Provincial Museum of Alberta, 2003), 20.
33 Government of Alberta, "Provincial Museum of Alberta Launches Wild Alberta," press release, Edmonton, Alberta Community Development, 22 September 2003, 1.
34 Provincial Museum of Alberta, "Wild Alberta."
35 Davis, *Museums and the Natural Environment,* 74-75.
36 This, of course, is not always the result. In Canada, exhibitions such as *The Spirit Sings* (Glenbow Museum, 1988), *Into the Heart of Africa* (Royal Ontario Museum, 1989), and *Land, Spirit, Power* (National Gallery of Canada, 1992) became sites of controversy and protest. For more on these exhibitions, see Frances W. Kaye, *Hiding the Audience: Viewing Art and Arts Institutions on the Prairies* (Edmonton: University of Alberta Press, 2003); Carol Tator, Frances Henry, and Winston Mattis, *Challenging Racism in the Arts: Case Studies of Controversy and Conflict* (Toronto: University of Toronto Press, 1998); and Charlotte Townsend-Gault, "Having Voices and Using Them: First Nations Artists and 'Native Art,'" *Arts Magazine* 65 (1991): 65-70.

37 "FRIAA News," press release, Edmonton, Forest Resource Improvement Association of Alberta (FRIAA) and Royal Alberta Museum (RAM), 23 July 2007.

38 Government of Alberta, "Provincial Museum of Alberta Launches Wild Alberta," 1.

39 Allan Schnaiberg and Kenneth Alan Gould, *Environment and Society: The Enduring Conflict* (Caldwell, NJ: Blackburn Press, 2000), 69, 205.

40 Weyerhaeuser, "Weyerhaeuser – About Us," n.d., http://www.weyerhaeuser.com/.

41 Weyerhaeuser, "Weyerhaeuser Forestry in Canada," n.d., http://www.weyerhaeuser.com/.

42 Greg Melnechuk, "Weyerhaeuser Pulp Mill Continues to Pollute," *BC Environmental Report* 3, 3 (1992): 26. Melnechuk points out that chlorine dioxide is a "deadly poisonous gas" and that sulphur dioxide is "a major contributor to acid rain."

43 Rainforest Action Network, "Wake up Weyerhaeuser: Protect Forests Now!" 19 February 2004, http://www.ran.org/; Rainforest Action Network, "Old Growth: Targeting Weyerhaeuser," n.d., http://ran.org/.

44 Melnechuk, "Weyerhaeuser Pulp Mill Continues to Pollute."

45 Weyerhaeuser, "Caribou Display Brings the Wild to Life at Wild Alberta Gallery," March 2004, http://www.wyl-leader.ca/.

46 Weyerhauser was among the twenty-one companies represented by the Forest Products Association of Canada who, in the spring of 2010, struck a historic agreement with Canadian environmental groups (including the Canadian Parks and Wilderness Society, the David Suzuki Foundation, and Greenpeace) over operations in the boreal forest. This agreement will see logging operations in 29 million hectares of boreal forest suspended in the coming years. The deal is intended to protect species such as the Woodland Caribou and has been celebrated as a "globally significant effort." Hanneke Brooymans, "Boreal Efforts Draw Praise, Canada on Track to Create World's Best Protected Wilderness," *Edmonton Journal*, 4 July 2010, A1; "Forest Industry, Green Groups Strike Deal," *CBC News*, 18 May 2010, http://www.cbc.ca.

47 Greenpeace, "Unbearable Truth about Toronto Dominion Bank's Role in Rainforest Destruction Revealed," 22 February 2001, http://archive.greenpeace.org/.

48 Joan Sherman and Michael Gismondi, "Jock Talk, Goldfish, Horse Loggings, and Star Wars: How a Pulp Company Communicates a Green Image," *Alternatives Journal* 23, 1 (1997): 14.

49 Davallon, Grandmont, and Schiele, *The Rise of Environmentalism in Museums*, 142.

50 Donna Haraway, "Teddy Bear Patriarchy: Taxidermy in the Garden of Eden, New York City, 1908-1936," in *Cultures of United States Imperialism*, ed. Amy Kaplan and Donald E. Pease (Durham: Duke University Press, 1993), 237-91.

51 Kay Anderson, "Animals, Science, and Spectacle in the City," in *Animal Geographies: Place, Politics, and Identity in the Nature-Culture Borderlands*, ed. Jennifer Wolch and Jody Emel (London: Verso, 1998), 33.

52 Davallon, Grandmont, and Schiele, *The Rise of Environmentalism in Museums*, 143.

53 Eco, *Travels in Hyperreality*, 51.

54 Gluckman, "The Great Indoors," 117.

55 Davis, *Spectacular Nature*, 238.

CONCLUSION

1 Steven Hoelscher, "The Photographic Construction of Tourist Space in Victorian America," *Geographical Review* 88, 4 (1998): 549.

2 Susan G. Davis, *Spectacular Nature: Corporate Culture and the Sea World Experience* (Berkeley: University of California Press, 1997), 11.
3 Andrew Ross, "The Ecology of Images," in *Visual Culture: Images and Interpretations,* ed. Norman Bryson, Michael Ann Holly, and Keith Moxey (Hanover, NH: University of New England Press, 1994), 325-46.
4 For a more detailed discussion of this point, see J. Keri Cronin, "A Tale of Two Parks: Photography, Pollution, and 'the Pecuniary Canons of Taste,'" in *Thorstein Veblen's Contributions to Environmental Sociology: Essays in the Political Ecology of Wasteful Industrialism,* ed. Ross Mitchell (Lewiston, NY: Edwin Mellen Press, 2007), 257-86.
5 For more on the Council of Elders of the Descendants of Jasper Park, see Richard A. Ouellet, "Tales of Empowerment: Cultural Continuity within an Evolving Identity in the Upper Athabasca Valley" (MA thesis, Simon Fraser University, 2006).
6 Margot Francis, "The Lesbian National Parks and Services: Reading Sex, Race, and the Nation in Artistic Performance," *Canadian Woman Studies* 20, 2 (2000): 131-36; Gallery TPW, "Subversive Souvenirs: Questioning the Institutional View in the Imagery of Tourism and Surveillance," 2006, http://www.virtualmuseum.ca/.
7 Nicole Hill, "Tourists on the March: Martin Parr Uses His Camera to Capture the Absurd Moments of Global Tourism," *Christian Science Monitor,* 27 November 2007, http://www.csmonitor.com/. See also Peter Osborne, *Travelling Light: Photography, Travel, and Visual Culture* (Manchester: Manchester University Press, 2000), 70-71.
8 For more information, see http://bridgland.sunsite.ualberta.ca/ and Chapter 5 in I.S. MacLaren, Eric S. Higgs, and Gabrielle Zezulka-Mailloux, *Mapper of Mountains: M.P. Bridgland in the Canadian Rockies* (Edmonton: University of Alberta Press, 2005).
9 Eric Higgs, "Twinning Reality, or How Taking History Seriously Changes How We Understand Ecological Restoration in Jasper National Park," in *Culturing Wilderness in Jasper National Park: Studies in Two Centuries of Human History in the Upper Athabasca River Watershed,* ed. I.S. MacLaren (Edmonton: University of Alberta Press, 2007), 299.
10 Cliff White and E.J. (Ted) Hart, *The Lens of Time: A Repeat Photography of Landscape Change in the Canadian Rockies* (Calgary: University of Calgary Press, 2007), 184-85.
11 Ibid., 224-25.
12 Charlie Gillis, "A Ranger in Wolf's Clothing," *National Post,* 11 April 2002, A8.
13 Ibid.
14 Ibid.
15 Brenda Dobson et al., *The Effectiveness of Wildlife Corridor Restoration: Fairmont Jasper Park Lodge Golf Course, Jasper National Park* (Ottawa: Parks Canada, 2004).
16 Ibid., 53-54.
17 Ibid., 9.
18 Richard White, "'Are You an Environmentalist or Do You Work for a Living?'" in *Uncommon Ground: Rethinking the Human Place in Nature,* ed. William Cronon (New York: W.W. Norton and Company, 1995), 185.

Bibliography

Action on Smoking and Health (ASH). "Graphic Health Warnings Needed to Deter Smokers." http://www.ashaust.org.au/.

Adams, I.C. "Good Post Cards Still Profitable." *Camera Craft* 10, 11 (1913): 501-3.

Alberta Economic Development, and Travel Alberta. *Tourism – Alberta, Canada*. February 2004. http://industry.travelalberta.com.

Alberta Provincial Tourist and Publicity Bureau. *See Alberta First.* Edmonton: Provincial Tourist and Publicity Bureau, 1938.

–. *Alberta.* Edmonton: Provincial Tourist and Publicity Bureau, 1939.

Alberta Publicity and Travel Bureau. *The Alberta Vacation Cruise.* Edmonton: Publicity and Travel Bureau, 1942.

Alleyne, Richard. "Wildlife Documentaries Invade Animal Privacy Rights, Claims Leading Academic." *Telegraph,* 29 April 2010: http://www.telegraph.co.uk.

Allmand, Warren. "W.J. Oliver Photographer, 1887-1954." In *Footloose in the National Parks: W.J. Oliver* (exhibition catalogue), 1. Ottawa: Parks Canada, 1978.

Altmeyer, George. "Three Ideas of Nature in Canada." In *Consuming Canada: Readings in Environmental History,* ed. Chad Gaffield and Pam Gaffield, 96-118. Toronto: Copp Clark, 1995.

Anderson, Kay. "Animals, Science, and Spectacle in the City." In *Animal Geographies: Place, Politics, and Identity in the Nature-Culture Borderlands,* ed. Jennifer Wolch and Jody Emel, 27-50. London: Verso, 1998.

Andrews, Malcolm. *Landscape and Western Art.* Oxford: Oxford University Press, 1999.

Armstrong, Christopher, Matthew Evenden, and H.V. Nelles. *The River Returns: An Environmental History of the Bow.* Montreal: McGill-Queen's University Press, 2009.

Attridge, Ian. "Canadian Parks Legislation: Past, Present, and Prospects." In *Changing Parks: The History, Future, and Cultural Contexts of Parks and Heritage Landscapes,* ed. John S. Marsh and Bruce W. Hodgins, 221-37. Toronto: Natural Heritage/Natural History, 1998.

Atwood, Margaret. *Survival: A Thematic Guide to Canadian Literature.* Toronto: Anansi, 1972.

Baillargen, Claude, ed. *Imaging a Shattering Earth: Contemporary Photography and the Environmental Debate.* Rochester, MI: Meadow Brook Art Gallery (in association with CONTACT Toronto Photography Festival), 2006.

Baker, Steve. "Animals, Representation, and Reality." *Society and Animals* 9 (2001): 189-201.

–. *Picturing the Beast: Animals, Identity, and Representation.* 1993. Reprint, Urbana: University of Illinois Press, 2001.

Bale, John. "Parks and Gardens: Metaphors for the Modern Places of Sport." In *Leisure/Tourism Geographies: Practices and Geographical Knowledge,* ed. David Crouch, 46-58. London: Routledge, 1999.

Barclay, James A. *Golf in Canada: A History.* Toronto: McClelland and Stewart, 1992.

Barrell, John. *The Dark Side of the Landscape: The Rural Poor in English Painting, 1730-1840.* Cambridge, UK: Cambridge University Press, 1980.

Beardsley, John. *Earthworks and Beyond.* New York: Abbeville Press, 1989.

Beaudreau, Sylvie. "The Changing Faces of Canada: Images of Canada in *National Geographic.*" *American Review of Canadian Studies* 32, 4 (2002): 517-46.

Bekoff, Marc. *The Animal Manifesto: Six Reasons for Expanding Our Compassion Footprint.* Novato, CA: New World Library, 2010.

Bennett, Tony. *The Birth of the Museum: History, Theory, Politics.* London: Routledge, 1995.

Benton, Janetta Rebold. *The Medieval Menagerie: Animals in the Art of the Middle Ages.* New York: Abbeville Press, 1992.

Benton, Lisa M., and John Rennie Short. *Environmental Discourse and Practice.* Oxford: Blackwell Publishers, 1999.

Barringer, Mark Daniel. *Selling Yellowstone: Capitalism and the Construction of Nature.* Lawrence, KS: University Press of Kansas, 2002.

Bertwistle, Jim. "A Description and Analysis of Wildlife Mortality on Transportation Corridors in Jasper National Park, Canada." MSc thesis, University of Alberta, 2002.

Blundell, Valda. "Aboriginal Empowerment and the Souvenir Trade in Canada." *Annals of Tourism Research* 20 (1993): 64-87.

Bohlen, Jim. *Making Waves: The Origins and Future of Greenpeace.* Montreal: Black Rose Books, 2001.

Bonyhady, Tim. "Artists with Axes." *Environment and History* 1, 2 (1995): 221-39.

–. *The Colonial Earth.* Melbourne: Melbourne University Press, 2002.

Bordo, Jonathan. "Jack Pine – Wilderness Sublime or the Erasure of the Aboriginal Presence from the Landscape." *Journal of Canadian Studies* 27 (1992): 98-128.

Boswell, Randy. "Two of Canada's Natural Wonders, Nahanni, Rocky Mountain Parks, under Threat, Says UNESCO." *CanWest News,* 29 August 2006, 1.

Botkin, Daniel. *Discordant Harmonies: A New Ecology for the Twenty-First Century.* Oxford: Oxford University Press, 1990.

Boyle, David. *Authenticity: Brands, Fakes, Spin, and the Lust for Real Life.* London: HarperCollins, 2003.

Braddock, Alan C., and Christoph Irmscher. *A Keener Perception: Ecocritical Studies in American Art History.* Tuscaloosa: University of Alabama Press, 2009.

Braun, Bruce. *The Intemperate Rainforest: Nature, Culture, and Power on Canada's West Coast.* Minneapolis: University of Minnesota Press, 2002.

Braun, Marta, and Elizabeth Whitcombe. "Marey, Muybridge, and Londe: The Photography of Pathological Locomotion." *History of Photography* 23, 3 (1999): 218-24.

Bright, Deborah. "The Machine in the Garden Revisited: American Environmentalism and Photographic Aesthetics." *Art Journal* 51 (1992): 60-71.

–. "Of Mother Nature and Marlboro Men: An Inquiry into Cultural Meanings of Landscape Photography." In *The Contest of Meaning: Critical Histories of Photography*, ed. Richard Bolton, 125-43. Cambridge, MA: MIT Press, 1992.

Brooymans, Hanneke. "Jasper Hopes to Open Gates to More Visitors." *Edmonton Journal*, 25 November 2009, B2.

–. "Boreal Efforts Draw Praise, Canada on Track to Create World's Best Protected Wilderness." *Edmonton Journal*, 4 July 2010, A1.

Brower, Matthew. "Trophy Shots: Early North American Photographs of Nonhuman Animals and the Display of Masculine Prowess." *Society and Animals* 13, 1 (2005): 13-31.

Brown, R. Craig. "The Doctrine of Usefulness: Natural Resources and National Park Policy in Canada, 1887-1914." In *Conference on the National Parks Today and Tomorrow: Proceedings*, ed. J.G. Nelson and R.C. Scace, 94-110. Calgary: University of Calgary, 1968.

Brown, Stewardson. *Alpine Flora of the Canadian Rocky Mountains. Illustrated with Water-Colour Drawings and Photographs by Mrs Charles Schäffer*. New York and London: GP Putnam and Sons/The Knickerbocker Press, 1907.

Brownlow, Alec. "A Wolf in the Garden: Ideology and Change in the Adirondack Landscape." In *Animal Spaces, Beastly Places: New Geographies of Human-Animal Relations*, ed. Chris Philo and Chris Wilbert, 141-58. London: Routledge, 2000.

"By Motor and Pack Horse through Cloud Wonderland." *Banff Crag and Canyon*, 12 July 1924, 8.

Canada. Department of the Interior. *Vacations in Canada: A Handbook of Information for Tourists and Sportsmen*. 2nd ed. Ottawa: Department of the Interior/Natural Resources Intelligence Service, 1929.

–. *The National Parks of Canada: A Brief Description of Their Scenic and Recreational Attractions*. Ottawa: Department of the Interior, 1936.

Canada. Department of Mines and Resources. *Jasper National Park in the Canadian Rockies*. Ottawa: National Parks Bureau, [1940s].

Canada. Department of Resources and Development. *Banff and Jasper National Parks*. Ottawa: Department of Resources and Development, 1951.

Canadian National Railways. *Jasper National Park*. Montreal: Canadian National Railways, 1927.

–. "Choose a Canadian National Vacation This Year – Vacation at Jasper National Park." *World's Work Magazine* (April 1927): n. pag.

–. *What to Do at Jasper and Mount Robson*. Montreal: Canadian National Railways, 1930.

–. *Canadian Rockies: Jasper, Mount Robson, and the Fiords of the North Pacific*. Montreal: Canadian National Railways, 1934.

–. "Magnificent Jasper Park in the Heart of the Canadian Rockies." *Maclean's Magazine*, 1 May 1934, 57.

–. *What to Do in Jasper National Park*. Montreal: Canadian National Railways, 1935.

–. *Canadian Rockies and the Pacific Coast*. Montreal: Canadian National Railways, 1938.

–. *Jasper National Park in the Canadian Rockies*. Montreal: Canadian National Railways, 1938.

–. "Jasper: Gem of the Canadian Rockies." *Canadian National Magazine* 24, 5 (May 1938): 1.

–. *Jasper National Park in the Canadian Rockies.* Montreal: Canadian National Railways, 1939.
–. *Jasper National Park in the Canadian Rockies.* Montreal: Canadian National Railways, 1940.
–. *Jasper National Park, Canadian Rockies.* Montreal: Canadian National Railways, 1942.
–. *Jasper National Park.* Montreal: Canadian National Railways, 1946.
–. *Jasper National Park, Canadian Rockies.* Montreal: Canadian National Railways, 1953.
–. *Through Your Picture Window.* Montreal: Canadian National Railways, 1960.
–. *Across Canada: The Canadian Scene in Map and Pictures.* Montreal: Canadian National Railways, 1961.
Canadian Parks and Wilderness Society. *What's Happening in Our Mountain Parks?* Calgary: Canadian Parks and Wilderness Society, 2002.
"Canadian Rockies." *Your Official Alberta Vacation Guide,* 25-38. 2002.
Castonguay, Stéphane. "Naturalizing Federalism: Insect Outbreaks and the Centralization of Entomological Research in Canada, 1884-1914." *Canadian Historical Review* 85, 1 (2004): 1-34.
Cautley, R.W. "Jasper National Park." *Canadian Geographical Journal* 1, 6 (1930): 466-80.
Cavell, Edward, and John Whyte. *Rocky Mountain Madness: A Historical Miscellany.* Canmore, AB: Altitude Publishing, 2001.
Clifford, Hal. *Downhill Slide: Why the Corporate Ski Industry Is Bad for Skiing, Ski Towns, and the Environment.* San Francisco: Sierra Club Books, 2002.
–. "Downhill Slide." *Sierra Magazine,* January-February 2003. http://www.sierraclub.org/.
Coleman, Annie Gilbert. "From Snow Bunnies to Shred Betties: Gender, Consumption, and the Skiing Landscape." In *Seeing Nature through Gender,* ed. Virginia Scharff, 194-217. Lawrence: University Press of Kansas, 2003.
Collinson, Helen. *One Man's Mountains: Joe Weiss in Jasper.* Edmonton: University of Alberta Collections, 1979.
Colpitts, George. "Wildlife Promotions, Western Canada Boosterism, and the Conservation Movement, 1890-1914." *American Review of Canadian Studies* 28, 1-2 (1998): 103-30.
Connelly, Joel. "A Growing Awareness: Environmental Groups and the Media." *Aperture* 120 (1990): 36-43.
Cory, Harper. "W.J. Oliver, Cameraman to Nature." *Photography* 6, 62 (1937): 6-7.
Cosgrove, Denis. *Apollo's Eye: A Cartographic Genealogy of the Earth in the Western Imagination.* Baltimore: Johns Hopkins University Press, 2001.
–. "Images and Imagination in 20th Century Environmentalism: From the Sierras to the Poles." *Environment and Planning A* 40, 8 (2008): 1862-80.
Cotter, John. "Canada's Mountain Parks Try Different Ways to Reduce Wildlife Carnage." *Canadian Press NewsWire,* 6 February 2005, 1.
"Court Defends Harlequins and Parks." *Sierra Legal Defence Fund Newsletter* 24 (1999): 1.
CPAWS, Northern Alberta Chapter. "The Future of Jasper National Park." http://cpawsnab.org/.
Crang, Mike. "Knowing, Tourism, and Practices of Vision." In *Leisure/Tourism Geographies: Practices and Geographical Knowledge,* ed. David Crouch, 238-56. London: Routledge, 1999.
Crawshaw, Carol, and John Urry. "Tourism and the Photographic Eye." In *Touring Cultures: Transformations of Travel and Theory,* ed. Chris Rojek and John Urry, 176-95. London: Routledge, 1997.

Croft, Stephanie. "Pin-Up Protest: Salt Spring Women Bared All in a Fundraising Calendar." *Alternatives Journal* 27, 2 (2001): 28.

Cronin, J. Keri. "'The Bears Are Plentiful and Frequently Good Camera Subjects': Picture Postcards and the Framing of Interspecific Encounters in Canada's Rocky Mountain Parks." *Mosaic* 39, 4 (2006): 77-92.

–. "A Tale of Two Parks: Photography, Pollution, and 'the Pecuniary Canons of Taste.'" In *Thorstein Veblen's Contributions to Environmental Sociology: Essays in the Political Ecology of Wasteful Industrialism*, ed. Ross Mitchell, 257-86. Lewiston, NY: Edwin Mellen Press, 2007.

Cronon, William. "Foreword." In *Uncommon Ground: Rethinking the Human Place in Nature*, ed. William Cronon, 19-22. New York: W.W. Norton and Company, 1995.

–. "The Trouble with Wilderness; Or, Getting Back to the Wrong Nature." In *Uncommon Ground: Rethinking the Human Place in Nature*, ed. William Cronon, 69-90. New York: W.W. Norton and Company, 1995.

–. "The Trouble with Wilderness; or, Getting Back to the Wrong Nature." *Environmental History* 1 (1996): 7-28.

–. "Foreword: Why Worry about Roads?" In *Driven Wild: How the Fight against Automobiles Launched the Modern Wilderness Movement*, ed. Paul S. Sutter, vii-xii. Seattle: University of Washington Press, 2002.

–, ed. *Uncommon Ground: Rethinking the Human Place in Nature*. New York: W.W. Norton and Company, 1995.

Cross, Michael S., ed., *The Frontier Thesis and the Canadas: The Debate on the Impact of the Canadian Environment*. Toronto: Copp Clark Publishing, 1970.

Curry, Shannon. "UNESCO Questions Cheviot Mine Approval." *Alternatives Journal* 24, 4 (1998): 2.

Dale, Stephen. *McLuhan's Children: The Greenpeace Message and the Media*. Toronto: Between the Lines, 1996.

Davallon, Jean, Gérald Grandmont, and Bernard Schiele. *The Rise of Environmentalism in Museums*. Quebec: Museé de la Civilisation, 1992.

Davis, Peter. *Museums and the Natural Environment*. London: Leicester University Press, 1996.

Davis, Susan G. *Spectacular Nature: Corporate Culture and the Sea World Experience*. Berkeley: University of California Press, 1997.

Dawson, Donald. "Plans for Ten New Canada Parks Met with Skepticism." *National Geographic News*, 10 October 2002. http://news.nationalgeographic.com/.

Dearden, Philip. "Endangered Species and Terrestrial Protected Areas." In *Politics of the Wild: Canada and Endangered Species*, ed. Karen Beazley and Robert Boardman, 75-93. Oxford: Oxford University Press, 2001.

Dekker, Dick. "The Not-So-Natural History of Jasper National Park." *Park News* 23, 4 (1987-88): 26-29.

Diehl, Carol. "The Toxic Sublime." *Art in America* 94, 2 (2006): 118-23.

Dobson, Brenda, Jesse Whittington, Robert St. Clair, and Mike Wesbrook. *The Effectiveness of Wildlife Corridor Restoration: Fairmont Jasper Park Lodge Golf Course, Jasper National Park*. Ottawa: Parks Canada, 2004.

Donald, Diana. "'Beastly Sights': The Treatment of Animals as a Moral Theme in Representations of London, c. 1820-1850." *Art History* 22, 4 (1999): 514-44.

Dryzek, John S., and David Schlosberg. "Introduction." In *Debating the Earth: The Environmental Politics Reader,* ed. John S. Dryzek and David Schlosberg, 1-3. Oxford: Oxford University Press, 1998.

Ducks Unlimited Canada. "Our Position on Hunting." http://www.ducks.ca/.

Dunaway, Finis. *Natural Visions: The Power of Images in American Environmental Reform.* Chicago: University of Chicago Press, 2005.

–. "Gas Masks, Pogo, and the Ecological Indian: Earth Day and the Visual Politics of American Environmentalism." *American Quarterly* 60, 1 (2008): 67-99.

Dunlap, R.E., and R.B. Heffernan. "Outdoor Recreation and Environmental Concern: An Empirical Examination." *Rural Sociology* 40 (1975): 18-30.

Dunlap, Thomas R. "Ecology, Nature, and Canadian National Park Policy: Wolves, Elk, and Bison as a Case Study." *Canadian Issues* 13 (1991): 139-47.

Eco, Umberto. *Travels in Hyperreality.* New York: Harcourt Brace Jovanovich, 1986.

Ellis, Cathy. "Golf Stars Event Dismays Conservationists; 2010 Skins Game OK'd for Banff." *Calgary Herald,* 3 July 2009, A16.

Emberley, Julia V. *The Cultural Politics of Fur.* Ithaca: Cornell University Press, 1997.

Emel, Jody, and Jennifer Wolch. "Witnessing the Animal Moment." In *Animal Geographies: Place, Politics, and Identity in the Nature-Culture Borderlands,* ed. Jennifer Wolch and Jody Emel, 1-24. London: Verso, 1998.

Evernden, Neil. *The Social Creation of Nature.* Baltimore: Johns Hopkins University Press, 1992.

Fagone, Vittorio. *Art in Nature.* Milan: Mazzotta, 1996.

Faris, John T. *Seeing Canada.* Philadelphia: J.B. Lippincott Company, 1924.

"Finds Jasper Waters Teeming with Fine Fish." *Calgary Herald,* n.d. Library and Archives Canada, William J. Oliver Fonds, MG30-D402, vol. 1, file Scrapbook of Clippings, 1918-47.

Finnegan, Ardith. "CPAWS to Fight for National Parks." *Banff Crag and Canyon,* 10 June 1992, 5.

Fiske, John. "The Progress from Brute to Man." *North American Review* 117, 241 (1873): 251-319.

Fitzgerald, F. Scott. *The Great Gatsby.* New York: Charles Scribner's Sons, 1925.

Foer, Jonathan Safran. *Eating Animals.* New York: Little, Brown, and Company, 2009.

"Forest Industry, Green Groups Strike Deal." *CBC News,* 18 May 2010. http://www.cbc.ca.

Foster, Janet. *Working for Wildlife: The Beginnings of Preservation in Canada.* Toronto: University of Toronto Press, 1978, 1998.

Francis, Daniel. *National Dreams: Myth, Memory, and Canadian History.* Vancouver: Arsenal Pulp Press, 1997.

Francis, Margot. "The Lesbian National Parks and Services: Reading Sex, Race, and the Nation in Artistic Performance." *Canadian Woman Studies* 20, 2 (2000): 131-36.

Franklin, Adrian. *Animals and Modern Culture: A Sociology of Human-Animal Relations in Modernity.* London: Sage Publications, 1999.

French, Cameron. "Environmentalists Applaud Canadian Parks Plan." Reuters News Service, 4 September 2002. http://www.enn.com/.

Friends of Jasper National Park. "Drivers for Wildlife." *Nature Calls* (newsletter of the Friends of Jasper National Park) (fall-winter 2003): 2.

–. "Jasper Institute: Natural History Field Courses in the Canadian Rockies." N.d. http://www.friendsofjasper.com/.

Frow, Jonathan. "Tourism and the Semiotics of Nostalgia." *October* 57 (1991): 123-51.

Fudge, Erica. *Animal.* London: Reaktion Books, 2002.

–, ed. *Renaissance Beasts: Of Animals, Humans, and Other Wonderful Creatures.* Champaign: University of Illinois Press, 2003.

Gachelin-Ribault, Christiane. "Skiing, Culture, and the Environment: Mountains Are Not Made for Crowds, Some Say, but Can Mountain Communities Live without Tourism?" *Ecodecision* 20 (1996): 49.

Gadd, Ben. "Why Ski Areas Don't Belong in National Parks." Jasper Environmental Association, 2006. http://www.jasperenvironmental.org/.

Gallery TPW. "Subversive Souvenirs: Questioning the Institutional View in the Imagery of Tourism and Surveillance." *Virtual Museum of Canada,* 2006. http://www.virtualmuseum.ca/.

Garb, Yaakov Jerome. "The Use and Misuse of the Whole Earth Image." *Whole Earth Review* 45 (1985): 18-25.

Gelfand, Judy. "Nature Canada Takes Mining Company and Feds to Court over Cheviot Mine." *Nature Canada* 33, 4 (2004-5): 35.

Gibbon, John Murray. *The Romance of the Canadian Canoe.* Toronto: Ryerson Press, 1951.

Gibbons, Bill. *Photographing the Canadian Rockies.* Banff: British Photographic Laboratories of Canada, 1948.

Gillespie, Greg. "'I Was Well Pleased with Our Sport among the Buffalo': Big-Game Hunters, Travel Writing, and Cultural Imperialism in the British North American West, 1847-72." *Canadian Historical Review* 83, 4 (2002): 555-85.

Gillis, Charlie. "A Ranger in Wolf's Clothing." *National Post,* 11 April 2002, A8.

Gluckman, Ron. "The Great Indoors." In *In Search of Wild Adventure: A Wild Travel Anthology,* ed. Brad Olsen, 117-20. San Francisco: CCC Publishing, 1999.

Government of Alberta. "Provincial Museum of Alberta Launches Wild Alberta." Press release, Edmonton, Alberta Community Development, 22 September 2003.

Government of Canada. "National Historic Parks Wildlife and Domestic Animals Regulation (SOR/81-613)." *Canada Gazette Part II* 115, 15 (23 July 1981): 2316-20.

Goyette, Linda. "Jasper by Starlight." *Canadian Geographic Travel* (May 2007): 68-78.

Grande, John K. *Balance: Art and Nature.* Montreal: Black Rose Books, 1994.

Greenpeace. "Unbearable Truth about Toronto Dominion Bank's Role in Rainforest Destruction Revealed," 22 February 2001. http://archive.greenpeace.org/.

Gullo, Andrea, Unna Lassiter, and Jennifer Wolch. "The Cougar's Tale." In *Animal Geographies: Place, Politics, and Identity in the Nature-Culture Borderlands,* ed. Jennifer Wolch and Jody Emel, 139-61. London: Verso, 1998.

Hadley, Margery Tanner. "Photography, Tourism, and the CPR." In *Essays on the Historical Geography of the Canadian West: Regional Perspectives on the Settlement Process,* ed. L.A. Rosenvall and S.M. Evans, 48-69. Calgary: University of Calgary, 1987.

Hall, C. Michael, and John Shultis. "Railways, Tourism, and Worthless Lands: The Establishment of National Parks in Australia, Canada, New Zealand, and the United States." *Australian-Canadian Studies* 8, 2 (1991): 57-74.

Haraway, Donna. "Teddy Bear Patriarchy: Taxidermy in the Garden of Eden, New York City, 1908-1936." In *Cultures of United States Imperialism,* ed. Amy Kaplan and Donald E. Pease, 237-91. Durham: Duke University Press, 1993.

[Harkin, J.B.]. "Report of the Commissioner of Dominion Parks." In Canada, Department of the Interior, *Annual Report of the Department of the Interior for the Fiscal Year ending March 31, 1914,* 4. Ottawa: 1915.

"Harmon's Images of Civilization and Wilderness." *Banff Crag and Canyon,* 24 August 1988, 3.

"Harmon's Photographs Published in England." *Banff Crag and Canyon,* 5 June 1925, 1.

Harris, R. Cole, and John Warkentin. "Conclusion." In *Canada before Confederation: A Study in Historical Geography,* 312-330. New York: Oxford University Press, 1974.

Hart, E.J. *The Selling of Canada: The CPR and the Beginnings of Canadian Tourism.* Banff: Altitude Publishing, 1983.

–. *Trains, Peaks, and Tourists: The Golden Age of Canadian Travel.* Banff: EJH Literary Enterprises, 2000.

–. *J.B. Harkin: Father of Canada's National Parks.* Edmonton: University of Alberta Press, 2010.

–, ed. *A Hunter of Peace: Mary T.S. Schäffer's Old Indian Trails of the Canadian Rockies: Incidents of Camp and Trail Life, Covering Two Years Exploration through the Rocky Mountains of Canada.* Banff: Whyte Museum of the Canadian Rockies, 1980.

Herrero, Stephen. *Bear Attacks: Their Causes and Avoidance.* Guilford, CT: Lyons Press, 1988.

Higgs, Eric. *Nature by Design: People, Natural Processes, and Ecological Restoration.* Cambridge, MA: MIT Press, 2003.

–. "Twinning Reality, or How Taking History Seriously Changes How We Understand Ecological Restoration in Jasper National Park." In *Culturing Wilderness in Jasper National Park: Studies in Two Centuries of Human History in the Upper Athabasca River Watershed,* ed. I.S. MacLaren, 289-316. Edmonton: University of Alberta Press, 2007.

Hill, Nicole. "Tourists on the March: Martin Parr Uses His Camera to Capture the Absurd Moments of Global Tourism." *Christian Science Monitor,* 27 November 2007. http://www.csmonitor.com/.

Hoelscher, Steven. "The Photographic Construction of Tourist Space in Victorian America." *Geographical Review* 88, 4 (1998): 548-70.

Howay, F.W. "A Short Historical Sketch of Jasper Park Region." *Sierra Club Bulletin* 14 (1929): 28-33.

Hryciuk, Dennis. "Get Rid of Ski Hills in Parks, Jasper Environmentalist Says." *Edmonton Journal,* 15 December 1998, A5.

Jaimet, Kate. "Ignoring Nature's Call." *Ottawa Citizen,* 9 December 2006, B1.

Jameson, Sheilagh S. *W.J. Oliver: Life through a Master's Lens.* Calgary: Glenbow Museum, 1984.

Jasen, Patricia. *Wild Things: Nature, Culture, and Tourism in Ontario, 1790-1914.* Toronto: University of Toronto Press, 1995.

Jasper Chamber of Commerce. *Jasper Tourist News.* Jasper: Jasper Chamber of Commerce, 1960.

–. "Animals Are the Funniest People." In *Jasper Tourist News – Your Companion in Jasper,* 13. Jasper: Jasper Chamber of Commerce, 1965.

–. "Bing Crosby's Victory in Totem Golf Rivalled Best Hollywood Scripts." In *Jasper Tourist News – Your Companion in Jasper,* 14. Jasper: Jasper Chamber of Commerce, 1965.

–. "Canadian Rockies Driving and Sight-Seeing Lead in Popularity." In *Jasper Tourist News – Your Companion in Jasper,* 7. Jasper: Jasper Chamber of Commerce, 1965.

–. "Fishermen Best When It Comes to Relaxing." In *Jasper Tourist News – Your Companion in Jasper,* 3. Jasper: Jasper Chamber of Commerce, 1965.

–. "Jasper Park Moves into Skiing's Big Leagues." In *Jasper Tourist News – Your Companion in Jasper,* 17. Jasper: Jasper Chamber of Commerce, 1965.

–. *Jasper Tourist News.* Jasper: Jasper Chamber of Commerce, 1965.

–. *Jasper Tourist News – Your Companion in Jasper.* Jasper: Jasper Chamber of Commerce, 1965.

–. "Rivers Are Swift but Lakes Romantic." In *Jasper Tourist News – Your Companion in Jasper,* 14. Jasper: Jasper Chamber of Commerce, 1965.

Jasper Environmental Association (JEA). "*Canis Lupus:* Architect of Prey Species." http://www.jasperenvironmental.org/.

–. "Cheviot Mine: Grizzlies vs. Coal." http://www.jasperenvironmental.org/.

–. "Environmental Assessments: Mitigation Magic." http://www.jasperenvironmental.org/.

–. "Funding for Parks: What Price Canada's Heritage?" http://www.jasperenvironmental.org/.

–. "Marmot Basin Ski Hill: A Slippery Slope for Wildlife." http://www.jasperenvironmental.org/.

–. *Report to Parks Canada and the Public on the Current State of Jasper National Park, with Reference to Observations and Recommendations from 2002,* 29 January 2007. http://www.jasperenvironmental.org/.

Jasper Environmental Association, Nature Canada, Pembina Institute for Appropriate Development, Sierra Club of Canada, and Sierra Legal Defence Fund. "Conservation Groups Shift Focus in Tacking Mine Next-Door to Jasper National Park." 30 September 2005. http://www.sierraclub.ca/.

Jasper in June: A Vacationtime Superb in the Canadian Rockies. Edmonton: Hamly Press, n.d.

"Jasper National Park Update." *News for the Wild (Canadian Parks and Wilderness Society Newsletter)* (summer 2002): 8.

"Jasper Park Must Step up Pace of Development." *Banff Crag and Canyon,* 21 September 1988, 12.

"Jasper Scenery Hollywood's Choice." *Jasper Tourist News* (summer 1960): 6.

"Jasper's Early Visitors Knew 'Togetherness.'" *Jasper Tourist News* (summer 1960), 1.

"Jasper Seeks Policy for Filmmakers in Park." *Bow Valley This Week,* 3 August-10 August 1993, 1.

Jasper's Marmot Basin 25th Anniversary. Jasper: Marmot Basin Ski Lifts, 1989.

Jasper: Visitor's Choice, Winter 2002/2003. Vancouver: Visitor's Choice Publications, 2002.

Jessup, Lynda. "The Group of Seven and the Tourist Landscape in Western Canada, or the More Things Change ..." *Journal of Canadian Studies* 37 (2002): 144-79.

–. "Landscapes of Sport, Landscapes of Exclusion: The 'Sportsman's Paradise' in Late-Nineteenth-Century Canadian Painting." *Journal of Canadian Studies* 40, 1 (2006): 71-123.

Johnsrude, Larry. "Cheviot Road Illegal – Activists." *Edmonton Journal,* 25 January 2005, A6.

–. "Cheviot Road Less Damaging than Rail Line: Mine Official." *Edmonton Journal,* 26 January 2005, B6.

Jonaitis, Aldona. "Northwest Coast Totem Poles." In *Unpacking Culture: Art and Commodity in Colonial and Postcolonial Worlds,* ed. Ruth B. Phillips and Christopher B. Steiner, 104-21. Berkeley: University of California Press, 1999.

Jones, Karen R. *Wolf Mountains: A History of Wolves along the Great Divide.* Calgary: University of Calgary Press, 2002.

Kane, Paul. *Wanderings of an Artist among the Indians of North America, from Canada to Vancouver's Island and Oregon, through the Hudson's Bay Company's Territory and Back Again.* London: Longman, Brown, Green, Longmans, and Roberts, 1859.

Karlberg, Michael. "News and Conflict: How Adversarial News Frames Limit Public Understanding of Environmental Issues." *Alternatives Journal* 23, 1 (1997): 22-27.

Karp, Ivan, and Steven D. Lavine, eds. *Exhibiting Cultures: The Poetics and Politics of Museum Display.* Washington, DC: Smithsonian Institution Press, 1991.

Kastner, Jeffrey, ed. *Land and Environmental Art.* London: Phaidon Press, 1998.

Kaye, Frances W. *Hiding the Audience: Viewing Art and Arts Institutions on the Prairies.* Edmonton: University of Alberta Press, 2003.

Kendall, Brian. "Go Ahead, Tree Huggers, Hit the Links." *Globe and Mail,* 30 April 2010, T11.

Kennedy, Kathy. "It Pays to Stay off the Beaten Track." *Edmonton Journal,* 19 June 1976, 37.

–. "Jasper Overcrowding Brings Hiking Quotas." *Edmonton Journal,* 19 June 1976, 37.

Koch, George, and John Weissenberger. "Jumbo Controversy: A Visionary Architect Wants to Bring a World-Class Ski Resort to a Logged-Over B.C. Valley. Eco-Freaks Respond with 'Grizzlies Not Gondolas' Bumper Stickers." *National Post,* 19 December 2003, FP11.

"Kodak Is Taking Kodachrome Film Away." 22 June 2009. http://www.cbc.ca/.

Kopas, Paul. *Taking the Air: Ideas and Change in Canada's National Parks.* Vancouver: UBC Press, 2007.

Korobanik, John. "Restroom for Campers No Longer Maligned; Powered by Six Solar Panels, New Jasper Facility Is Virtually a Self-Contained Sewage Treatment Plant." *Edmonton Journal,* 30 August 2007, F2.

Lears, T.J. Jackson. *No Place of Grace: Antimodernism and the Transformation of American Culture, 1880-1920.* New York: Pantheon Books, 1981.

Legault, Stephen. "Coal Miner's Fodder." *Canadian Geographic* 117, 2 (1997): 20.

–. "Making Waves: Commercial Rafters on Alberta's Maligne River Are Crowding out the Harlequin Ducks." *Outdoor Canada* 25, 3 (1997): 13.

"Let's Develop the Parks: Alberta Gov't." *Banff Crag and Canyon,* 25 November 1987, 1-2.

Lewis, Margaret. *To Conserve a Heritage.* Calgary: Alberta Fish and Game Association, 1979.

Lippard, Lucy. *On the Beaten Track: Tourism, Art, and Place.* New York: New Press, 1999.

Locke, Harvey. "Is Banff an Endangered Space?" *Borealis (Magazine of the Canadian Parks and Wilderness Society)* 4, 1 (1993): 3.

Loo, Tina. "Making a Modern Wilderness: Conserving Wildlife in Twentieth-Century Canada." *Canadian Historical Review* 82 (2001): 91-121.

–. *States of Nature: Conserving Canada's Wildlife in the Twentieth Century.* Vancouver: UBC Press, 2006.

Lothian, W.F. *A History of Canada's National Parks – Volume II.* Ottawa: Parks Canada, 1977.

–. *A History of Canada's National Parks – Volume III.* Ottawa: Parks Canada, 1979.

–. *A Brief History of Canada's National Parks.* Ottawa: Environment Canada, Parks Canada, 1987.

Louter, David. *Windshield Wilderness: Cars, Roads, and Nature in Washington's National Parks.* Seattle: University of Washington Press, 2006.

Lowe, Meaghan. "Dreamworld and Reality: An Exploration of Environmental Aesthetics in Contemporary Photography." *Topia* 21 (2009): 105-20.

Luke, Timothy W. "Nature Protection or Nature Projection: A Cultural Critique of the Sierra Club." *Capitalism, Nature, Socialism* 8, 1 (1997): 37-63.

Macdonald, Sharon. "Introduction." In *Theorizing Museums,* ed. Sharon Macdonald and Gordon Fyfe, 1-18. Oxford: Blackwell Publishers, 1996.

MacEachern, Alan. *Natural Selections: National Parks in Atlantic Canada.* Montreal: McGill-Queen's University Press, 2001.

–. "Voices Crying in the Wilderness: Recent Works in Canadian Environmental History." *Acadiensis* 31, 2 (2002): 215-26.

MacGregor, J.G. *Overland by the Yellowhead.* Saskatoon: Western Producer Book Service, 1974.

MacLaren, I.S. "Cultured Wilderness in Jasper National Park." *Journal of Canadian Studies* 34, 3 (1999): 7-58.

–. "Henry James Warre's and Paul Kane's Sketches in the Athabasca Watershed, 1846." In *Culturing Wilderness in Jasper National Park: Studies in Two Centuries of Human History in the Upper Athabasca River Watershed,* ed. I.S. MacLaren, 41-70. Edmonton: University of Alberta Press, 2007.

–, ed. *Culturing Wilderness in Jasper National Park: Studies in Two Centuries of Human History in the Upper Athabasca River Watershed.* Edmonton: University of Alberta Press, 2007.

MacLaren, I.S., Eric S. Higgs, and Gabrielle Zezulka-Mailloux. *Mapper of Mountains: M.P. Bridgland in the Canadian Rockies.* Edmonton: University of Alberta Press, 2005.

Marmot Basin Ski Hill. "Ski Marmot Basin: Skiing and Snowboarding in Jasper National Park." N.d. http://www.skimarmot.com/.

Marsh, W. Ward. "Travel Pictures Prompt the Old Vacation Urge." *Cleveland Plain Dealer,* [1932], n.p. Library and Archives Canada, MG30-D402, vol. 1.

Martens, Debra. "Graphic Tobacco Warnings Have Desired Effect." *Canadian Medical Association Journal* 166 (2002): 1453.

Marty, Sid. *A Grand and Fabulous Notion: The First Century of Canada's Parks.* Toronto: NC Press, 1984.

McNamee, Kevin. "Canadian Nature Federation Intervenes in Cheviot Mine Hearings." *Nature Canada* 26, 1 (1997): 23.

–. "Prime Minister Protects Two Candidate National Parks." *Nature Alert* 7, 1 (1997): 4.

–. "The World's Treasures." *Nature Canada* 29, 1 (2000): 18-23.

Melnechuk, Greg. "Weyerhaeuser Pulp Mill Continues to Pollute." *BC Environmental Report* 3, 3 (1992): 26.

Milton, William Fitzwilliam, and W.B. Cheadle. *The North-West Passage by Land.* 6th ed. London: Cassell, Petter, Galpin, [1870].

Mitchell, Ross E., ed. "Thorstein Veblen: Pioneer in Environmental Sociology." *Organization and Environment* 14, 4 (2001): 389-409.

–. *Thorstein Veblen's Contribution to Environmental Sociology: Essays in the Political Ecology of Wasteful Industrialism.* Lewiston, NY: Edwin Mellen Press, 2007.

Mitchell, W.J.T. "Interdisciplinarity and Visual Culture." *Art Bulletin* 76 (1995): 540-44.

Mowat, Farley. *Rescue the Earth! Conversations with the Green Crusaders.* Toronto: McClelland and Stewart, 1990.

"Mrs. Schäffer's Discovery and Survey of Lake Maligne, Canadian Rockies." *Geographical Journal* 39, 4 (April 1912): 397-81.

Mugford, Michael. "Wildlife Protection: Parks Canada Joins Forces with Photofinishers." *Photo Life* 24, 5 (1999): 22.

Murphy, Peter J. "'Following the Base of the Foothills': Tracing the Boundaries of Jasper Park and its Adjacent Rocky Mountains Forest Reserve." In *Culturing Wilderness in Jasper National Park Studies in Two Centuries of Human History in the Upper Athabasca River Watershed,* ed. I.S. MacLaren, 87-88. Edmonton: University of Alberta Press, 2007.

–. "Homesteading in the Athabasca Valley to 1910: An Interview with Edward Wilson Moberly, Prairie Creek, Alberta, 29 August 1980." In *Culturing Wilderness in Jasper National Park: Studies in Two Centuries of Human History in the Upper Athabasca River Watershed,* ed. I.S. MacLaren, 123-53. Edmonton: University of Alberta Press, 2007.

Nadeau, Chantal. *Fur Nation: From the Beaver to Bridgitte Bardot.* London: Routledge, 2001.

Nash, Roderick. *Wilderness and the American Mind.* New Haven: Yale University Press, 1967.

Nelson, J.G. "Parks and Protected Areas and Sustainable Development." In *Changing Parks: The History, Future, and Cultural Context of Parks and Heritage Landscapes,* ed. John S. Marsh and Bruce W. Hodgins, 279-94. Toronto: Natural History/Natural Heritage, 1998.

Nord, Douglas C. "Canada Perceived: The Impact of Canadian Tourism Advertising in the U.S.A." *Journal of American Culture* 9 (1986): 23-30.

Nord, Mark, A.E. Luloff, and Jeffrey C. Bridger. "The Association of Forest Recreation with Environmentalism." *Environment and Behavior* 30, 2 (1998): 235-46.

Nye, David. "Technologies of Landscape." In *Technologies of Landscape: From Reaping to Recycling,* ed. David Nye, 1-17. Amherst: University of Massachusetts Press, 1999.

"Open Season on Poachers." *Canadian Geographic* 112, 1 (1992): 10-11.

Osborne, Peter. *Travelling Light: Photography, Travel, and Visual Culture.* Manchester: Manchester University Press, 2000.

Ouellet, Richard A. "Tales of Empowerment: Cultural Continuity within an Evolving Identity in the Upper Athabasca Valley." MA thesis, Simon Fraser University, 2006.

Our Jasper (promotional brochure). Jasper: Mountain Park Lodges, c. 2003.

Parker, Dayle. "Ski Resorts Take the High Road on Environmental Protection." *Edmonton Journal,* 2 March 2006, E2.

Parks Canada. "Jasper – National Parks of Canada: Natural Wonders and Cultural Treasures." n.d. http://www.pc.gc.ca/.

–. *Welcome to National Parks.* Ottawa: Parks Canada, 1986.

–. *Parks Canada: First Priority. Progress Report on the Implementation of the Recommendations of the Panel on the Ecological Integrity of Canada's National Parks.* Ottawa: Parks Canada, 2001.

–. "Evolution of Bear Management in the Mountain National Parks." 2003. http://www. pc.gc.ca/.

–. *The Icefields Parkway.* Ottawa: Parks Canada, 2003.

–. *The Mountain Guide to Banff, Jasper, Kootenay, Yoho, Glacier, and Mount Revelstoke National Parks of Canada.* Ottawa: Parks Canada, 2003.

–. "Jasper National Park of Canada: One Hundred Years of History in Jasper National Park." 2007. http://www.pc.gc.ca/.

–. *Jasper National Park of Canada: State of the Park Report.* Ottawa: Parks Canada, 2008.

–. *Jasper National Park Management Plan.* Updated 15 April, 2009. http://www.pc.gc.ca.

–. *Jasper National Park of Canada Management Plan.* Ottawa: Parks Canada, 2010.

–. "Jasper Raven Totem Pole Returns to Haida Gwaii." 21 June 2010. http://news.gc.ca.

Payne, Michael. "The Fur Trade on the Upper Athabasca River, 1810-1910." In *Culturing Wilderness in Jasper National Park: Studies in Two Centuries of Human History in the Upper Athabasca River Watershed*, ed. I.S. MacLaren, 1-39. Edmonton: University of Alberta Press, 2007.

Peck, William H. "Animal Symbolism in Ancient Egyptian Art." *Sculpture Review* 52, 2 (2003): 8-15.

Phoenix Seagaia Resort. "Announcement of Termination of Ocean Dome Operations on October 1, 2007." 7 August 2007. http://www.seagaia.co.jp/.

Pickles, Katie. *Transnational Outrage: The Death and Commemoration of Edith Cavell.* Basingstoke and New York: Palgrave MacMillan, 2007.

Pleasurable Places in the Wide Open Spaces. Vancouver: Traveller's Digest, 1944.

Pollan, Michael. *The Omnivore's Dilemma: A Natural History of Four Meals.* New York: Penguin Press, 2006.

Price, Jennifer. *Flight Maps: Adventures with Nature in Modern America.* New York: Basic Books, 1999.

Provincial Museum of Alberta. "Wild Alberta at the Museum." 2003. http://www.pma. edmonton.ab.ca/.

–. *Wild Alberta Media Kit.* Edmonton: Provincial Museum of Alberta, 2003.

Pyne, Stephen J. *How the Grand Canyon Became Grand: A Short History.* New York: Viking Penguin, 1998.

"Rafters Oppose River Closure." *Banff Crag and Canyon,* 14 July 1993, 3.

Rainforest Action Network. "Wake up Weyerhaeuser: Protect Forests Now!" 19 February 2004. http://www.ran.org/.

–. "Old Growth: Targeting Weyerhaeuser." N.d. http://ran.org/.

Reichwein, PearlAnn. "'Hands off Our National Parks': The Alpine Club of Canada and Hydro-Development Controversies in the Canadian Rockies, 1922-1930." *Journal of the Canadian Historical Association* 6 (1995): 129-55.

Reichwein, PearlAnn, and Lisa McDermott. "Opening the Secret Garden: Mary Schäffer, Jasper Park Conservation, and the Survey of Maligne Lake, 1911." In *Culturing Wilderness in Jasper National Park Studies in Two Centuries of Human History in the Upper Athabasca River Watershed*, ed. I.S. McLaren, 155-98. Edmonton: University of Alberta Press, 2007.

Reid, Dennis. *"Our Own Country Canada": Being an Account of the National Aspirations of the Principal Landscape Artists in Montreal and Toronto, 1860-1890.* Ottawa: National Gallery of Canada, 1979.

Reiger, John F. *American Sportsmen and the Origins of Conservation.* 3rd ed. Corvallis: Oregon State University Press, 2001.

"Rocky Mountains." In *Our Alberta: Driving Guide for Travellers,* 19. 2008.

Ross, Alec. "The Ecology of Images." In *Visual Culture: Images and Interpretations,* ed. Norman Bryson, Michael Ann Holly, and Keith Moxey, 325-46. Hanover, NH: University of New England Press, 1994.

Rothfels, Nigel, ed. *Representing Animals.* Bloomington: Indiana University Press, 2002.

Rubin, Cynthia Elyse, and Morgan Williams. *Larger than Life: The American Tall-Tale Postcard, 1905-1915.* New York: Abbeville Press, 1990.

Ryan, James R. "'Hunting with the Camera': Photography, Wildlife, and Colonialism in Africa." In *Animal Spaces, Beastly Places: New Geographies of Human-Animal Relations,* ed. Chris Philo and Chris Wilbert, 203-21. London: Routledge, 2000.

Said, Edward. "Imaginative Geography and Its Representations: Orientalizing the Oriental." In *Orientalism,* by Edward Said, 49-73. New York: Pantheon Books, 1978.

Sandilands, Catriona. "Ecological Integrity and National Narrative: Cleaning up Canada's National Parks." *Canadian Woman Studies* 20 (2000): 137-42.

Sandlos, John. *Hunters at the Margin: Native People and Wildlife Conservation in the Northwest Territories.* Vancouver: UBC Press, 2007.

Saunders, Doug. "The Simple Pleasures of Fake Nature." *Globe and Mail,* 16 August 2003, F3.

Sawyer, Jill. "The Ultimate Alberta." *Our Alberta* 20, 1 (2002): 6-11.

Schäffer, Mary T.S. *Old Indian Trails of the Canadian Rockies.* Vancouver: Rocky Mountain Books, 2007.

Schama, Simon. *Landscape and Memory.* Toronto: Random House, 1995.

Schindler, David W. "The Eastern Slopes of the Canadian Rockies: Must We Follow the American Blueprint?" In *Rocky Mountain Futures: An Ecological Perspective,* ed. Jill S. Baron, 285-99. Washington, DC: Island Press, 2002.

Schnaiberg, Allan, and Kenneth Alan Gould. *Environment and Society: The Enduring Conflict.* Caldwell, NJ: Blackburn Press, 2000.

Schwartz, Joan M. "The Geography Lesson: Photographs and the Construction of Imaginative Geographies." *Journal of Historical Geography* 22, 1 (1996): 16-45.

Schwartz, Joan M., and James R. Ryan. "Introduction: Photography and the Geographical Imagination." In *Picturing Place: Photography and the Geographical Imagination,* ed. Joan M. Schwartz and James R. Ryan, 1-18. London: I.B. Tauris, 2003.

Searle, Rick. *Phantom Parks: The Struggle to Save Canada's National Parks.* Toronto: Key Porter Books, 2000.

Seaton, Jill. "Jasper on the Brink." *Nature Alert* 7, 1 (1997): 2.

–. "Bogged down in the Tonquin Valley." *Prairie Sierran* 1, 4 (1997-98): 5-6.

Sellars, Richard West. "Science or Scenery? A Conflict of Values in the National Parks." *Wilderness* 52 (1989): 29-38.

Seth (Gregory Gallant). "Jasper the Bear Sheds a Tear." *National Post,* 11 February 2004, AL08.

Setting a New Direction for Canada's National Parks. Vol. 2 of *"Unimpaired for Future Generations"? Protecting Ecological Integrity within Canada's National Parks.* Ottawa: Parks Canada Agency, 2000.

Shaffer, Marguerite. *See America First: Tourism and National Identity.* Washington, DC: Smithsonian Institution Press, 2001.

Shepherd, Brenda, and Jesse Whittington. "Response of Wolves to Corridor Restoration and Human Use Management." *Ecology and Society* 2 (2006): http://www.ecologyandsociety.org/.

Sherlock, Maureen P. "The Accidental Tourist." In *Eye of Nature,* ed. Daina Augaitis and Helga Pakasaa, 123-37. Banff: Walter Phillips Gallery, 1991.

–. "Parks Canada Guiding Principles and Operational Policies: Preface; Early History." Modified 15 April 2009. http://www.pc.gc.ca/.

Sherman, Joan, and Michael Gismondi. "Jock Talk, Goldfish, Horse Loggings, and Star Wars: How a Pulp Company Communicates a Green Image." *Alternatives Journal* 23, 1 (1997): 14-20.

Shultis, John. "Recreational Values of Protected Areas." In *The Full Value of Parks: From Economics to the Intangible,* ed. David Harmon and Allen D. Putney, 59-75. Lanham, MD: Rowman and Littlefield, 2003.

Silversides, Brock. *Waiting for the Light: Early Mountain Photography in British Columbia and Alberta, 1865-1939.* Saskatoon: Fifth House Publishers, 1995.

Ski Jasper's Marmot Basin. Jasper: Marmot Basin Ski Lifts, 1995.

Skidmore, Colleen. *This Wild Spirit: Women in the Rocky Mountains of Canada.* Edmonton: University of Alberta Press, 2006.

Smith, Cyndi. *People, Places, and Events: A History of Jasper National Park.* Jasper: Jasper-Yellowhead Historical Society, 1983.

—. *Jasper Park Lodge: In the Heart of the Canadian Rockies.* Rev. ed. Waterton Park, AB: Coyote Books, 2000.

Smith, John. *The Generall Historie of Virginia, New-England, and the Summer Isles: With the Names of the Adventurers, Planters, and Governours from Their First Beginning Ano: 1584 to This Present 1624. With the Proceedings of Those Severall Colonies and the Accidents That Befell Them in All Their Journyes and Discoveries. Also the Maps and Descriptions of All Those Countryes, Their Commodities, People, Government, Customes, and Religion Yet Knowne. Divided Into Six Bookes. By Captaine John Smith, Sometymes Governour in Those Countryes and Admirall of New England.* London: Printed by I.D. and I.H. for Michael Sparkes, 1624.

Solman, V.E.F., J.P. Currier, and W.C. Cable. "Why Have Fish Hatcheries in Canada's National Parks?" In *Transactions of the 17th North American Wildlife Conference,* 226-33. Washington, DC: Wildlife Management Institute, 1952.

Spence, Mark David. "Dispossessing the Wilderness: Yosemite Indians and the National Park Ideal, 1864-1930." *Pacific Historical Review* 65, 1 (1996): 27-59.

Squire, Shelagh J. "Rewriting Languages of Geography and Tourism: Cultural Discourses of Destinations, Gender, and Tourism History in the Canadian Rockies." In *Destinations: Cultural Landscapes of Tourism,* ed. Greg Ringer, 80-100. London: Routledge, 1998.

Standeven, Joy, and Paul DeKnop. *Sport Tourism.* Champaign, IL: Human Kinetics, 1999.

Stead, Robert J.C. *Canada's Mountain Playgrounds.* Ottawa: Department of Mines and Resources, c. 1935.

Steiner, Christopher B. "Authenticity, Repetition, and the Aesthetics of Seriality: The Work of Tourist Art in the Age of Mechanical Reproduction." In *Unpacking Culture: Art and Commodity in Colonial and Postcolonial Worlds,* ed. Ruth B. Phillips and Christopher B. Steiner, 87-103. Berkeley: University of California Press, 1999.

Stoneham, Gordon. "Film Probes 'Bad Guy' Reputation of Wolves." *Saturday Citizen,* 25 September 1971, 29.

Struzik, Ed. "Sierra Club Opposes Cheviot Mine Project; U.S. Conservation Lobby Urges PM to Say No." *Edmonton Journal,* 10 September 1997, B5.

—. "Did You Get My Good Side? A Picture Is Worth a Thousand Wildlife Studies in Jasper National Park." *Outdoor Canada* 27, 2 (1999): 10.

—. "Is It Possible to Restore Altered Fish Populations to Their Natural State? A New Study in Jasper National Park May Provide an Answer." *Outdoor Canada* 29, 1 (2001): 11.

—. "New Plan to Open Cheviot Coal Mine: Controversial Mine Borders Jasper National Park." *Edmonton Journal,* 15 June 2002, A1.

—. "Can Our Parks Be Saved?" *Edmonton Journal,* 26 December 2004, F5.

—. "Call of the Wild Once Again Echoes through Jasper; Since Culls Virtually Killed Off the Predators, Park Elk Have Spiralled out of Control – So that Today, Wolves Are Welcome Once More." *Edmonton Journal,* 25 May 2008, E6.

"Surfing Indoors." *The Economist,* 18 December 1993, 86.

Sutter, Paul S. *Driven Wild: How the Fight Against Automobiles Launched the Modern Wilderness Movement.* Seattle: University of Washington Press, 2002.

Suvantola, Jaakko. *Tourist's Experience of Place.* Burlington, VT: Ashgate, 2002.

Suzuki, David, and Dave Robert Taylor. *The Big Picture: Reflections on Science, Humanity, and a Quickly Changing Planet.* Vancouver: Greystone Books, 2009.

Tator, Carol, Frances Henry, and Winston Mattis. *Challenging Racism in the Arts: Case Studies of Controversy and Conflict.* Toronto: University of Toronto Press, 1998.

Taylor, C.J. *Negotiating the Past: The Making of Canada's National Historic Parks and Sites.* Montreal: McGill-Queen's University Press, 1990.

–. "Legislating Nature: The National Park Act of 1930." In *To See Ourselves/To Save Ourselves: Ecology and Culture in Canada,* ed. R. Lorimer, M. M'Gonigle, J-P. Revéret, and S. Ross. Montreal: Association for Canadian Studies, 1991.

–. "The Changing Habitat of Jasper Tourism." In *Culturing Wilderness in Jasper National Park: Studies in Two Centuries of Human History in the Upper Athabasca River Watershed,* ed. I.S. MacLaren, 199-231. Edmonton: University of Alberta Press, 2007.

The Fairmont Jasper Park Lodge Golf Club: The Wild Side of the Rockies. Jasper, AB: The Fairmont Jasper Park Lodge and the Jasper Park Lodge Golf Club, 2009.

Thomas, Greg. *Art and Ecology in Nineteenth Century France: The Landscapes of Théodore Rousseau.* Princeton: Princeton University Press, 2000.

"To Advertise Banff." *Banff Crag and Canyon,* 13 October 1917, 8.

Townsend-Gault, Charlotte. "Having Voices and Using Them: First Nations Artists and 'Native Art.'" *Arts Magazine* 65 (1991): 65-70.

Travel Alberta. *Canadian Rockies Tourism Destination Region – Marketing Plan, 2003/2004.* Edmonton: Travel Alberta, 2003.

–. *Maximum Opportunity Regions: Travel Alberta Partnership Planner, 2003-2005.* Edmonton: Travel Alberta, 2003.

–. "Marketing Opportunities – In Province." N.d. http://industry.travelalberta.com/.

Tresidder, Richard. "Tourism and Sacred Landscapes." In *Leisure/Tourism Geographies: Practices and Geographical Knowledge,* ed. David Crouch, 137-48. London: Routledge, 1999.

Urquhart, Ian, ed. *Assault on the Rockies: Environmental Controversies in Alberta.* Edmonton: Rowan Books, 1998.

Urry, John. *The Tourist Gaze: Leisure and Travel in Contemporary Societies.* London: Sage Publications, 1990.

–. *Consuming Places.* London: Routledge, 1995.

–. "Sensing Leisure Spaces." In *Leisure/Tourism Geographies: Practices and Geographical Knowledge,* ed. David Crouch, 34-45. London: Routledge, 1999.

van den Broek, Gerard J. "The Sign of the Fly: A Semiotic Approach to Fly Fishing." *American Journal of Semiotics* 3, 1 (1984): 71-78.

Van Tighem, Kevin. "Parks at Risk (Book Review of Rick Searle's *Phantom Parks*)." *Alternatives Journal* 27, 3 (2001): 38.

Veblen, Thorstein. *The Theory of the Leisure Class.* 1899. Reprint, New York: Dover Thrift Editions, 1994.

Volpé, Catherine, and Paul E. Burton. *Tourism: New Realities – A Canadian Perspective.* Toronto: Prentice Hall, 2000.

Voorhis, Ernest. "Fishing in Canada." *Canadian Travel* 13, 2 (1928): 29-40.

Waiser, Bill. *Park Prisoners: The Untold Story of Western Canada's National Parks, 1915-1946.* Saskatoon: Fifth House Publishers, 1995.

Walker, Dustin. "Groups Worried about Mining Road's Impact on Grizzlies." *Jasper Booster,* 24 March 2004. http://www.jasperbooster.com/.

Wall, Geoff. "Outdoor Recreation and the Canadian Identity." In *Recreational Land Use: Perspectives on Its Evolution in Canada,* ed. G. Wall and J. Marsh, 419-34. Ottawa: Carleton University Press, 1982.

Walt Disney World Resort. "Disney's Wilderness Lodge." N.d. http://disneyworld.disney. go.com/.

Walter, J.A. "Social Limits to Tourism." *Leisure Studies* 1 (1982): 295-304.

Waugh, Jeff. *Cheadle and Milton's Northwest Passage.* 1996. http://www.jaspernationalpark. com/.

Westling, Louise H. *The Green Breast of the New World: Landscape, Gender and American Fiction.* Athens, GA: University of Georgia Press, 1996.

Weyerhaeuser. "Weyerhaeuser – About Us." N.d. http://www.weyerhaeuser.com/.

–. "Weyerhaeuser Forestry in Canada." N.d. http://www.weyerhaeuser.com/.

–. "Caribou Display Brings the Wild to Life at Wild Alberta Gallery." March 2004. http://www.wyl-leader.ca/.

Wharton, Thomas. *Icefields.* Edmonton: NeWest Publishers, 1995.

White, Cliff, and E.J. (Ted) Hart. *The Lens of Time: A Repeat Photography of Landscape Change in the Canadian Rockies.* Calgary: University of Calgary Press, 2007.

White, Richard. "'Are You an Environmentalist or Do You Work for a Living?'" In *Uncommon Ground: Rethinking the Human Place in Nature,* ed. William Cronon, 171-85. New York: W.W. Norton and Company, 1995.

–. *The Organic Machine: The Remaking of the Columbia River.* New York: Hill and Wang, 1995.

–. "The New Western History and the National Parks." *George Wright Forum* 13, 3 (1996): 31.

"Wildlife of the Mountain Parks." In *Experience the Mountain Parks: A Visitor's Guide to Alberta and British Columbia,* 47. 2009-10.

Williams, M.B. *Jasper National Park.* Ottawa: Department of the Interior, 1928.

–. *Jasper Trails.* Ottawa: National and Historic Resources Branch, [1930].

–. *The Banff Jasper Highway: Descriptive Guide.* Saskatoon: H.R. Larson Publishing Company, 1948.

Wilson, Alexander. "The View from the Road: Nature Tourism in the Postwar Years." *Border/Lines* 12 (1988): 10-14.

–. *The Culture of Nature: North American Landscape from Disney to the* Exxon Valdez. Toronto: Between the Lines, 1991.

"Wolves Close in on Moose for Kill." *Globe and Mail,* 6 May 1944, 4.

Wonders, Karen. *Habitat Dioramas: Illusions of Wilderness in Museums of Natural History.* Uppsala: Uppsala University, 1993.

Woods, Michael. "Fantastic Mr. Fox? Representing Animals in the Hunting Debate." In *Animal Spaces, Beastly Places: New Geographies of Human-Animal Relations,* ed. Chris Philo and Chris Wilbert, 182-202. London: Routledge, 2000.

Wylie, Liz. "Canoeing and Canadian Art." *Queen's Quarterly* 103, 3 (1996): 615-27.

Wynn, Graeme. "'Shall We Linger along Ambitionless?' Environmental Perspectives on British Columbia." *B.C. Studies* 142-43 (2004): 5-67.

Zezulka-Mailloux, Gabrielle. "Laying the Tracks for Tourism: Paradoxical Promotions and the Development of Jasper National Park." In *Culturing Wilderness in Jasper National Park: Studies in Two Centuries of Human History in the Upper Athabasca River Watershed,* ed. I.S. MacLaren, 233-59. Edmonton: University of Alberta Press, 2007.

Zickefoose, Sherri. "National Park Fees Frozen." *Calgary Herald,* 10 May 2009, B3.
Zukin, Sharon, Robert Baskerville, Miriam Greenberg, Courtney Guthreau, Jean Halley, Mark Halling, Kristin Lawler, Ron Nerio, Rebecca Stack, Alex Vitale, and Betsey Wissinger. "From Coney Island to Las Vegas in the Urban Imaginary: Discursive Practices of Growth and Decline." *Urban Affairs Review* 33, 5 (1998): 627-54.

Index

Printed and bound in Canada by Friesens

Set in Garamond by Artegraphica Design Co. Ltd.

Copy editor: Dallas Harrison

Proofreader: Stephanie VanderMeulen